Mary Barnard

Mary Barnard

Complete Poems and Selected Translations

Edited and with an introduction by

SARAH BARNSLEY

Cover credit: Facsimile sketch of Mary Barnard by Charlotte Heaton-Sessions. Collection of Elizabeth J. Bell, Vancouver, Washington. Also available in the Mary Barnard Papers, Yale Collection of American Literature, Beinecke Rare Book and Manuscript Library, New Haven, CT.

Published by State University of New York Press, Albany

EU GPSR Authorised Representative:
Logos Europe, 9 rue Nicolas Poussin, 17000, La Rochelle, France
contact@logoseurope.eu

For information, contact State University of New York Press, Albany, NY
www.sunypress.edu

Library of Congress Cataloging-in-Publication Data

Names: Barnard, Mary, 1909–2001, author. | Barnsley, Sarah, 1974– editor.
Title: Mary Barnard : complete poems and selected translations / Mary
    Barnard ; edited and with an introduction by Sarah Barnsley.
Description: Albany : State University of New York Press, [2025]. | Includes
    bibliographical references and index.
Identifiers: LCCN 2024049482 | ISBN 9798855802641 (hardcover : alk. paper) |
    ISBN 9798855802665 (ebook) | ISBN 9798855802658 (pbk. : alk. paper)
Subjects: LCGFT: Poetry. | Literary criticism. | Essays.
Classification: LCC PS3503.A5825 M37 2025 | DDC 811/.54—dc23/eng/20250101
LC record available at https://lccn.loc.gov/2024049482

Playroom

Wheel of sorrow, centerless.
Voices, sad without cause.
Slope upward, expiring on grave summits.
Mournfulness of muddy playgrounds,
Raw smell of rubbers and wrapped lunches
When little girls stand in a circle singing
Of windows and of lovers.

Hearing them, no one could tell
Why they sing sadly, but there is in their voices
The pathos of all handed-down garments
Hanging loosely on small bodies.

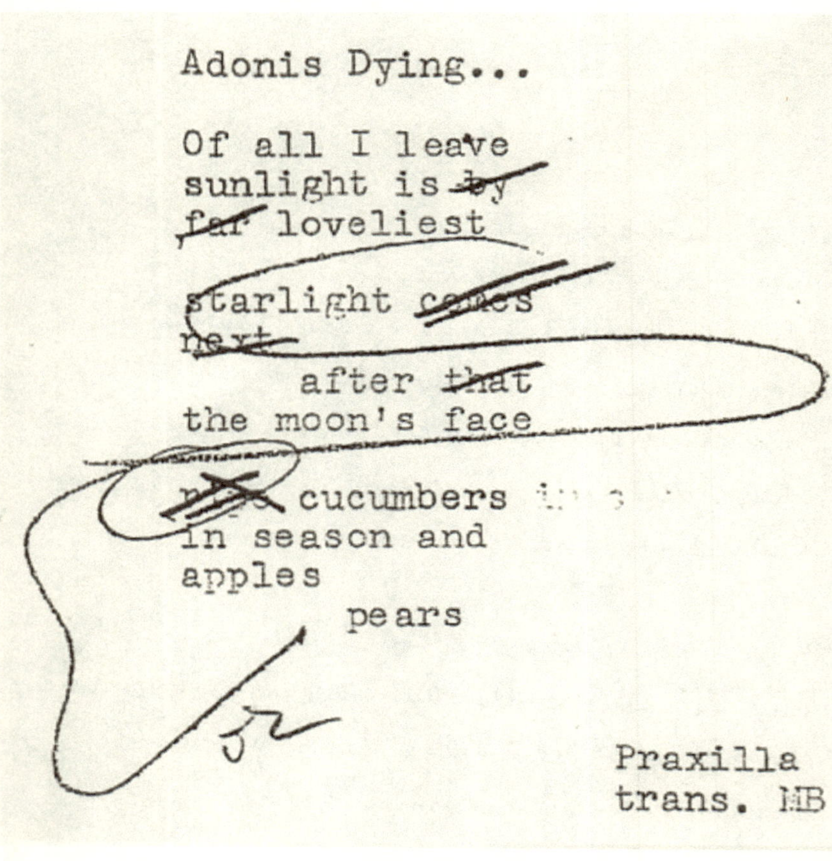
Adonis Dying...

Of all I leave
sunlight is by
far loveliest

starlight comes
next
        after that
the moon's face

        cucumbers
in season and
apples
        pears

Praxilla
trans. MB

Contents

I. POEMS

List of Illustrations and Facsimiles

Acknowledgments

My deepest thanks go to Elizabeth J. Bell, Mary Barnard's literary executor, and her husband Bruce, without whom this book would not have been possible. Thank you for the immeasurable generosity, endless kindness, and wholehearted warmth over the many years we have known each other. Betty, you have done a remarkable service to American Letters in making the full extent of Mary Barnard's poetic achievement available to the world. Thank you for asking me to do it—and for trusting in me so entirely. It's been the greatest honor and privilege.

Thank you to Mary de Rachewiltz for a golden foreword and also to Siegfried de Rachewiltz for kind correspondence in relation to this. Thank you to Helen Carr for the sharpest of insights and comments on the introduction. Thank you to Mary Barnard's dear collaborators, her publisher James Anderson and illustrator Anita Bigelow, for immense warmth and generosity. Thank you to Sue Hennum for another scoop of wonderful Barnard conversation, this time over dinner during my last visit to Vancouver in April 2022, including art history guidance for the notes to Barnard's poem "Eternal She." Thank you to Margaret Halpin for forensic research assistance and patience with my countless book queries. At Reed College, thank you to the professor who introduced me to Mary Barnard's work, Ellen K Stauder: you are a legend. Thank you also to Reed's Robin Tovey and Reed Womack-Hoffman for *Dr Who* levels of wizardry with archives. Thank you to other academics and writers who have contributed to my thinking on this book: Chris Baldick, Walter Baumann, Ian F. Bell, Jane Desmarais, Maura Dooley, James Gifford, Isobel Hurst, and Padraig Kirwan.

Thank you to my magnificent editor and fellow modernist Rebecca Colesworthy: your unwavering faith in this book, good humor and Herculean patience has meant the world to me. Thank you also to Editor-in-Chief James

Peltz for wisdom just when it was needed, and again to the tremendous team at SUNY Press, especially Julia Cosacchi and Céline Parent. I couldn't have wished for a better home for the work of SUNY Buffalo's first Poetry Curator than SUNY Press.

For all travel assistance, thank you to the Mary Barnard Literary Estate, to Goldsmiths, University of London, and to the British Association of American Studies (BAAS) for the Founder's Research Travel Award (2019–2020).

Thank you to the beautiful friends I made at Reed over 1994–1995, fellow travelers in "Uzzlot": Angela Buxton, Sally McManus, and Natasha Moscovici. Thank you to Charlotte Gann for allyship and owl wisdom. Thank you to Di Shields: you lit the way.

Thank you to the two people I love the most: Louise and Zachary.

Finally, thank you to Mary Barnard: may this book find you "standing high, high" on Mount Helicon.

—Sarah Barnsley, Editor

Grateful acknowledgments are due to James Anderson, for permission to reprint Mary Barnard's poetry previously published by Breitenbush Books; to Elizabeth J. Bell, for permission to reprint from published and unpublished material by Mary Barnard, including illustrative material, under copyright by Barnardworks; to Elizabeth J. Bell, for permission to reprint from her unpublished correspondence and material relating to Mary Barnard; to Anita Bigelow, for permission to print facsimiles of diagrams and line drawings featured in the notes section to Mary Barnard, *Time and the White Tigress* (Portland, OR: Breitenbush, 1986); to Reed College, for permission to reprint Mary Barnard's poetry previously published by the Graphic Arts Workshop and the *Gawdawfulers Anthology 1928–1929*; to University of California Press Books, for permission to reprint selections from Mary Barnard, *Sappho: A New Translation*; and to Hamish Whyte, for assistance with translating a line in Greek in Mary Barnard's "Storm" and permission to print quotations from email correspondence related to this.

Permission for the use of the 6/30/1936 letter from Marianne C. Moore to Mary Barnard is granted by the Literary Estate of Marianne C. Moore by the successor executor, David M. Moore, Esq. All rights reserved. Previously unpublished letters and annotations by Ezra Pound, copyright © (2025) by Mary de Rachewiltz and the Estate of Omar S. Pound. Used by permission of

New Directions Publishing Corporation. A previously unpublished letter by May Sarton is reprinted by the permission of Russell & Volkening as agents for the author. Copyright © 1984 by May Sarton. Unpublished letters by William Carlos Williams are used by permission of the William Carlos Williams MD Estate in care of the Jean V. Naggar Literary Agency, Inc. (permissions@jvnla.com).

"A Communication on Greek Metric, Ezra Pound, and *Sappho*" was first published in *Agenda* and is reprinted from how it appeared in *Paideuma*; "Meeting Marianne" was first published by *The Iowa Review*; "Ezra Pound, Sappho and My Assault on Mount Helicon" was first published by *The Malahat Review*; "Song for the Northern Quarter" was first published by *The Paris Review*; "Song for the New Year" was first published by The University Libraries, State University of New York at Buffalo, 1985 (number seven of the second series of Christmas Broadsides).

Every effort has been made to obtain permissions from holders of copyrighted material published herein. The editor would like to apologize for any omissions and will be pleased to incorporate any missing acknowledgments in any future editions.

Foreword

Mary Barnard—American Imagist

Mary de Rachewiltz

Little did the eminent Flower Professor of Astronomy and founding director of the Flower Observatory at the University of Pennsylvania know of the influence stars and planets may have on poets when he called young Ezra, the son of Homer Loomis Pound, a "nomad," implying more or less he was not worthy company for his daughter Hilda. Or was it simply the word, as definition, to cause havoc among comets and falling stars? His daughter Hilda followed the exile and is now known as H. D. Imagist.

Mary Barnard's father, on the other hand, managed a sawmill, opened a lumber company in Vancouver, and like Homer, the nomad's father, looked at trees growing and knew "hand saws, buck saws, rotary saws, band saws, jig saws, hang saws, bone saws [. . .] an endless combination of sharp saws." He drank Hiawatha's spring water and his daughter stayed rooted in *Cool Country*.

Mary Barnard was the only woman among the *Five Young American Poets*, published in 1940, when New Directions was still at Norfolk, Connecticut. John Berryman and Randall Jarrell can hardly keep up with her in those pages for the landscape is full of rapids, rocks, and trestles and, in "Storm," "The radio brings [. . .] The well-plumed music" in the Greek alphabet.

In 1952 she published *A Few Poems*, printed in Portland, Oregon: in a dozen poems she demonstrates that her "Inheritance" is memory. She pays homage to the hardworking and willful women, her kin. "Persephone" and "Anadyomene" are a strong presence and in the last poem, "The Field," we find: "Mortal stirrings demand / Horoscopes of the stars."

Mary joined the Mythmakers and made the gods laugh "out of simple delight in rhythmic movement" (Editor's note—see *TM* 53). Tibor Serly set "The Pleiades" to music, but it is her metric that sets the tone. She knew her Greek and brought Sappho alive into our modernist world. Goethe wrote of Wahlverwandtschaft, not of a double helix. Mary Barnard was a seer: *Erato Agonistes* shows that she read like angels read, she made her Confession and stated her Creed.[1]

In 1988 she published *Nantucket Genesis: The Tale of My Tribe*. It was all one big family. Almost every person mentioned in the Nantucket part of the book is kin in some degree—except Wanack-Mamack. I read the poetry interwoven with legal documents as an oblique sequel or addenda to Pound's Cantos LXII–LXXI, also referred to as "The Adams Cantos," which open by quoting his grandson Charles Francis Adams: "Acquit of evil intention." This "Purgatory" section was written before 1939, ready for the printer the year Barnard and Pound met in New York. They had been in correspondence since 1933, when Pound wrote "Eleven New Cantos—XXXI–XLI" and Mary had started translating Sappho. In her *Assault on Mount Helicon* she tells of the meeting with her first mentor in New York. Pound asked her to take tea with him at the Restaurant Robert, she was on tenterhooks and the older poet was "punctilious." She stressed the word *punctilious* and added she too, like E. E. Cummings, had sensed that her host felt lonely, in need of friends. Public opinion was misled by the Press. As late in the Cantos as *Thrones—CV,* Pound reminds himself and his readers:

> I shall have to learn a little Greek to keep up with this
> but so will you, dratt you.
> "They want to bust out of kosmos"

In 1986 Mary published *Time and the White Tigress*; she did not follow in Pound's footsteps through China into Tibet. She knew her measure, stood still, in her star-maze, watching the shadows with great sensibility. Not only did she know her Greek and her Latin fables, but also *The Divine Comedy* and the *Panchasiddhantika*—a truly learned lady, able to sing of astronomical phenomena. And one of her greatest accomplishments was the cultivation of friendships.

---

1. Editor's note: see "Confessional" and "Creed," reprinted in this edition in section III.

List of Abbreviations

The following abbreviations are used throughout this volume:

Manuscripts, Typescripts, Printings, and Performances of Poems

AFEST A Festschrift for Lloyd J. Reynolds (Portland, OR, 1966), 60.

AFP Mary Barnard, *A Few Poems* (Portland, OR: Graphics Arts Workshop, Reed College, 1952). (300 print copies signed by the poet; the editor has referred to copy 170).

AP *American Prefaces* 1.4 (January 1936): 61.

APGIF Mary Barnard, *A Pagan's Guide to Italian Frescoes* (Mary Barnard Papers, Yale Collection of American Literature, Beinecke Rare Book and Manuscript Library, New Haven, CT).

AP V2 *American Poetry: The Twentieth Century*, Vol. 2, compiled by Robert Hass, John Hollander, Carolyn Kizer, Nathaniel Mackey, and Marjorie Perloff (Library of America, 2000).

BKNB Black Notebook (Collection of Elizabeth J. Bell, Vancouver, Washington. Also available in the Mary Barnard Papers, Yale Collection of American Literature, Beinecke Rare Book and Manuscript Library, New Haven, CT). Referenced by Bell in her records as both "Bk. N. B." and "BKK.N.B."

CC Mary Barnard, *Cool Country*, in *Five Young American Poets*, ed. James Laughlin (Norfolk, CT: New Directions, 1940), 3–40.

CP   Mary Barnard, *Collected Poems* (Portland, OR: Breitenbush, 1979).

CPR   *Cincinnati Poetry Review* 8 (Spring 1981): 47.

CV 2.1   *College Verse* 2.1 (November 1932): 12–13.

CV 2.3   *College Verse* 2.3 (January 1933): 16–17.

CV 2.6   *College Verse* 2.6 (April 1933): 17.

CV 2.7   *College Verse* 2.7 (May 1933): 17.

ENC   *Encore* 2.4 (February–March 1978): 6–9.

G   *Gawdawfulers Anthology 1928–1929* (Portland: OR, 1929).

H   Mary Barnard, "The Horae of Mary Ethel Barnard" (senior thesis, Reed College, 1932).

HAT   *Homespun: A Tribute to Mary Barnard*, eds. Douglas Spangle and Brian Christopher Hamilton (Portland, OR: Quiet Lion Press, 1994).

JUV   Folder marked "Juv." [for Juvenilia] (Collection of Elizabeth J. Bell, Vancouver, Washington. Also available in the Mary Barnard Papers, Yale Collection of American Literature, Beinecke Rare Book and Manuscript Library, New Haven, CT).

KBOO   Mary Barnard, poetry reading, KBOO Community Radio, Portland, OR, April 1, 1975. Recording provided by Thomas J. Donovan.

LBN   Little Brown Notebook (Collection of Elizabeth J. Bell, Vancouver, Washington. Also available in the Mary Barnard Papers, Yale Collection of American Literature, Beinecke Rare Book and Manuscript Library, New Haven, CT). In an email to the editor of 9 June 2020, Bell reports:

It looks like the size of the pages are 5" wide by 7 ¾" high. I noted [. . .] that there were some loose papers folded in the back of it and I have copies of those. They are "On Your Birthday" hand-written in Mary's hand; also a little handwritten note "I was delighted to hear of the inclusion of Mary Barnard. I regard her work as of exceptional ability—in fact, I know of no other young woman who is writing verse nearly so good as hers. I plan to include a considerable amount of her work in the anthology I mentioned. T.C. Wilson is written perpendicularly on the side; typed out are 2 working versions of "Noon Hour" with a third that is not marked up; "Kronos" (signed MB (solo) and "Late Roman" signed (ditto) [*sic*].

MC	Mary Barnard poetry manuscript in Mildred Cline Papers (Collection of Elizabeth J. Bell, Vancouver, Washington. Also available in Reed College, Portland, OR).
ND	*New Democracy* 5.12 (15 February 1936): 193–94 (Section entitled "New Directions" with a note "Edited by James Laughlin IV").
ND ONE	*New Directions 1*, ed. James Laughlin (Norfolk, CT: New Directions, 1936): No pag.
ND TWO	*New Directions 2*, ed. James Laughlin (Norfolk, CT: New Directions, 1937): No pag.
NEW	*New English Weekly* (London) 6.17 (7 February 1935): 354.
NG	Mary Barnard, *Nantucket Genesis: The Tale of My Tribe* (Portland, OR: Breitenbush, 1988).
NR	*Northwest Review* 17.2–3 (1979): 233–42.
ODY	*Odysseus* 1.5 (1972): No pag.
OE	*Oregon English* 11.2B (Fall 1989): 73.
P	*Poetry* 151, 1–2 (October–November 1987): 1–2.
PJ	*Providence Journal*, 15 June 1941, sec. 6.2.
S	Mary Barnard, *Sappho: A New Translation* (Berkeley: University of California Press, 1958).
TA	*The Arts in Clark County* (December 1978): No pag.
TG	*The Griffin* (Portland: OR, 1929): No pag.
TI	Typescript of *The Iliad*, unpublished translation by Mary Barnard (Collection of Elizabeth J. Bell, Vancouver, Washington.

Also available in the Mary Barnard Papers, Yale Collection of American Literature, Beinecke Rare Book and Manuscript Library, New Haven, CT).

TIME   Mary Barnard, *Time and the White Tigress* (Portland, OR: Breitenbush, 1986).

TSMS   Mary Barnard, "The Shadow" prose manuscript (Collection of Elizabeth J. Bell, Vancouver, Washington. Also available in the Mary Barnard Papers, Yale Collection of American Literature, Beinecke Rare Book and Manuscript Library, New Haven, CT).

U   Unknown TS/MS (in such instances the material is located among Barnard's papers without being connected to a specific TS/MS such as *LBN*) (Collection of Elizabeth J. Bell, Vancouver, Washington. Also available in the Mary Barnard Papers, Yale Collection of American Literature, Beinecke Rare Book and Manuscript Library, New Haven, CT).

UH   Unsubmitted portion of Mary Barnard, "The Horae of Mary Ethel Barnard" (Collection of Elizabeth J. Bell, Vancouver, Washington. Also available in the Mary Barnard Papers, Yale Collection of American Literature, Beinecke Rare Book and Manuscript Library, New Haven, CT).

WP   *Woman Poet: The West*, ed. Elaine Dallman (Reno, NV: Reno/Regional Editions, 1980), 34–35. [Anthology scheduled for publication before *CP*, but was actually published after it, in 1980].

WQ   *The Westminster Quarterly* 24.1 (Spring–Summer 1935) [An anthology of British and American Poetry edited by Ezra Pound, John Drummond, and T.C. Wilson]: 30–32, 38.

Memoirs, Letters, Notebooks, and Other Records

AMH   Mary Barnard, *Assault on Mount Helicon* (Berkeley: University of California Press, 1984).

BD/MB   Babette Deutsch letters to Mary Barnard (Collection of Elizabeth J. Bell, Vancouver, Washington. Also available in the Mary

Barnard Papers, Yale Collection of American Literature, Beinecke Rare Book and Manuscript Library, New Haven, CT).

DDP/MB   D. D. Paige letters to Mary Barnard (Mary Barnard Papers, Yale Collection of American Literature, Beinecke Rare Book and Manuscript Library, New Haven, CT).

DS   Mary Barnard, "The Distaff Side" (Mary Barnard Papers, Yale Collection of American Literature, Beinecke Rare Book and Manuscript Library, New Haven, CT).

EA   Mary Barnard, *Erato Agonistes: Writing a Creative Thesis at Reed College in the "Golden Age"* (Portland, OR: White Tigress Press, 1999).

EP/MB   Ezra Pound letters to Mary Barnard (Ezra Pound Papers, Yale Collection of American Literature, Beinecke Rare Book and Manuscript Library, New Haven, CT).

EP/MBEJB   Ezra Pound letters to Mary Barnard (transcribed by Barnard) (Collection of Elizabeth J. Bell, Vancouver, Washington).

FC/MB   Florence Codman letters to Mary Barnard (Mary Barnard Papers, Yale Collection of American Literature, Beinecke Rare Book and Manuscript Library, New Haven, CT). [Correspondence contains anonymous readers' report, which Codman sent Barnard on 8 May 1936].

JS/MB   Mary Barnard, interview by John Sheehy and Ellen Johnson, 13 September 1998, transcript, Electronic Oral History Project, The Reed Institute.

JSN   Jewel Steno Notebook (Collection of Elizabeth J. Bell, Vancouver, Washington. Also available in the Mary Barnard Papers, Yale Collection of American Literature, Beinecke Rare Book and Manuscript Library, New Haven, CT). In an email to the editor of 9 June 2020, Bell reports:

The "Jewel Steno NB" [. . .] bound at the top, as stenographers use so they can flip the page back really fast when taking dictation. On the cover is printed: JEWEL 200 page Note Book for Stenographers. From___________1933, To___________193_

(Mary has filled in the From line "December 1933," but did not fill in the To line. At bottom of cover in small print is No. 0101 Gregg Ruled With Centenaries Down Line. It's a daily journal [*sic*].

MB/BR Mary Barnard letters to Breitenbush, Breitenbush Folder #1 (Mary Barnard Papers, Yale Collection of American Literature, Beinecke Rare Book and Manuscript Library, New Haven, CT).

MB/EG Mary Barnard letter to Emily Grosholz (Collection of Elizabeth J. Bell, Vancouver, Washington. Also available in the Mary Barnard Papers, Yale Collection of American Literature, Beinecke Rare Book and Manuscript Library, New Haven, CT).

MB/EP Mary Barnard letters to Ezra Pound (Ezra Pound Papers, Yale Collection of American Literature, Beinecke Rare Book and Manuscript Library, New Haven, CT).

MB/F Mary Barnard letters to *Furioso* (*Furioso* Papers, Yale Collection of American Literature, Beinecke Rare Book and Manuscript Library, New Haven, CT).

MB/IC Mary Barnard Index Cards [a catalog by Mary Barnard of all her poems, both published and unpublished—with bibliographic details of published poems] (Collection of Elizabeth J. Bell, Vancouver, Washington).

MB/JA Mary Barnard letters to James Anderson (Mary Barnard Papers, Yale Collection of American Literature, Beinecke Rare Book and Manuscript Library, New Haven, CT).

MBJO Mary Barnard journal, 1932, marked in pencil "Mary Ethel Barnard, Reed," one of two sets (manufacturer: Chief. Student's Note Book No. 619) (Collection of Elizabeth J. Bell, Vancouver, Washington).

MB/JS Mary Barnard letters to John Sheehy (Mary Barnard Papers, Yale Collection of American Literature, Beinecke Rare Book and Manuscript Library, New Haven, CT).

MB/MEH Mary Barnard letters to Myrna and Erik Haugaard (Mary Barnard Papers, Yale Collection of American Literature, Beinecke Rare Book and Manuscript Library, New Haven, CT).

MB/OR Mary Barnard letters to Olga Rudge (Olga Rudge Papers, Yale Collection of American Literature, Beinecke Rare Book and Manuscript Library, New Haven, CT).

MB/Parents Mary Barnard letters to her parents (Samuel M. Barnard and Bertha H. Barnard) (Collection of Elizabeth J. Bell, Vancouver, Washington. Also available in the Mary Barnard Papers, Yale Collection of American Literature, Beinecke Rare Book and Manuscript Library, New Haven, CT).

MB/TD Mary Barnard/Thomas J. Donovan correspondence (Collection of Elizabeth J. Bell, Vancouver, Washington. Also available in the Mary Barnard Papers, Yale Collection of American Literature, Beinecke Rare Book and Manuscript Library, New Haven, CT).

MB/TW Mary Barnard letters to T. C. Wilson (T. C. Wilson Papers, Yale Collection of American Literature, Beinecke Rare Book and Manuscript Library, New Haven, CT).

MB/WS Mary Barnard letters to William Stafford (Mary Barnard Papers, Yale Collection of American Literature, Beinecke Rare Book and Manuscript Library, New Haven, CT).

MS/MB May Sarton letters to Mary Barnard (Mary Barnard Papers, Yale Collection of American Literature, Beinecke Rare Book and Manuscript Library, New Haven, CT).

PNC Poem notecard index created by Elizabeth J. Bell, one notecard per poem recording data and observations on poems (Collection of Elizabeth J. Bell, Vancouver, Washington).

WCW/MB William Carlos Williams letters to Mary Barnard (Collection of Elizabeth J. Bell, Vancouver, Washington).

Prose by Mary Barnard

ACOG Mary Barnard, "A Communication on Greek Metric, Ezra Pound, and *Sappho*," *Agenda* (London) 16.3–4 (Autumn–Winter 1978–79): 62–68. Reprinted in *Paideuma* 23, no. 1 (Spring 1994): 147–52.

BTS   Mary Barnard, "Boundaries: The Shadow," *Harper's Bazaar* 2820 (December 1946): 164–65, 278 ff.

EPS   Mary Barnard, "Ezra Pound, Sappho and My Assault on Mount Helicon," *The Malahat Review* 66 (October 1983): 140–44.

FN   Mary Barnard, "Further Notes on Metric," *Paideuma* 23, no. 1 (Spring 1994): 153–57.

MM   Mary Barnard, "Meeting Marianne," *The Iowa Review* 13.1 (Winter 1982): 96–100.

TF   Mary Barnard, *Three Fables* (Portland, OR: Breitenbush, 1983). First published in *The Kenyon Review* 10.1 (Winter 1948): [109]–124. Subsequently reprinted in *From Timberline to Tidepool: Contemporary Fiction from the Northwest*, ed. Rich Ives (Missoula, MT: Owl Creek Press, 1986), 10–16.

TM   Mary Barnard, *The Mythmakers* (Athens: Ohio University Press, 1966).

WCW   Mary Barnard, "William Carlos Williams and the Poetry Archive at Buffalo," in *William Carlos Williams: Man and Poet*, ed. Carroll F. Terrell (Orono, ME: The National Poetry Foundation, University of Maine, 1983), 83–88.

Criticism and Other

AC   Angela Christy, "The Mary Barnard Translation of Sappho," *Paideuma* 23, no. 1 (Spring 1994): 25–63.

BAR   Greg Barnhisel, "Ezra Pound, James Laughlin and New Directions: The Publisher as Spin Doctor," *Paideuma* 29, no. 3 (Winter 2000): 165–78.

BER   Charles Bernstein, "Objectivist Blues: Scoring Speech in Second-Wave Modernist Poetry and Lyrics," *American Literary History* (February 2008): 346–68.

BIB   Elizabeth J. Bell and Mary Barnard, "Bibliographic Record of Periodical and Book Production," *Paideuma* 23, no. 1 (Spring 1994): 187–98.

COR   Cid Corman, *Sappho: Wee Ones* (Green River, VT: Longhouse Publishers and Booksellers, 2004).

DG   David Gordon, "Ezra Pound to Mary Barnard: An ABC of Metrics," *Paideuma* 23, no. 1 (Spring 1994): 159–79.

EME   Ralph Waldo Emerson, "The Poet," in *Selected Essays* (London: Penguin, 1985), 259–84.

FSF   F. S. Flint, "Imagisme," *Poetry*, 1.6 (March 1913): 198–200.

FUS   Paul Fussell, "Whitman's Curious Warble: Reminiscence and Reconciliation," in *The Presence of Walt Whitman: Selected Papers from the English Institute*, ed. R. W. B. Lewis (New York and London: Columbia University Press, 1962), 28–51.

GA   *The Greek Anthology*, Volume 3, trans. W. R. Paton (London: Heinemann, 1916).

HEL   Anita Helle, "The Odysseys of Mary Barnard," *Encore* 2.4 (February–March 1978): 6–9.

LE   Ezra Pound, *Literary Essays*, ed. T. S. Eliot (Norfolk, CT: New Directions, 1954).

MIL   Tyrus Miller, *Late Modernism: Politics, Fiction, and the Arts between the World Wars* (Berkeley: University of California Press, 1999).

MOHE   Molly O' Hara Ewing, "The Poetry of Mary Barnard: A Study in Voice and Verse," *Paideuma* 23, no. 1 (Spring 1994): 65–108.

PER   Ezra Pound, *Personae*, rev. by Lea Baechlar and A. Walton Litz (New York: New Directions, 1990).

PLINY   Pliny, *Natural History*, Vol. IX, Libri XXXIII–XXXV, trans. H. Rackham (Cambridge, MA: Harvard University Press, 1952. Loeb Classical Library).

OLS   Charles Olson, "Projective Verse," in *The New American Poetry 1945–1960*, ed. Donald Allen (Berkeley: University of California Press, 1999).

OX   *The Oxford History of the Classical World*, ed. John Boardman, Jasper Griffin, and Oswyn Murray (Oxford University Press, 1994 edition).

RL   Richard Lattimore, *Greek Lyrics* (University of Chicago, 1955).

RUE   William Rueckert, "Literature and Ecology: An Experiment in Ecocriticism," in *The Ecocriticism Reader: Landmarks in Literary Ecology*, eds. Cheryll Glotfelty and Harold Fromm (Athens and London: University of Georgia Press, 1996), 105–23.

SB/MBAI   Sarah Barnsley, *Mary Barnard, American Imagist* (Albany: State University of New York Press, 2013).

SB/P   Sarah Barnsley, "'She *would* write about forest fires at a time like this!'—Mary Barnard at the Lockwood Memorial Library, University of Buffalo, September 1939," *Paideuma: Modern and Contemporary Poetry and Poetics*, 44 (2017; published 2019): 9–18.

SB/PhD   Sarah Barnsley, "Mary Barnard, Late Imagist: A study of her poetry 1927–1952" (PhD diss., Goldsmiths College, University of London, 2006).

SB/W   Sarah Barnsley, "Late Modernism in Manhattan: Mary Barnard and May Swenson," *Women: A Cultural Review*, 26, no. 3 (2016): 254–69.

TFH   *The Oxford Book of Greek Verse in Translation*, eds. T. F. Higham and C. M. Bowra (Oxford University Press, 1938).

TGM   Robert Graves, *The Greek Myths*, ed. Kenneth McLeish (First Folio Society edition 1996—Sixteenth Printing [two volumes] 2003. First published in 1955 by Penguin Books).

TGL   David Campbell, *The Golden Lyre: The Themes of the Greek Lyric Poets* (London: Duckworth, 1983).

TREAT   Longinus, *A Treatise on the Sublime*, trans. Frank Granger (London: Stanley Nott, 1935).

WHI   Walt Whitman, *Complete Prose Works: Specimen Days and Collect, November Boughs and Good Bye My Family* (New York and London: D. Appleton, 1909).

WCW/ZUK   *The Correspondence of William Carlos Williams and Louis Zukofsky*, ed. Barry Ahearn (Middletown, CT: Wesleyan University Press, 2003).

ZUK   *Prepositions: The Collected Critical Essays of Louis Zukofsky* (London: Rapp & Carroll, 1967).

NORTH WINDOW

A book with a green binding

And snow dropping out of shallow sky:

The falling away of light and blood,

Of all yellow and rose

Leaves only

Forced passage to another country,

To a beach without wharf, quiet

Like a lake beach.

    Green cloth and polished horn,

      Stairways of unstained wood.

We sit among grasses,

Among bloodless stones

Or lie at night upon white fur

Watching mist gather under the rafters,

Speaking of the queen's emeralds.

Introduction

SARAH BARNSLEY

Mary Barnard: The Life

In February 1936 Mary Barnard drafted an Imagist gem of a poem called "North Window." While the poem has its fantastical qualities—in a snow-laden green-roofed cabin in the woods its personae "lie at night upon white fur [. . .] [s]peaking of the queen's emeralds"—it is also rooted in the real, in Barnard's Pacific Northwest. Descendants of one of the first Nantucket purchasers, her family had undergone "passage to another country" numerous times as her father's line moved from England to Nantucket then to North Carolina, Indiana, Kentucky, and finally to Vancouver, Washington, where Barnard was born on 6 December 1909. With the compass point of "NW" etched into the poem's title, "North Window" puts into frame the northwestern forests and lumber camp clearings of Barnard's childhood following her father's appointment to the Pittock and Leadbetter Lumber Company in 1908.

Barnard spent her early childhood in rural Buxton and started school in nearby Hillsboro. In 1918 her father Samuel opened the Barnard Lumber Company, triggering deeper passage into "another country" as the new business necessitated regular journeys into the mountains to purchase lumber; if not in school, Barnard accompanied him. "We went in all seasons, and in all kinds of weather except snow, when the mills would be shut down for lack of logs," Barnard recalled in her literary memoir *Assault on Mount Helicon (AMH)*; "the pleasure given by mountains, rivers, woods, wildflowers, baby lambs, waterfalls, and the like was sheer golden bonus" (*AMH* 13). The mill stops—"most often long ones" (*AMH* 14)—gave her plenty of opportunities to sit in the car and read or make sketches of the mills.

But Barnard was also charting another country in her imagination, that of the Greek dramatists, making her first attempts at translation while in high school. This she continued at Reed College, a small liberal arts college recently founded across the Columbia River in Portland fast gaining a reputation because of its nondenominational status, unsupervised dormitories, and the unusual freedom women had to smoke anywhere on campus. "[R]umor persisted that the principal subjects taught at Reed were 'atheism, communism, and free love'" (*AMH* 31), Barnard recalled. For her, it was a place where there were "proper desks, the desks loaded with books"—none of the "great flying about in dressing gowns, pealing telephones, and a general hurly-burly" that Barnard had observed on prospective visits elsewhere. At Reed she was in "seventh heaven" (*AMH* 32). From the beginning, Barnard was enchanted by readings given by Classics professor Barry Cerf: "I had had no idea of taking Greek until I heard the sound of it when he [Cerf] read one line of Homer in a freshman lit. lecture. It was a tiny seed that took root. Sometimes a small group of students would assemble in the evening to hear him read Homer aloud, in Greek. I was always present" (*AMH* 34–35).

Barnard excelled at Greek—this was to help her later—but she was also immersed in the Reed literary scene. She joined the Gawd-Awful writers' group, meeting monthly on Saturday nights at Professor Victor Chittick's home "to read our Gawd-Awful poetry and our Gawd-Awful prose" (*AMH* 35), her freshman poems appearing in one of the group's anthologies. But the traditional character of this early work was to take a distinctly modernist turn by the time Barnard enrolled in Lloyd Reynolds' creative writing class in her junior year. There Barnard began reading T. S. Eliot, H. D., Edith Sitwell, Hart Crane, and E. E. Cummings and the one poet who was to steer her from one north window to another—Ezra Pound. Recalling this decisive moment, Barnard wrote:

I no longer know which came first, the day I wrote a poem liberated, at least, from a whalebone corset, or the day when Lloyd wrote out several lines of Pound's poetry on the blackboard, waved his arms about, and proclaimed, "The man who could do that could do anything!" [. . .] I copied the lines in my notebook, feeling skeptical, yet intrigued. The lines were from the "Homage to Sextus Propertius" [. . .] They bit deep. I returned to Gill's bookstore the copy of the Harriet Monroe anthology that my mother gave me for my birthday, and brought home [Pound's] *Personae* instead. I was beginning to know at last the country I wanted to explore. (*AMH* 39)

Graduating into the Depression, Barnard returned home to Vancouver where, jobless, she formed a study club to keep up her spirits. As part of this she read "A Few Don'ts by an Imagist"—"the only really worthwhile piece of poetry criticism I had ever read" (*AMH* 51). Realizing that Pound had done so much for other poets and that he had an appetite, like her, for classical Greek, Barnard went to Vancouver's public library, looked up Pound's address in the *Who's Who* and, in October 1933, sent him six poems with a request for advice or assistance.

Impressed by her work, which reminded him of early H. D., and hearing "the shattering wail of the segregated and lone poet on the far, far coast" (*AMH* 73), Pound replied swiftly with a postcard asking "Age? intentions? intention? how MUCH intention? I mean how hard and for how long are you willing to work at it?" (*EP/MBEJB*, 29 October 1933; also *AMH* 53). The following summer he wrote "I don't see any other *occupation* for you than WORK on metre, rhythm, melodic line, and to set round watchin' and waitin' " before proclaiming that "[y]ou are probably more abundant than such of the younger males of yr/ generation as I know of." ([*sic*]; *EP/MBEJB*, 13 August 1934; also *AMH* 71). As with others, Barnard became Pound's protégé and joined the "Ezuversity"—a kind of epistolary "one-man symposium of sorts in which Pound taught his special body of knowledge to the few students who sat through it," as Greg Barnhisel described it (*BAR* 165). Barnard told Pound about her interest in Sappho; he told her to try writing American-language poems in Sapphics; Barnard obliged. Just as Pound had made himself "Foreign Correspondent" for Harriet Monroe's early days of *Poetry*, so he saw Barnard fulfilling that role for him, a kind of "American Correspondent" for the American poet in Europe. While Barnard rejected it—"[y]ou might as a well ask an unborn infant whether there is any mobilizable energy in this country as to ask me" (*MB/EP*, 11 November 1934)—her subsequent immersion in literary life through other "north windows" never failed to interest Pound. By the time Barnard was visiting Pound in St. Elizabeths Hospital in Washington, DC, their mutual friend D. D. Paige (editor of Pound's letters) told Barnard that Pound had "made you his ambassador" (*DDP/MB*, 14 October 1950).

One "north window" Pound opened for Barnard was New York. In April of 1936, ground down by stints as a social worker for the Emergency Relief Administration, Barnard took Pound up on his advice to get into a group, traveling cross-country by train then up from New Orleans on the SS *Dixie* on the back of her winnings from *Poetry*'s Levinson Prize awarded the previous year. The "Pound connection," as she called it (*MB/EG*, 8 January 1989) was to induct Barnard into the Manhattan literary scene, meeting William Carlos

Williams and Marianne Moore, who, like Pound, were to become lifelong friends and mentors. She met E. E. Cummings, Ford Madox Ford, poet and editor T. C. Wilson, and Florence Codman of Arrow Editions, who introduced her to another member of the "Ezuversity," James Laughlin, whose New Directions outfit would go on to publish her debut collection *Cool Country* (*CC*) in 1940. On one trip home she stopped by the *Poetry* offices in Chicago where she had sherry and dinner with Harriet Monroe who, just before her untimely death, told Barnard she expected "great things of our Levinson Award winners" (*AMH* 110).

It was another Levinson winner who opened the next north window. Barnard was at Greenwich Village hangout Café Brevoort with Codman and translator Robert Fitzgerald when Muriel Rukeyser pulled up in her car (*MB/Parents*, 10 May 1936). A friendship quickly sprang up, from which came an invitation to Yaddo, the artists' colony in upstate New York. Barnard spent the summers of 1936 and 1938 at Yaddo, meeting Malcolm Cowley and Babette Deutsch, as well as the composer Edwin Gerschefksi who set one of her first American-language poems in Sapphics, "Lai," to music. At Pound's encouragement, Barnard took *The Iliad* with her to translate during her 1938 residency. The following May, Pound himself was in New York. After taking tea together, Pound insisted Barnard accompany him to the Museum of Modern Art to see Iris Barry, then curator of the Film Library, whom he had known when she was a young poet in London struggling, like Barnard, to secure work to support her writing. There, Barry "handed Pound some mail that had come for him, care of the Museum. As he took it, he said casually, 'Now while I look over my mail, give Mary a job'" (*AMH* 161). While Barry had no work for Barnard at the museum, her brother-in-law Charles Abbott did. Director of Libraries at the University of Buffalo, Abbott had recently begun collecting poetry volumes and manuscripts by twentieth-century poets writing in English and was in need of an assistant. Duly appointed first Curator of the Poetry Collection at the Lockwood Memorial Library, another north window opened.

The Buffalo years (1939–1943) did much to expand Barnard's associations with the modern poets of the day, be it through correspondence, library visits, or readings, but it was also a time she branched out into fiction as she began writing mystery stories. After Buffalo, she took up long-term residence in Greenwich Village, where she had an apartment on Minetta Street, and published her mysteries in popular magazines like *Harper's Bazaar*. Barnard published a set of Greek/Pacific northwestern-themed modern fables (*TF*) in *The Kenyon Review* and began work on a novel (*Ashe Knoll*), a novella (*Swamp*

Lake), and a verse drama with Greek chorus (*The Trap*). While none of these attracted much attention other than Williams' admiration for *The Trap*, Barnard's curator's skills kept her in paid work; she became a researcher, an indexer to Mark Van Doren, and later assisted his brother Carl with his biography of Benjamin Franklin.

Then came what Barnard called her "watershed years": 1949 to 1951 (*AMH* 249). In 1949 she traveled to Pound's Italy on an itinerary he had drawn up for her, meeting his lover Olga Rudge and her daughter Mary along the way. That same year she became financially independent, Samuel Barnard having sold his business and investing a third of the money in his daughter's name. But then things took a turn for the worse—or so it seemed. Falling seriously ill and being hospitalized in 1951—first in New York then in Vancouver—Barnard was discharged to her parents' care only to find herself in a new nightmare: confinement to bed. Allowed to sit up for just fifteen minutes a day for one month, then half an hour a day for the next, Barnard chillingly figured that it would be many months before she would be able to live a semblance of a normal life again. "I felt that I must do something to make this catastrophe *pay*," she recalled; "something I would *not* have done if I had been on my feet [. . .] something I could do comfortably while propped up by pillows" (*AMH* 280, italics Barnard's). As she reflected:

> I had thought and said repeatedly that if I ever had time I would like to take up my Greek again. During my [prior] summer vacations at home I had occasionally taken my Homer out into the garden and read a bit, but the tools were definitely rusty. This was my chance to do something about it [. . .] I went to work immediately. Since I had two beginner's grammars in the house, I began by working my way through both of them. I then read twelve books of the *Iliad*, but because I was unable at that time to get the text of the last twelve books, I switched to the *Odyssey*, which happened to be available, and read twelve books of that. (*AMH* 280–81)

Paige topped up Barnard's bedside book pile with a copy of Quasimodo's *Lirici Greci*, containing Sappho. The gift brought another gift, a project she could carry on even when not propped up by pillows—translation: "I could lie there rolling [Sappho's fragments] around and around in my mind, trying different words and different arrangements of words, asking myself over and over: what did she *mean*? why did she say gold *sandals*? is she speaking or is someone else speaking? why would peace be difficult to endure? When I sat up for my allotted hour or two, I typed the versions I had been trying in my head" ([*sic*]; *AMH* 283).

Upon recovery Barnard had a manuscript of what would become *Sappho: A New Translation* (*S*), but also a second volume of her own, *A Few Poems* (*AFP*). Returning to New York with a degree of financial freedom, Barnard was a frequent caller on Pound in St. Elizabeths and undertook further European travel, including Greece where she spent the winter of 1953 having arrived there via London, Paris, and Mary de Rachewiltz's Brunnenburg Castle in northern Italy. In 1955 Barnard gave up the Minetta Street apartment—New York was by now just too fast for her and she worried about her ageing parents—and returned to Vancouver for good. She visited Pound in Italy in 1959, shortly after his release from St. Elizabeths, then again in 1961 and 1964, the latter two trips poignantly captured in "Two Visits" where "The masks have all slipped off / except a death-mask stark / as marble" (*CP* 44). It would be the last time Barnard would see Pound in person.

By her later decades, *Poetry*'s 1935 Levinson Award winner had certainly made good on Harriet Monroe's call for "great things." Barnard's acclaimed *Sappho: A New Translation* (*S*) has been in continuous print since its first publication in 1958. Her research for the translation's famous "footnote" (actually an essay) led Barnard to produce a study of mythology, *The Mythmakers* (*TM*), in 1966, which anticipated Levi-Strauss' work on myth and was also an investigation into the use of intoxicants in sacred rituals coincident with work on the hallucinogenic mushroom by Gordon Wasson, with whom she had a correspondence. Her *Collected Poems* (*CP*) of 1979 won Barnard the Elliston Award that same year; she added to her awards shelf the Washington State Governor's Award for achievement in the literary arts in 1982 and the Western States Book Award for Poetry for *Time and the White Tigress* (*TIME*) in 1986, which saw Barnard expanding her repertoire to the essay-in-verse, here featuring "two imaginary observers [. . .] viewing the heavens from somewhere in the north temperate zone"—a north window out into the stars, as it were (*TIME* 63). The prize-winning streak was rounded off by the May Sarton Award in 1987. Sarton herself had earlier commended Barnard in private correspondence for *Assault on Mount Helicon*. "[W]onderful . . . acute, generous, modest, exact like your poems," it was a book, Sarton thought, that "does [Pound] a service in that he comes through as such a life-giver—all that getting poets to meet each other and the cogent severe eye" ([*sic*]; *MS/MB*, 4 May 1984; ellipses Sarton's).

But *Assault on Mount Helicon* was also a book Barnard wrote for today's emergent creative writers, searching, as she had once been, for a way to break through. Her chief reason for writing it was "the hope of writing a useful book," explaining:

> I do not mean a book useful to scholars who might be able to establish a date or identify a would-be poet in a walk-on part, but useful to young writers who read literary biography or autobiography much as a young explorer whose goal was the South Pole might read the journals of Scott's or Shackleton's expeditions. The magnitude of the success or the fact of the failure is of less interest than the day-to-day account of what happened: the equipment, the rations, the precautions, the errors and accidents. (*AMH* XVIII)

Barnard's last volume came out in 1988, a return to an ancestral "north window" in the genealogical, hybrid verse essay *Nantucket Genesis: The Tale of My Tribe* (*NG*), tracing her family's "almost invisible strand / in three hundred years of history" (*NG* 49). The Pound journal, *Paideuma*, dedicated a special issue to Barnard in 1994, and younger Pound enthusiasts dedicated that year's Portland Poetry Festival to her. In 1999, aged ninety, Barnard published a short retrospective of her last year at Reed, *Erato Agonistes: Writing a Creative Thesis at Reed College in the "Golden Age"* (*EA*). Two years later, on 25 August 2001, Barnard passed away from complications of cancer in her "north window" home overlooking the Columbia River. "[D]ead, I / won't be forgotten," she had translated from Sappho some fifty years earlier (*S* 93); time, now, to recount the ways in which the poems and translation in this volume might accomplish the same for Barnard herself.

Mary Barnard: The Poems

"Things have a certain starkness about them in an autumn rain. I should like my writing to be like that—hard substantial colors, *on* something, not transparent" wrote Barnard in her notebook on 31 October 1932 (*MBJO*; emphasis Barnard's). The fusion of an Imagist aesthetic with her experience of the local—northwestern climate, geographies, and logging industry—was always important to her, as I explored in *Mary Barnard, American Imagist* (2013). When fellow northwestern poet William Stafford came to write the introduction for *Collected Poems*, Barnard told him a number of her early poems drew on her experiences of making those trips with her father to the region's sawmills—"Cool Country,"

"Roots," "The Axe," "Logging Trestle," "Highway Bridge," "Planks," and "The Orchard Spring"—but so did much later poems like "The Pump" and "Noon Hour" (*MB/WS*, 15 October 1978). There were other poems written from these experiences, which she never published but appear here for the first time—the magnificent "North Window," of course, but also "Reverdie," "Thirst," and so many that evoke variations of a particular scene typified by "Letter from the Country" where the "wooded cones of the hills stand close," poems that have all the cutting clarity ("starkness") and compacted density ("hard substantial") of that region's forests of Douglas firs—"the green," "the enveloping color" of "forest heavy" land to quote "Cool Country" (*CC* 10).

The northwestern coast was important too, in particular an area of the Long Beach Peninsula, which Barnard described in another previously unpublished poem as "that listening place / Of mud-flat and sea-pasture" ("Gourmand Before an Oyster Can"). That "listening place" was Ocean Park, a resort where the Barnards frequently holidayed ("Utopia," as Barnard called it—see note to "Shoreline"), which inspired many early poems such as the previously unpublished "Estuary," "An Evening by the Sea," "Moonstone," and "Uninspired to the Uninspiring," as well as the previously uncollected "The Silk Leaf," which all appear here, and also a number of poems that appeared in *Cool Country*—"Wine Ship," "Lai," and the poems that saw her launched nationally in *Poetry*, such as "Ondine" and "Shoreline." Together they engage what Whitman saw figured in the American seashore—"that suggesting, dividing line, contact, junction, the solid marrying the liquid—that curious, lurking something [. . .] which means far more than its mere first sight" (*WHI* 88), which Paul Fussell conceptualized as initiating its own genre: "*The American Shore Ode*" (*FUS* 31, italics Fussell's). To Fussell's shore ode canon—including H. D.'s "Sea Gods," Marianne Moore's "A Grave," Wallace Stevens' "The Idea of Order at Key West," and poems by Barnard's more immediate peers (Elizabeth Bishop's "At the Fishhouses," Amy Clampitt's "Beach Glass," and A. R. Ammons' "Corsons Inlet")—we can surely add Barnard's shoreline poetics, which ask questions about the relation of self to others, nation, and world. After all, "Sand is the beginning and the end / Of our dominion," she wrote in "Shoreline."

It would be easy to conclude that Barnard spent a lifetime trying to find a language for this region. She was the first major poet of colonial American ancestry to set the "cool country" of this local into verse, doing for the Northwest what Robinson Jeffers had done for California. But the project was more complex—and more prescient—than simply an extension of Emerson's call to find poetic forms for an American geography that "dazzles the imagination" (*EME* 281). Like the best of Williams' and Moore's anti-romantic nature poems, Barnard's cool country poems were ahead of the eco-poetry curve that came to prominence in the US in the second half of the twentieth century through younger poets like fellow Reed alumnus Gary Snyder. As she put it in "Fable from the Cayoosh Country," written following a hiking trip in British Columbia in the 1930s, Barnard was deeply mindful of "feet pointing northwest" where "thought pushed forwards into the margins of silence." The "fable" of the poem is that the speaker, having taken "the grammars of all languages" into the "nameless mountains" and "flung [. . .] textbooks into a rocky pool," confronts then learns from the stream she finds there. The stream "turned through the volumes" before "speaking clearly." What the stream says, in Barnard's fable, is precisely what we find her poems say:

> "Where my monologue runs, there was once the debate of the beasts.
> The burrows bubbled with words, conversation
> Issued from the mouths of caves.
> Where there was speech there is now only my voice.
>
> "Had the mountain goat need of his eloquence
> To make of his native rocks a rostrum?
> Did the beaver's young learn industrious ways of a proverb?
> The humming bird was a fiction. What legend could please her?
>
> "The blade of this tool, useless for digging, chopping,
> Shearing, they used against each other with such zeal
> They all but accomplished their own extermination.
> Then—they abandoned speech!
> They retained cries expressive of emotion,
> As rage, or love. That was all.
> That was eons ago.
> Consider this thing," said the stream, in six languages. (*CC* 37)

That is, in place of "speech," "debate," "conversation," "eloquence," "proverb[s]," "fiction," and "legend[s]"—associated with the human—Barnard wanted to hear, respect, and give space to the land's "voice," to give up imposing some kind of story, scaffold, or containment around it, not too unlike Charles Olson's "Objectism"—a "getting rid of the lyrical interference of the individual as ego" (*OLS* 395). It was what she had wanted when she read Sappho, too; she wrote in "Static" of wanting to hear Sappho's "laughter / and the speech of her stringed shell" without the almost-electrical interference (to consider the poem's punning title) of the "whiskered mumble- / ment" of "grammarians." The commitment to an unframed, unvanquished environment, to her own brand of eco-poetics (although Barnard didn't use this term herself) never left her, as later poems like "Real Estate" and "The River Under Different Lights" make plain.

In her interactions with the land in her poetry, Barnard "retained cries expressive of emotion, / As rage, or love," for the northwestern landscape was almost always an emotionally charged arena, one that did not so much speak *for* her often lonely, lovelorn personae, but *with* them—prescient of what eco-critic William Rueckert was to say in a seminal essay of 1978, that "[e]verything is connected to everything else" (*RUE* 108). "The railroad depot stands deserted," Barnard wrote in "Crossroads," in a poem that neither names nor specifies any human presence. And yet the abandonment enacted in this spare railroad scene resurfaces in countless presentations of a Northwest that also suggest countless presentations of Barnard's own life such as that first daring move to New York, such as that in another poem that makes metaphor from a railroad scene:

> The slenderly poised clean shaft of your fir,
> Arrowy and yet still, might have stood in the station,
> Beside the Great Northern rails and the wilful water
> Of my life, flowing so contrarily eastward.

The conditionality of that fir, that it "*might* have stood in the station" (italics mine) to see off the eastbound traveler, is heartbreaking—we infer that, after all, it *didn't*. There's also the "abandoned wharf extended into wind" of "Logging Trestle;" this is heartbreak, too (*CC* 8). Here, then, are poems that reverberate with stories of lovers who forget and those (the "abandoned") who don't—or *can't*. Memory is a recurring theme, from the poem Pound singled out for praise in response to the very first letter she wrote him (" 'Lethe' the best because there is more IN it," *EP/MBEJB*, 29 October 1933; also *AMH* 53), to others making their first appearance in print here, such as "Against Lethe," "The Colored Stone," and "Bay Beach" where "the sea turns and moans / and will never forget."

Nevertheless, "the [. . .] water / Of my life, flowing so contrarily eastward," as Barnard settled in New York, was "wilful." Once she knew what she wanted for her poetry, she pursued it whether she be alone in that quest or not. Never mind that Imagism, as a movement, had long since finished—Barnard's orientation towards Imagism's prescriptions was sure and deployed with intelligence. Exactness of perception, as articulated in her youthful "Creed" (reprinted in this volume and as good a writer's manifesto as any), is always in abundance in Barnard's poems, be it at the level of language, or image, or both. So vital was this attentiveness to "direct presentation" in her work, for a while she contemplated a whole host of section titles for *Cool Country* to evoke this sense of seeing clearly, of seeing hard objects in plain light, as she told her parents: "Yesterday morning I worked more on titles + think I got somewhere. I made four groups [. . .] Title to 1st section—<u>Landscape in a Glass Vessel</u>. 2nd—<u>Reflected Hands</u> [. . .] 3rd—<u>The Chipped Edge</u>. 4th—<u>The Transparent Word</u>. I thought of using the last also for the book title, but it seems just a bit too pretentious or serious, or something" (*MB/Parents*, 31 August 1938, underlining Barnard's).

Barnard dropped the section titles and went with *Cool Country,* but not before she confessed to her parents the depth of her affinity to Pound: "The first choice seems to be a very old idea—<u>The Poet's Apprentice</u>" (*MB/Parents*, 31 August 1938, underlining Barnard's). Like Pound, Barnard developed a keen interest in the French troubadour poets early on. Her senior thesis (in creative writing) had begun life as "a play about Marie de France—a 12th century French poet at the court of Henry II of England" (*EA* 14), while other early poems filtered a troubadour consciousness through images of opulent objects and grand architecture, from the "white fur" and "the queen's emeralds" of "North Window" to "the purple lid of a box" of "A cloud comes down . . . ," through to the various medieval "towers" of "Lai," "Letter from the Country," "Sonnet for Dorothy," and "The Tears of Princesses," or even that of "Curly Locks" where a speaker is "walled [. . .] in with cushions," the wall "mortared with a sticky mortar / The troubadours I believe / Are held responsible for."

After leaving Buffalo, Barnard told her parents she had a "fifteen-year-plan" [*sic*], explaining:

I don't know exactly what it will turn into, but it is now a card-file (the librarian in me coming out) and into it go all kinds of jottings, anecdotes, characterizations, ideas for poems, quotations, ideas for plots (the short story I wrote went down first on a card) [. . .] I've written over sixty cards already. Some of the results, of course, will be fragmentary, and will emerge (like the short story) in the course of the fifteen years, but what I really have in mind is a longer work, prose or poetry, or a group of works on the same theme, or related, are going to emerge from the jumble, as the card file begins to fall into shape. (*MB/Parents,* 30 October 1944)

It was, in the end, much more than a fifteen-year plan; and the "shape" was a rich group of texts whose common themes and questions seemed almost effortlessly to concertina one out of the other with important cross-references, like a well-kept card file system. *A Few Poems* (1952) explored in just twelve poems topics that Barnard would expand on in later works—ancestry, biography, deaths, extinction, the processes of history and time. Those poems, which had first seen publication in the 1940s ("Beds," "Inheritance," and "Midnight" for instance), as well as newer poems such as "The Field" and "Dick" (later "Carillon" in *Collected Poems*), combined in *A Few Poems* to create a scheme of potent images, of "earlier darkness," of evenings spent wondering "what [. . .] will we remember?," of the "armour" of an inheritance that is "stronger than silver / Against time and men and women" where "the flesh of the field" is "lit by stars" (*AFP* No pag.).

Sappho: A New Translation came next, in 1958—fourteen years into the fifteen-year project—with Barnard sequencing the fragments into another time-oriented cycle, opening the book at dawn, closing it at night as death arrives. Soon she was cross-referencing to another "card" in her cardfile. "The poems of Sappho had raised questions in my mind concerning her religion" (*AMH* 294), Barnard realized, and she became hooked on exploring further:

> If, as it appeared, she was a priestess of Aphrodite, I felt I should explain something about her cult in the essay that ultimately became a Footnote to my translation [. . .] the poems themselves had given me certain ideas about the cult—its probable origin in Crete, the importance of the moon, the possible use of a drug in ceremonies—but everything I read contradicted my conclusions. I kept on reading, becoming more and more determined to correct the picture. I worked some of my ideas into my Footnote, but the Press asked me to remove that part of the essay, and I obliged. By that time I was deep in my maze. (*AMH* 294–95)

One turn of the maze led to *The Mythmakers*, the collection of essays that innovatively forged astronomy with anthropology. "One astronomer told me that *no* astronomer was interested in ancient astronomy. One anthropologist told me that we did not know and could not know the origin of any myth" (*AMH* 296; emphasis Barnard's). Another turn of the maze marshalled Barnard's research for *The Mythmakers* into *Time and the White Tigress*. A long poem just short of nine hundred lines concerned with time and its traditions, she told her publisher:

Historically and geographically the work has a wide sweep because all peoples in all ages have observed the same celestial phenomena with results that are often parallel. The moon, as the earliest Teller of Time for most of humankind, has a major role, but the scope of the poem extends beyond the solar and lunar movements to take in the wheeling Dipper and the dripping water-clock, the moving solstices and equinoxes, [suggesting] possible origins for some of the Zodiacal constellations. (*MB/BR*, 15 July 1986)

Time and the White Tigress dug backward in a search for the origins of time myths in a way that was conversant, say, with Olson's own mature work recovering lost origins (in his case, of pre-Western holism, as a salve against Eliot's pessimistic vision of a fragmented world). Barnard's salve was that she found the world is unified by the very existence of such myths, as told by the fifth fytte (or canto)—out of ten that comprise the work—that lies at the very core of the work:

> Time as a constant seeping away is at once
> indistinct and unbearable, a thin high sound
> never swelling or breaking, continuous to the world's end,
> stretching our nerves like a bowstring.
> > Ebb without flow.
>
> But time-counts marked by a stamp of the foot
> release the string to be drawn again.
> A rhythm established by moon after moon,
> tide after tide, and year after year
> has formed a framework for all our cultures,
> a pattern of custom that echoes the pattern
> woven by time in the heavens . . . (*TIME* 30)

That the rudimentary methods of early timekeeping (using the foot, stake, and string on leveled earth to record and measure shadows) parallel those of keeping time in poetry ("a stamp of the foot") is important: in *Time and the White Tigress* Barnard is offering us another "framework," her musical rhythms providing a salve against the "a thin high sound / never swelling or breaking" and creating a "pattern of custom" in the poem—in short, bringing order to chaos. Such impulse to make patterns reminds of what was said about Barnard's debut manuscript when she sent it to Arrow Editions fifty years prior—her poems were made out of "statements [. . .] freshly perceptive," she was told, which were "arranged in a particularly open, detached sequence: the effect of particles reflectively dropped to make a pattern" (*FC/MB*, 8 May 1936). Arrow's reader could have been talking about the constellations that are the focus of much of *Time and the White Tigress*; stunning star-patterns, each thoroughly unique and detectable to "sky-watchers" across thousands and thousands of years (*TIME* 1), are metaphors for free verse poetry itself.

Two years after *Time and the White Tigress*, in 1988, the "sweep" of Barnard's research poetics was narrowed from "all peoples" to Barnard's people ("my tribe") in *Nantucket Genesis: The Tale of My Tribe*—but not the form. Here, Barnard collaged long-form poetry with an array of source documents from early American history resonant with Susan Howe's enquiries into historical-personal New England pasts. In the "jumble," of course, Barnard finds "shape": "[t]he constriction of the metric disciplined my narrative" (*NG* 20). At "[f]ourteen miles in length" (*NG* 31), Nantucket perhaps conjured up parallels with the slender Long Beach Peninsula of Barnard's beloved Ocean Park, for it appears as "[a] few sand dunes surrounded by ocean" (*NG* 27) or, as the poem goes on to quote Melville's Ishmael, " 'a mere hillock and elbow of sand [. . .] without a background' " (*NG* 31). It's another space in which again to ask "shore ode" questions, here about the genesis of histories, kinships, families, and the idea of "the line" that is by turns personal as it is poetic. "What moving keel remembers / Such things as here buried under sand," Barnard had asked in "Shoreline" in 1935; fifty-three years later the metrically disciplined, sweeping long lines of *Nantucket Genesis: The Tale of My Tribe* provide such a keel. The "fifteen-year-plan," then, was more a fifty-year plan, one intent on stretching hundreds and thousands of years back in time across the globe. If Pound's *Cantos* were a "poem containing history" (*LE* 86), then Barnard's later oeuvre worked for the poem containing history *and* geography

Mary Barnard: The Translations

The "Pound connection" was preceded by what we might call Barnard's "Sappho connection." It began before Pound urged her to try Greek translation in 1933, before she took a Greek class at Reed, before she wrote an article on Sappho (deemed "so impassioned and rather intimate") for the Reed *Quest* (*MB/Parents*, 17 December 1930), even before Barnard signed off as "A Would-Be Sappho" in a letter to her mother (*MB/Parents*, 27 October 1930), for Sappho was there in one of the Would-Be Sappho's earliest poems, "Impassioned Sonnet," from around 1927. Composed in her teens, Barnard wrote of wanting "singing lines," closing the poem with a declaration that sounded as if sung from the heights of Sappho's Leucadian rock itself: "Let it be thus or let my voice / Sing ever these small tunes, unheard, unknown." Sappho's Aphrodite appears in as many of Barnard's earlier poems as she does in the fragments Barnard eventually translated, either directly ("Anadyomene," "Departure," "Love Poem") or allusively through the color associations of purple and gold ("A cloud comes down . . . ," "Fire, snow, and the night . . .") or through the images of the sea foam from which Aphrodite was said to have risen from the sea ("Blanchefleur," "Departure," and "The Fool's Serenade" to name but a few).

By the time Barnard was translating Sappho in the early 1950s, she was, like other "second-wave modernists [. . .] born between 1889 and 1909" to quote Charles Bernstein (*BER* 348), refining her response to Poundian-Williams modernism even further. If another of Pound's New York-based protégés, Louis Zukofsky, was pursuing a poetics where writing is an activity "of seeing, of thinking with the things as they exist, and of directing them along a line of melody" (*ZUK* 20) with reference to the structure of the baroque fugue in his long poem "*A*," Barnard's Sappho connection was tending similar ground. "Rudiments music???" Pound had barked in that first postcard to her in 1933 (*EP/MBEJB*, 29 October 1933; also *AMH* 53). "So far as music was concerned, I was hopeless. I couldn't carry a tune," she confessed in the early days of their correspondence; "I did not know then that both he and Yeats had the same difficulty" (*AMH* 53–54). But music, Pound said, was essential to Barnard's attempt to translate Sapphics; and he insisted she read the chapter on Greek metric in the *Encyclopedie de la Musique* edited by Albert Lavignac and Lionel de la Laurencie. As with Zukofsky—and Pound before him—the fugue held a particular power:

> I don't think I ever told you that I got a book of Bach preludes and fugues for beginners, and found I could play better than I thought, which is saying very little. I can't tell whether they have improved my sense of rhythm. In any case, I have received a great deal of pleasure from working at them. I need another one of those superlatives here. It is not only that I enjoy playing them myself, but that I enjoy listening to Bach music so much more than I ever could have, otherwise. (*MB/EP*, 20 April 1935)

Pound replied in the May: "O/K/ keep at it till you get *your* basic [. . .] so into yr/ head that you have no more difficulty about picking up quantitative dactyl, trochee or spondee, than J. S./B wd/ in knowing intervals of 3d, 4th and 5th and what they wd/ sound like before hand, not merely as intervals, but as intervals in transit" (Pound in *AMH* 80; emphasis Pound's).

Barnard's prosody, her "basic"—comprising what she called "the weighted syllable" and the "balanced line" derived from her work with the variable duration of English-language syllables akin to the duration of the musical note—is extensively explored in an essay reprinted here, "A Communication on Greek Metric, Ezra Pound, and *Sappho*" (*ACOG*), as well as in chapter 4 of *SB/MBAI*. Of pertinence here is how Barnard's Pound-driven work with music, combined with her knowledge of Italian, opened a door into a means of translating Sappho into American idiom. Paige's gift of Quasimodo's *Lirici Greci* gave her the freedom "to balance between the Greek phrase and the Italian phrase while I searched for the truly equivalent phrase in living, not lexicon English" (*EPS* 142). In this search she found her method, as she explains in "Ezra Pound, Sappho and My Assault on Mount Helicon" (*EPS*) reprinted in section III: "I found here in Sappho's Greek, as revealed to me through the medium of the Italian, the style I had been groping toward [. . .] It was spare but musical and had, besides, the sound of the speaking voice making a simple but emotionally loaded statement. It is never 'tinkling' as Bill Williams's friend A. P. characterized it. Neither is it 'strident' as Rexroth described it: it is resonant although unmistakeably in the female register"(*EPS* 142).

This late modernist (to use a term from *MIL*), late Imagist aesthetic of the "spare but musical" was itself a crisp compression of the pivotal three Imagist principles ("Direct treatment [. . .] to compose in the sequence of the musical phrase") (*FSF* 199) that have maintained influence over successive generations of poets working in free verse and open form. Emerging at the same time as the poetics of Olson (to whom Pound directed Barnard in 1946), Robert Creeley, and Robert Duncan, Barnard's speech-based translation poetics held some influence within their circles. The work was to inspire Cid Corman, another Olson associate, to produce his own chapbook *Sappho: Wee Ones* (*COR*) and his *Origin* magazine to publish Barnard alongside other seminal mid-century American avant-garde poets.

Barnard's interest in the Greek classical poets was not limited to Sappho; Homer was important too, first in mind then later in practice when Barnard translated (but did not publish) Books I–V of *The Iliad* (Book I is reprinted here.) Like Sappho, the project was, as Barnard told Anita Helle at the time of composition, "a metric adaptation [. . .] into modern English" (*ENC* 6). Like Sappho, Homer had become somehow entwined in the "voice" of Ocean Park. Writing in a letter during one of her summer stays there with Reed friends, Barnard told her parents:

The wind drove a fog in across the ocean suddenly a few minutes
ago, so Millie [Mildred Cline] + I scampered in. We have found a
nice sheltered dune where nobody ever comes. Mildred toasts and
reads <u>Ulysses</u>, + I pull up socks [. . .] retire under my hat brim, +
do Greek sporadically [. . .] I think when I'm alone I'll start mem-
orizing Homer. Can't you imagine me intoning hexameters with the
accompaniment of sea water + a boiling tea-kettle? ([*sic*]; *MB/Parents*,
no date; Barnard marks the letter as written "Saturday" and appears
to have added "Aug? 1935" as if having dated it in retrospect)

And so she did chant Homer into the sea, recalling in her memoir that "I
liked best roaming the beach and the dunes by myself [. . .] reciting poems
that seemed appropriate to the place [. . .] after I learned Greek it was Homer
shouted into the noisy breakers" (*AMH* 19). Just as these breakers became
entwined with reimaginings of Sappho's Aphrodite emerging from the foam in
Barnard's poetry, so too did they recall Thetis, goddess of water and mother of
the hero of *The Iliad*, Achilles, evoked in poems like "Anadyomene," "The Fool's
Serenade," "The Pathetic Fallacy" and the group of four fragments beginning
"In the bridal . . ."

As with Sappho, it was, of course, Pound who provided the necessary
nudge for Barnard to go forward in actually translating Homer. In his letter
to her of 18 February 1938, at a time when Barnard was feeling particularly
deflated and listless with regards to her own writing, Pound wrote:

There is Catullus' "Collis O Heliconii"
still untranslated / well over a century since any female
tackled Homer / and Rouse has made bread and butter of it ([*sic*];
    Pound in *AMH* 117)

"Rouse" was the classical scholar W. H. D. Rouse, whom Pound encouraged
her to contact when she was first attempting Sapphics, as Barnard discusses in
"A Communication on Greek Metric, Ezra Pound, and *Sappho*." Importantly,
Pound cautioned in the same letter:

As to the AUTHOR; you will want a SUBJECT by the time
you are 40 / may as well pick it NOW so that you will then
know something about it.
No real work been done on Chinese sound sequence /
If that is too difficult / there is always the Odyssey and the
Catullus longer impossibles. ([*sic*]; Pound in *AMH* 117)

That it would take Barnard some decades to buckle down to her Homer project had something to do with the kind of development, in retrospect, she felt she needed. Just as she had said of Sappho (that her poems "are not the work of a young woman [. . .] I could not have translated her poems 20 years earlier," cited in *DG* 171), so the same was probably true of Homer: "I'm not a scholar and never gave any promise of being one. I can struggle along with Greek for my own pleasure and edification, but I can't imagine translating Homer," Barnard told Pound in a letter of 7 March 1938 (*MB/EP*). Pound snapped back:

> Also you needn't set out translate the WHOLE of the Iliad /
> but you CAN work on the juicier bits / Iliad for exercise and the
> Odyssy as an aim. no lady has since Mme Dacier and yrs / wd.
> be different.
>
> OR Catullus . . . at any rate METRE" ([*sic*]; *EP/MB*,
> 21 March 1938; see also *AMH* 118, which corrects the spelling
> of "Odyssy")

Having spent time with Homer translator Robert Fitzgerald while on a visit to Mary de Rachewiltz at Brunnenburg in 1954 where they "[read] each other's manuscripts: his *Odyssey*, Book 1, and my Sappho translation" (*AMH* 99), Barnard was beginning to change her mind. In 1966 she published the short poem "Odysseus Speaking" (with the accompanying note "from the *Odyssey*, opening of Book IX"), but was still working on the "Iliad for exercise" into the 1970s. In a letter to Olga Rudge a few months before Pound's death Barnard wrote about how cut off she felt, how she was caring for her mother who "is very frail, but still on her feet, and able to go out occasionally." "When I have time," she confided, "I'm translating Homer" (*MB/OR*, 12 June 1972). Perhaps Pound was right after all: "the Odyssy [was] an aim"—one she simply ended up having no time for, in translation, but whose story nevertheless haunted her from as early as her debut collection in poems like "Cassandra," "Storm," and "Wine Ship."

❧

It was fitting, then, that the selection made of Barnard's poems for the Library of America's fine two-volume anthology, *American Poetry: The Twentieth Century* (*AP V2*), published in the last year of Barnard's life, showcased poems that spanned the range of Barnard's interests—the land ("The Field") and self in the natural world ("The Solitary," "Probably Nobody"), the American shore ("Shoreline"), northwestern industry ("Logging Trestle"), myth ("Lethe"), archaeastronomy ("The Pleaides"), and translation ("Static"). And it was equally fitting that Bernstein identified that anthology as "[p]erhaps the best representation" of the "epic collage [. . .] of innovative and traditional poetry" he sees as fundamental, retrospectively, to both first- and second-wave modernist poetry (*BER* 346). Barnard broke new ground for sure, but she had no interest in what she called "modernist pyrotechnics" despite any common lines of influence (*AMH* 112)—Zukofsky's work, she told Pound, "leaves me speechless. Nothing in the western wildernesses aids me to a comprehension of his poems" (*MB/EP*, 1 April 1934). As Williams said in a letter encouraging Zukofsky to look up "a certain Mary Barnard, one of Ezra's string of ponies (he seems to like 'em long) now in New York from Portland, Oregon," her work possessed a "more or less conventional surface," but was no less integral to the cause; "[w]e've got to make her welcome" (*WCW/ZUK* 232).

And as Bernstein says, citing himself in an earlier interview about the anthology, "perhaps even more intriguing is how the players with the small parts now look so indispensable" (*BER* 347). Certainly Barnard has been viewed, in the past, by some as having a bit part in modernism—Valerie Trueblood's review of her *Collected Poems* said her "uncategorizable" work was "something people will [. . .] not *want* the way they want a Black Mountain poet or a copy of Laforgue. Writers of this kind are lightly noticed, especially when their output is small or irregular, even when they number Pound and Williams among their admirers" (Trueblood cited in *MOHE* 67; italics Trueblood's). *Complete Poems and Selected Translations* emphatically overturns this view, assembling, for the first time, a full and as complete a collection of Mary Barnard's entire oeuvre as it's possible to make. It's a collection that illustrates why Pound, Williams, Moore, and others so rated her—"[i]t is all there; the new is all there," Williams pronounced, upon publication of her *A Few Poems*, recognizing her work (and particularly her American metrics) as emblematic of "what we have been about all these years" (*WCW/MB*, 31 December 1952). Barnard's "basic" of the "weighted syllable" and "balanced line" was crucial not just to her *Sappho: A New Translation* or to her own free verse, but to the (long) modernist period itself as Bernstein frames it, a period that saw "reaccenting of English, but not by the English. Indeed, one of the primary sites of poetic invention in this period involved novel ways of [. . .] representing, or refusing, accentuated speech" (*BER* 348).

Also included is previously uncollected work from a range of periodicals, largely modernist in their leanings, but not always. Another important inclusion is a selection from Barnard's unpublished poems, some of which she shared privately with Pound, Williams, and Moore and all of which critically complement her published output, as the notes explore. Where copyright restrictions mean that this volume can only present selections from Barnard's critically acclaimed *Sappho: A New Translation*, the interested reader will hopefully be rewarded by the addition of Barnard's numerous poems written after Sappho's example in both Sapphics and free verse, many drawn directly from Barnard's archives. With such archives now fully available at Yale University's Beinecke Library, it's clear that Barnard's work as a translator was not confined to Sappho, as inclusions here from her translations of Homer and Sophocles testify. The volume is supplemented by a small number of related critical writings Barnard wrote concerning her poetry and metrics. Likely to be of interest to her own readers and, more broadly, scholars of the American free verse movement, Barnard's "Creed" and "A Note on Poetry" may also be of particular interest to those working in creative writing.

In a letter of 2 July 1978 to her editor James Anderson, Barnard confided "I wanted to call my Sappho translation 'They Say She Said,' but [the University of] California would have none of it" (*MB/JA*). *Complete Poems and Selected Translations* is informed by my thirty or so years spent with Barnard's poems—the fullest account yet of what "She—Barnard—Said." And, if future scholars tell it another way, then to quote Barnard's own words from *Time and the White Tigress*, "[w]hy / should we cease to make myths?" (*TIME* 5).

—Sarah Barnsley, Goldsmiths,
University of London, May 2024

Notes on the Text of This Edition

This edition strives to offer an overview of Mary Barnard's published work in chronological order, supplemented by a selection of previously unpublished poems deserving of wider attention and/or that lend insight and augment the published work in some way—often both, such as Barnard's many poems modeled after Sappho. In the case of uncollected work, the dates of first publication have been taken as the relevant chronological marker. In the case of previously unpublished work, every attempt has been made to establish the final date of the manuscript from which the poem is taken. In some cases, Barnard assisted with this process through dating the manuscript herself. In others, educated guesses have been made based on the evidence available. The rationale for each of these decisions has been explained in the relevant note to each poem.

In the spirit of showing chronological development and fully placing this work within the wider trajectory of twentieth-century American poetry,[1] Barnard's poems from her two collections, *Cool Country* and *A Few Poems*, appear as they were published in those collections, rather than as they first appeared (where relevant) in journals and magazines or as they later appeared in *Collected Poems*—although the notes detail variants in wording, punctuation, formatting, and so on for the interested reader. A key change is that by *Collected Poems* Barnard had switched from starting her run-on lines in upper case to lower case.

---

1. Some useful critical resources exploring this trajectory include Charles Altieri, *The Art of Twentieth-Century American Poetry: Modernism and After* (Oxford: Blackwell, 2006); Jennifer Ashton, ed., *The Cambridge Companion to American Poetry since 1945* (Cambridge University Press, 2015); and Alex Baker and Lee M Jenkins, eds., *A History of Modernist Poetry* (Cambridge University Press, 2015).

Details of subsequent printings of published poems have generally been collated from 1994's "Bibliographic Record of Periodical and Book Production" (*BIB*); the editor has made every effort to establish any post-1994 subsequent printings and include them here, but would be happy to include any omissions brought to her attention in any future edition.

A number of Barnard's previously unpublished poems appear in manuscripts without titles—these poems are thus presented by their first lines, in quotation marks, followed by ellipses. The same format is adopted in the table of contents for the fragments from *Sappho: A New Translation*. It is important to differentiate, from this, the poem entitled ". . . Without whose untender criticism this book . . ." In this unique instance, it is presented exactly as Barnard presented it herself in manuscript form, in quotation marks and bracketed by the pair of ellipses to signal that the title of the poem is itself a quotation.

One poem, "The Pleiades," is presented both as a stand-alone poem in section III, but also as it was subsequently incorporated into *Time and the White Tigress* as part of the third fytte. This dual inclusion is because the stand-alone poem has drawn wide attention in its own right, as noted by Mary de Rachewiltz in her foreword, but also to assist the interested reader curious about what the poem brings to *Time and the White Tigress*. Some material is excerpted from a larger work owing either to copyright restrictions (*S*) or volume (*TI* and *NG*); in the case of a hybrid work like *Nantucket Genesis: The Tale of My Tribe*, the rationale for selection is given in the notes.

I.

POEMS

COOL COUNTRY (1940)

Editor's note: Twenty-nine of these thirty-one poems were collected into Collected Poems *except for "Chanson Pathetique" and "Hot Broth."*

The Rapids

No country is so gracious to us
As that which kept its contours while we forgot them,
And whose valleys, closed under receding hills,
Open to our return.

The water we saw broken upon the rapids
Has dragged silt through marshland
And mingled with the embittered streams of the sea.
One might have kept sweet pailsful and kept nothing.

But the ungatherable blossoms floating by the same rock,
The chisel marks on a surface in full flight
Have flung light in my face, have made promises
In unceasing undertone.

Logging Trestle

Neither cloud nor rain casts
A chill into the valley
Like that of a trestle fallen into disuse.

The rails move out from the hillside,
Across the piling lengthening its stroke
Where ground slopes riverward.

Abruptly, the rails terminate.
Sky opens between the cross-ties lifted
Each upon five upright timbers. The gray wood

Leads the eye to nothing further.
The broken column stands against cloud
As though an abandoned wharf extended into wind.

Highway Bridge

When a hill stream enters a river at flood
It is abashed into stillness, welling
Between grass blades and small clover.
Its surface becomes the green of leaves obstructing light,
Tranquil between piers.

Although the bridge has a purpose other
Than the quiet under it, a peace
Exploded by the rapid wheels overhead,
After their passage this that we thought shattered
Absorbs the falling fragments of sound.
There is a deeper silence than before
Where two ruts dip under the river's border
And do not reappear.

Cool Country

This green is the pod,
The enveloping color of our triangular valleys
Where rivers still young spring
From the coast range into salt estuaries.

Mist blown between promontories
Saturates the earth's every crevice,
Making the grass deep and sweet in all seasons
And the forest heavy.

From these come the red cheeses,
The apricot-colored lumber, deckloads
Moving into the green like lanterns.
The pod is broken vermilion steaks of the salmon,
The chill wave itself opened
For the red-ripeness of harvest.

Shoreline

The sea has made a wall for its defence
Of falling water. Those whose impertinence
Leads them to its moving ledges
It rejects. Those who surrender
It will with the next wave drag under.

Sand is the beginning and the end
Of our dominion.

The way to the dunes is easy.
The shelving sand is stiffened in the rain
And loosened again in the sun's fingers.
Children, lustful of the glistening hours,
Drink and are insatiate. Wind under the eyelids,
Confusion walling the ears, their bodies glow
In the cold wash of the beach.

                And after,
They walk with rigid feet the planked street of the town.
They miss the slipping texture of the sand
And a sand pillow under the hollow instep.
They are unmoved by fears
That breed in darkening kitchens at sundown
Following storm, and they rebel
Against cold waiting in the wind and rain
For the late sail.

              Did you, as I,
Condemn the coastal fog and long for islands
Seen from a sail's shadow?
                  The dunes lie
More passive to the wind than water is.
This, then, the country of our choice.
It is infertile, narrow, prone
Under a dome of choral sound:
Water breaking upon water.

Litter of bare logs in the drift—
The sea has had its sharp word with them.
Wild roses, wild strawberries cover the dune shoulder.
It is a naked restless garden that descends
From the crouched pine
To shellfish caught in the reflecting sands.

We lose the childish avarice of horizons. The sea ends
Against another shore. The cracked ribs of a wreck
Project from the washed beach.
Under the shell-encrusted timbers
Dripping brine

Plucks at the silence of slant chambers
Opening seaward. What moving keel remembers
Such things as here are buried under sand?
The transitory ponds and smooth bar slice
Easily under the advancing tide
Emerging with the moon's
Turning.
          Clear lagoons
Behind the shattered hulk, thin
Movements of sea grass on the dune rim
Bending against cloud, these things are ours.
Submissive to the sea and wind,
Resistful of all else, sand
Is the beginning and the end
Of our dominion.

Provincial

Mossy stones, the quilted legends
Warming the villages like a sprigged comforter,
The dead like a smoke webbing the trees,
And all inviting dreaming:

These must be pleasant, but I never knew them,
Have no acquaintance with bronze monuments,
Have never spoken with a ghost on a bridge.
Our concrete piers are white and new in the water.

The dead are sparsely sown as yet.
The rain clouds rising above stumpland
Form no apparitions. Thin wheat by the fir roots,
Two potted geraniums on a stump
By the plank road receive the shower.

More beautiful than flowering moss
The naked rock rises,
Chipped columnar by the liquid
Blades of bright water.

Roots

Rain on the windshield,
Roads spongy with sawdust
Have meant in the end
A love of place that grows into the body.
Blood should be clear amber under tree bark.

Lacking that, there are the roads
Extending like root tendrils
Under the angles of mountains,
Rain sharpening on the windshield at evening.

Planks

Footsteps upon fine gravel drop into silence
Like pebbles into water at close intervals.
Circles of air break on the dark mountains.

Strange how hard it is to balance
In the pit of the evening, distances
Spreading upward, making the head light.
But walking feet have their own pleasure,
Touching rhythmically the hard earth.

Dry planks lying under the bank attract them.
The moment is completed neither
By fragrance of wild lilac, nor by
The presence of the darkening river,
But by the feel of wood underfoot
And the sound of stepping upon thick planks.

Prometheus Loved Us

I walk in a twilight half-drawn
Along the edge of the town,
Walk with rain on my coatsleeves,
Drops clinging upon the prongs of the wool.
Should I record anything?

Runnel of rain at the curb will
Drop down to the river. Vacant lots
Spill grass on the sidewalk
And I walk nowhere in particular.
Nothing.

Except that the merest match-wing
Of fire pricks through the rain
And the street is stung to life.
Heart leaps, like a fish striking.

Blood Ritual

Pestilence, violence, distress attendant
On the sharpening seasons
Are part of us and our incessant commotion.
The tree stems offer no remonstrance.
Does she who stood between them
Wait underground for peace again
As though the lilac should not bloom while hunger lasted?
Or is our passion acceptable as rain?

The pulp that swells the green skin of the grape
Is hard in its unripeness, indicating
A time before the violet eyes trembled
And the flesh knew his hunter.
The frozen mountain, falling as the road falls
Behind the scarlet leaf-burn of this season
Refers to it and to the curtains of quiet.
She will have a loveless peace then.

Adoring her in all her manifestations,
I think how Apollo without his sacrifice
Has lost his godhead. The flower will not sing on its stem,
Nor the fruit utter a cry as it falls.
Why should not the flesh of the innocent
While it endures, smoke on her altars?

The Axe

The axe lies in shadow at the house-root,
Hoarding its sharpness, menacing
As a nervous fang. Pause to search it out
While the eyes drink in darkness, then step
Carefully away from it into chips
By the frayed block, remembering:

How when the old lady drew off her gloves I saw,
In spite of myself, the three finger-stumps,
The sight cloaking me with a sickness.

Sheer off, back of the chimney. Creep
Over the wheelbarrow; keep clear of it.
If ever I have not enough kindling,
And the fire dies, I shall
Have to go cold.

But the woodcutter praises God for his fine days
In heavily-barked ricks by the wood-road.
The two tracks bright with chips
Meander through fern. His axe is the laughter
Made where hill warps against hill.
The swing of the axe-head in its arc
Has threaded his shoulders.
Ha! and the sound is tossed back, hill
To hill. Steel strikes a deep wound—
Ha! and the bearded lips of the hills
Are cracked with laughter—O, it's the merry axe-blade.

Carry, you with the weak wrists, your ten
Long cold fingers tucked in a shawl
Up basement stairs. Hark! It's the merry axe-blade!

Playroom

Wheel of sorrow, centerless.
Voices, sad without cause,
Slope upward, expiring on grave summits.
Mournfulness of muddy playgrounds,
Raw smell of rubbers and wrapped lunches
When little girls stand in a circle singing
Of windows and of lovers.

Hearing them, no one could tell
Why they sing sadly, but there is in their voices
The pathos of all handed-down garments
Hanging loosely on small bodies.

Storm

A vessel is breaking in half under the headland.
The ocean is swollen with storm and the lives
Of the drowned men. Foam drawn over them.

Above my left eye a pain burrows.
Conspirator, awaiting dangerous weather,
If I were there, you would be suffocation,
Pain and the ocean obliterating each other.

The radio brings Bach from Philadelphia.
Closer within than sickness and outside death,
The well-plumed music drives beyond the lighthouses
Toward the extreme coastland—
  ἀκτὰν πρὸς ἑσπέρου θεοῦ
         On our beaches
Dead sea birds under yellow curds of foam.

Cassandra

Write of her if you will, but never try
To speak as though in her person, "I, Cassandra—"
Speak of her as the least of the Trojan
Women might have spoken
After they learned that captives do not die,
But suffer inconveniences of exile.

If we knew how the world looked, turning
Into the shadow, if any woman stood
As she did by Apollo's shoulder
And caught the smell of burning
Even before night closed upon the towers—
She would have little care for what was said
In a city seven times buried.
Her mind would be a cauldron. She would have
No thought for the dead.

Winter Evening

In the mountains, it is said,
The deer are dying by hundreds.
We know nothing of that
In the suburbs.

           The cougar,
And death by being devoured,
The snow starving and shrouding
With one economical gesture
Are ancestral myth. Our century
clings to the novel.
Coffee and novels.

With all the town's usual
Stirrings muffled in snow,
The train whistles, only,
Howl against death
Over the plump white hills,
The billowing roofs—
Howl like Lear in his heartbreak,
Savage as a new myth.

Wine Ship

A mast askew in the surf.
Wood of another climate
Bedded forever in half-liquid sand.

The sharp-eared foreigner
Struggling out of the sea wrack
Felt his flesh wither in the cold winds of this coast.

Here were no myrtle groves,
No familiar shrines,
Only the splintered casks and the sweet wines
Spilt in the sea.

Here were no grapes,
But bitter berries grew in the marsh.

Here was no moss,
But sea worn logs and the harsh
Grass on the dune top.

In this forlorn meeting of sea and land
Mirth is lost over the stormy water
And the sand
Lies suddenly cold under the hand.

From this shore an exile learns
To keep where a fire burns,
But there is no disguise
In small hand or white throat
When still by night a disturbing rhythm returns
From groves forgotten.

When the long eyelids are lifted
Suddenly, outlandish lights appear
In the woman's eyes: we think we hear
The tap of hidden hooves
Somewhere in our closed corridors.

Lethe
Above the brink
Of that lamentable river I shall lean,
Hesitant, unwilling to drink,
As I remember there for the last time.

Will a few drops on the tongue,
Like a whirling flood submerge cities,
Like a sea, grind pillars to sand?
Will it wash the color from the lips and the eyes
Beloved? It were a thousand pities
Thus to dissolve
The delicate sculpture of a lifted hand,
To fade the dye
Of the world's color, to quench forever
The fires of earth in this river.

The living will forget
More quickly than I,
Dead, lingering with lips unwet
Above Lethe.

Chanson Pathetique

My mouth draws the candleflame
Straight and high with a cold breath.
But once utter my name.
Save me from this death.

Think that my hand stirs the smoke
Moving in no wind;
Then is the blade broken,
By so much is the poison thinned.

As I am by you forgotten—
And forget me you must—
By so much is my tongue rotten,
By so much is my hair dust.

My heart's under your staircase
In a tea canister.
Pray step lightly on that place
Or slide down the bannister.

Lai

Nothing availed then in the starless darkness with the sea giving
    a gray light.
Nothing availed then either by sea or by land
For the boats were filled with a shallow and unlit water, their sails riven.
But her hands spread upon the bolt of the door refused to believe
And the waves spoke for her since she had no voice.

I said, striving with her, "He is long since dead.
I have seen the queens who ride fast along dark roads
Bearing death upon their lips and love upon the palms of their hands.
I know they now have left the mired ways and channelled meadows.
Where blue roads echo under the stripped high-singing trees,
    tower-ward they bear him.
In the yellow tideland shallow water laps unheard."

But she shook her head and the waves spoke for her as they do still,
Sighing a furtive song in the spread foam
While the troubled stones of the beach turn in my heart.

Adversity and the Generations

Mules and mulish children,
The obstinacy of boulders
Embedded in arable soil,
The extreme tenaciousness
Of roots in the wrong places
And intractable weather
Were, we suppose, the scourges
Of Cain also, toiling before
Eden's east threshold.

But we were not content.
Full of ambition, with capacity
For increased exasperation,
We devise a pancake machine.
The pancake batter, as always,
Creating a delicate situation,
The electrically animated parts
Miscalculate exactly.

Thistles and thorns were nothing
To this dogged inaccurate motion
Producing lunch-counter chaos.
Cain was bitter, but his seed
Suffer hysteria.

Drama

There are those who watch the papers for her name:
She passed here, was seen on the beach.
They think that Drama is, herself, an actress,
Not the ever-present third in all rooms that hold two,
Not the drowsy guest that every hostess finds
Making a fifth at bridge, her head inert
Upon the table edge, her hair
Tangled among the cards. At dinner time the drone
Of conversation is a lullaby
And smoke an opium cloud about her head.
But if a clumsy sleeve should brush her dress
So that she stirs,
Silence bursts in the ears before the drone resumes,
Oh sleep, sleep. We're all dead. Sleep, dear.
In the candlelight we watch her palpitant lids
And prowl about her on tiptoes,
Fingers to lips. Oh, hush, hush.

To a Lie-Adept

In a shadowed corner
She rolled another's sorrow
Under her tongue like a sweet caramel.
Truth became obscene in her mouth.

From one like her I learn finally
To come back to you in all humbleness,
Knowing the shameful uses of truth,
Desiring to be taught the craft of liars
And how to prepare, as you do, fiction suitable
For a disordered appetite.

Nor shall I dispense
Occasional cinnamon drops.
Rather, I will lie as you do,
Urging whole succulent messes, whole platterfuls,
Upon the gluttonous guest.

Provincial II

The European made his appearance
Wearing velvet and the jewels
Of his inheritance
Gravely, without unbecoming pride.

He courteously made it plain to her
The silk she wore was paper.
Dismayed, caught in the shower
Of his disapproval, she bragged
In buckskin, which (he remarked)
Was outdated fully one hundred years.
At last, cowering in a few rags
Of homespun, she dried her tears with grass
And consoled herself with the large
Plums of the provinces.

The Tears of Princesses

The tears of princesses were cool as rain.
They wept purely into their unbound hair.
Tears were ornaments to be hung
At the pale eyelid like jewels
At the coral lobe of the ear.

Princesses had long beautiful names
And they always cried with perfect reasonableness
For lasting sorrow or bloody-hilted
Abhorrent wickedness
Presented at the unguarded breast.

Princesses melted, sugar-and-dew, in privacy,
In dungeons, towers, or lying on forest moss;
But never, never were their eyes scalded with hot salt,
Their chins dripping, their mouths swollen
Just anywhere, for nothing, for no reason
But having too many tears.

In Praise of Potted Plants

With the wet snow that falls
Before the beginning of spring,
The dark flowers put forth buds
In hearts which expect nothing.

Bring only flowers
Into the invalid's chamber.
Let no squirrel intrude
And although a marmot
Raise unanswerable questions
He does so without dignity.
He nibbles (God help him!)
At his tragedy.

Bring humorless flowers
To complement those we imagine
Dark in the heart. Surround us
With the grave perfume of plants.

Hot Broth

A smell of hot broth hung in the air
Over the chill clashing streams,
Among the wet twigs of the trees.
"Flesh is warm and rock is cold," said the aroma.

But the rock showed bubble shapes.
The cold volcano was at such peace,
Its flank icy, fading in still
Skyline older than the supper-smell:

I should stomp and yell around the kettle?
I should brag to snow-filled, gassy craters?
O my little coal, be modest, lest
There be laughter of avalanches!

The Orchard Spring

Not in the forest with its air of childhood—
The secret fern, the tree tops
Run through with wind—
But in an orchard planted and grown
In the traditions of men,
I heard for the first time
An ancient sequence of words, a rhyme
That like the fragrance of warm grass
Tempted an illusive appetite
But seemed meaningless.

A doorsill was buried in the dew
Of a steep orchard: from what quarter
Did the difference come
To unsettle that room?
A twelfth-century nightingale
Half-heard, still, in the western coast range
Of the continent, troubles
The dreams of little green children.
Doves, gold rings, words

Out of the English island.
Fresh delight of rain on our hillsides
And the earth answering with springs.

Fable from the Cayoosh Country

As we lay at the lake edge, feet pointing northwest,
Our thought pushed forward into the margins of silence.
There would be a crying of creeks, birds,
And animal young, but verbal silence.
A region crowded with nameless mountains.

Thorn branches sheltered the beach,
Graying the arrested twilight.
Indians passed at our feet,
Averted profiles moving against the clear lake,
Against the boundaries of an inarticulate world.

We slept, and our minds crawled with words.
Footloose words ran about in our dreams.

I went, a missionary, into the mountains,
Taking the grammars of all languages.
I preached the blessing of the noun and verb,
But all was lost in the furred ear of the bear,
In the expressive ear of the young doe.
What the doe said with her ear, I understood.
What I said, she obviously did not.

Despairing, I flung my textbooks into a rocky pool,
And the stream turned through the volumes, speaking clearly.
"Where my monologue runs, there was once the debate of the beasts.
The burrows bubbled with words, conversation
Issued from the mouths of caves.
Where there was speech there is now only my voice.

"Had the mountain goat need of his eloquence
To make of his native rocks a rostrum?
Did the beaver's young learn industrious ways of a proverb?
The humming bird was a fiction. What legend could please her?

"The blade of this tool, useless for digging, chopping,
Shearing, they used against each other with such zeal

They all but accomplished their own extermination.
Then—they abandoned speech!
They retained cries expressive of emotion,
As rage, or love. That was all.
That was eons ago.
Consider this thing," said the stream, in six languages.
"They have never seen any cause to repent their decision."

I dreamed then, of a tide in the lake.
It rose over us where we slept
And flooded southward into the settled country.
My consternation was that of a poet, whose love
If not his living was gravely endangered.

I awoke, and the lake was in place.
Perhaps that was a pity. A purification . . . ?
Perhaps if one rose now and bathed in the water?

Remarks on Poetry and the Physical World

After reading *Ash Wednesday*
She looked once at the baked beans
And fled. Luncheonless, poor girl,
She observed a kind of poetic Lent—
And I had thought I liked poetry
Better than she did.

I do. But to me its most endearing
Quality is its unsuitableness;
And, conversely, the chief wonder in heaven
(Whither I also am sometimes transported)
Is the kind of baggage I bring with me.

Surely there is no more exquisite jointure
In the anatomy of life than that at which
Poetry dovetails with the inevitable meal
And Mrs. B. sits murmuring of avocados.

Suggested Miracle

The fishing boats lie on the spring flood,
One motor awakening over the water, and soon quieted.
Fishing looks an idle occupation,
Idle as mine: gillnetting
At the confluence of two rivers
For fish of two colors.

My townspeople, my acquaintance, may I
Lower you under this river
Nose to nose with the salmon?
The silver and red fish of my catch
Do not tempt you. Salmon would be a preferable food
If interviewed before eaten.

Note to a Neapolitan

On shipboard or in Naples
Miranda still walked on her island.
The palace floors ebbed from her private beaches.
Thought, that could not swim,
Found no footing but on memory.

There is a green place in my mind
That paces my mind's conceptions.
The farthest-ranging of them
Run with that colored shadow
Under their sandals.
It gives them a foreign look
In brown places and gray places.

And Miranda emptied her shoes
Of little pools of sand.

A FEW POEMS (1952)

Beds

Sleep, to the chirruping incantations of night, rises
Like vapor in lowland pastures, clouding the eyes of children.
Lulla, lulla, will there be, will there
Always be a place to sleep when smoke gathers under the rafters?

The carved oak headboards of ancestral beds tilt
Like foundered decks from fog at the mouth of the river.
Lulla, lulla. Flood after flood. When the beds float
Downstream, will there be a place to sleep, Matthew, Mark?

Will new beds be sold in those aisles where soft-eyed brides
Are shopping with gift money for the bed of Odysseus?
Instead of the rooted olive: sham walnut, a bed in the wall,
A mattress on the shed floor. Will there be this?

The damp webs, answering, tangled against my face at nightfall
In the pink festival of fireweed and on pumice beaches.
The feathers of my grandmothers' beds melted into earlier darkness
As, bone to earth, I lay down. A trail that leads out, leads back.
Leads back, anyway, one night or another, bone to earth.
Bat wings traced the water and sleep was pure.

The Fitting

She is imprisoned among mirrors
While a trio of hags with the cold hands
Of elderly dressmakers entangle,
Bind and define her body with tape-measures.
They compress withered lips upon pins.

Again and again she will re-enact
This fitting. Censure will be a knuckle
Shocking the flushed skin; all women
These women, their muttered words
Breathing distortion upon the mirror's reflection.

The knocking of hammers comes
From beyond the still window curtain
But her hands will make nothing:
Her life is confined here, in this depth,
In the well of the mirrors, on the carpet
The pulled threads, at her heel the scissors
Making a soft snipping sound.

Dick

In the morning, early, sitting
Eating our loaves on weedgrown milestones
At the edge of the city, we hear the bells
Swinging, challenging the attentive air.

The four-leaved pattern of a quarter hour
Unfolds its conundrum; oh what
Will the day bring? What, when the bells
Ring evening, will we remember?
Of hours and quarter hours, which
Will be honey-tongued? Which echo
In the stroke of all hours forever?

At twilight the sphinx in the bell tower
Answers her riddle, ringing: Remember?
Remember wondering: oh what will the day bring?

Height Is the Distance Down

What's geography? What difference what mountain
It is? In the intimacy of this altitude
Its discolored snowfields overhang half the world.

On a knife-rim edge-up into whirlpools of sky,
Feet are no anchor. Gravity sucks at the mind
Spinning the blood-weighted body head downward.

The mountain that had become a known profile
On the day's horizon is a gesture of earth
Swinging us above falling spaces, above
A map of the world. Disturber of the unseen,
Provoker of the gusts in which we bend
Struggling up against destruction gaping eastward.
The wind fails. The breath held. The illusion of death.
The resisting shoulder unopposed lurches
West in innocent still air, as steep, as deep.

The Whisperer

Where the sea runs a cobalt wedge under the coast bridges
And rhododendrons burn cool above concrete piers, an eddy of air
At the bridgehead will be I, as much I as
Walks alone here between lawns at moonrise.

The eyes lie in daytime, that say these chairs, fields,
Faces, are I, who am a strand of air raveling in the sound of leaves.
If the winds of the soul be unconsumed, I am lost,
Left clinging at a bridgehead over sea water.

There is no reprieve in the touch of flowering trees.
Finger is sister to bark, both mute and solid, both
Independent in death. Pity the poor soul, the public wind
Imaged in language, proud to whirl papers down a littered street,
A draft at the floor whining for the bellows under your ribs.

Persephone

I lived like a mole. There were
Subterranean flat stone stairways
To columns supporting the earth and its
Daffodils. Or shall we say, to the facade
Of the hiding place of earth's treasure?

From there in any direction
One walked endlessly upon short grass tufts
Stiff as cactus in the aridity of cold.
The lake wharves were icebound;
The wind, unending, circling the earth's interior,
Brought no news.
                Homesickness here
Is for the raw working and scars of the surface:
Furrows, quarries, split wood . . .
Thirst drawing the throat is for warm blood,
Speech with the living. And hunger—to which
(the long table, the tentative offering
of fruit from lost orchards)
                    surrender is death.
How many times it is said to the living,
Conquer hunger! If you
Want to go back, up, up where the sun falls
Warm on flowering rock and make garlands again.

Fable of the Ant and the Word

Ink-black, but moving independently
Across the black and white parquet of print,
The ant cancels the author out. The page,
Translated to itself, bears hair-like legs
Disturbing the fine hairs of its fiber.
These are the feet of summer, pillaging meaning,
Destroying Alexandria. Sunlight is silence
Laying waste all languages, until, thinly,
The fictional dialogue begins again:
The page goes on telling another story.

Anadyomene

This is confusion of sea mist,
A white clot of it, bred of uncertain weather.

A cloud, that has no skeleton,
Skin, lips, or any defined
Outline, could not
Moving feel more wonder,
Moving without volition
Towards the bare mountain.

See where the sunlit headland
Changes! Light-dazzle on rock fades
And shadow softens. Cliffs, rising,
Widen in encircling vapor—
Cloudself, a nothingness which
Touching the warm stone
Distils radiance.

Far down, the sea,
Loud on the rocks.

Encounter in Buffalo

The country lies flat, expressionless as the face of a stranger.
Not one hillock shelters a buried bone. The city:
A scene thin as a theater curtain, where no doors open,
No streets extend beyond the view from the corner.

Only the railroad embankment is high, shaggy with grass.
Only the freight, knuckling a red sun under its wheels,
Drags familiar box-car shapes down long perspectives
Of childhood meals and all crossings at sunset.

With a look as deep as the continent, with the casual greeting
Of those who will meet again, it bestrides the viaduct.
Its span is the span of trestles above mountain gorges,
Its roar the echo of streams still wearing away stone.

Inheritance

I have no inheritance in
The only sense you know—one teaspoon
Out of a Virginian dozen
That twinkled after Boone's
Bold star into Kentucky.
Spoon-clink fell to axe-chink
Falling along the Ohio. Those women
Made their beds, God bless them,
In the wandering, dreamed, hoped-for
Hesperides, their graves
In permanent places.

And, dying, left no inheritance?
I call to witness those women,
(Mary Marshall, Mary Noel—
Did they leave me only their names?—
Polly Connor, Susan Carroll)
Whose daughters had a woman's value.
My own pride is theirs
Descended through that willful girl,
Proudest of all, who turned
Twenty on her death-bed—

And, dying, left me neither pride
Of place, nor pride of blood,
But memory of the pride of
Her love, and a night ride.
A thing easy to carry, the right
Thing to be found dead in:
Armor stronger than silver
Against time and men and women.

Midnight

Now the dead lend us
Peace for the dark hours.

At midnight the never-to-awaken
Sleep lightly; yet those who lay
In love at death-fall have quiet to lend.

Only the murdered must walk.
The murderer clutches at sleep
As at scant covers; wakes chilled.

Come now,
Comes now death-lent oblivion. I love
Her who died unknown to me.
I adjust my bones to the composure
Of hers.
Peace fall on my exile
From hers.

The Field

Sweep the mind
                clean
Like a field of dry stubble
When the constellations
Of daisies have been mown.

Let it be lit by stars
Rooted outside the seasons . . .

To the flesh of the field
Alive with worm and seed
Tomorrow is in the night wind;
While drought or rain
Spirals towards earth
Mortal stirrings demand
Horoscopes of the stars.

Weather is all.

from *COLLECTED POEMS* (1979)

Editor's note: Collected Poems *comprised seventy-two poems, including those first published in* Cool Country *or* A Few Poems, *presented earlier in this volume. The selection here comprises the remaining poems with the exception of those inspired by Sappho (these poems appear in the section* Poems Inspired by Sappho *later in this volume).*

Ondine

At supper time an ondine's narrow feet
made dark tracks on the hearth.
Like the heart of a yellow fruit was the fire's heat,
but they rubbed together quite blue with the cold.
The sandy hem of her skirt dripped on the floor.
She sat there with a silvered cedar knot
for a low stool; and I sat opposite,
my lips and eyelids hot
in the heat of the fire. Piling on dry bark,
seeing that no steam went up from her dark dress,
I felt uneasiness
as though firm sand had shifted under my feet
in the wash of a wave.

I brought her soup from the stove and she would not eat,
but sat there crying her cold tears,
her blue lips quivering with cold and grief.
She blamed me for a thief,
saying that I had burned a piece of wood
the tide washed up. And I said, No,
the tide had washed it out again; and even so,
a piece of sodden wood was not so rare
as polished agate stones or ambergris.

She stood and wrung her hair
so that the water made a sudden splash
on the round rug by the door. I saw her go
across the little footbridge to the beach.
After, I threw the knot on the hot coals.
It fell apart and burned with a white flash,
a crackling roar in the chimney and dark smoke.
I beat it out with a poker
in the soft ash.

Now I am frightened on the shore at night,
and all the phosphorescent swells that rise
come towards me with the threat of her dark eyes
with a cold firelight in them;

and crooked driftwood writhes
in dry sand when I pass.

Should she return and bring her sisters with her,
the withdrawing tide
Would leave a long pool in my bed.
There would be nothing more of me this side
the melting foamline of the latest wave.

The Pleiades

They are heard as a choir of seven
shining voices; they descend
like a flock of wild swans to the water.

The white wing plumage folds;
they float on the lake—seven
stars reflected among the reeds.

Tonight, the Seven Little Sisters,
daughters of the Moon, will come down
to bathe or wash their summer dresses.

They wear costumes of the seven
rainbow colors, they wear feather
mantles they can lift in sea winds

raised by their singing, and so rise
flying, soaring, until they fade
as the moon dawns; their voices dwindle

and die out in the North Woods, over
Australian bush, from Spartan
dancing grounds and African beaches.

They have returned to the sky
for the last time, and even
Electra's weeping over Troy is stilled.

What girl or star sings now
like a swan on the Yellow River?

They Are Excited

about

"ideas which they
apprehend but do
not comprehend."

Fog too settles
close over all
cabbage blue rain-

water patches
pondwater blue
cabbage patches

and up the hills.
On top—

six geese, distinct
as Chinese brushwork,
stretch their wings

in sunlight on
a misty field.

The Spring

The water whispers in a quick
flow out from under a boulder
to moisten the thick-standing mint.

It fills the pond, goes down over
the spillway and under the road.
It fills another small pond, then

falls quickly away between tall
cottonwoods, a mere trickle still,
to find its fate in the river.

Nameless, it has two little ponds
to its credit, like a poet
with two small collections of verse.

For this I celebrate it.

Noon Hour

The red-hatted mill
owners are eating
pears; their hunting
rifles trail dwarf
shadows through pine,
swinging in step;

longtailed puppies
yipping scamper
around slow boots.

The mill crew is one
merry old man wearing
a red rag on his hat:
a bearded Noah perched
on ark-lumber.

The stag sighted
at midmorning
was safe at noon.

The Solitary

The lone drake, upended,
nibbles the pond bottom,
red legs paddling the air.

He sleeps on the rock wall
by the spillway, balanced
on one foot, head hidden.

In the shadowed shallows
under sycamore boughs
the encircling ripples

have one center: himself.
Intruders, including
mallards of his own race,

beautiful strangers, drive
him to frenzied attack,
quacking, snapping, churning

the pond. When they have gone
bright wavelets unbroken
to the rim spread round him.

Probably Nobody

Twenty crows
(charred paper)
litter the
frosted ground.

Small yellow
apples gleam
nakedly through
bare twigs.

Who'll buy red
rose haws white
snowberries

or a crane
mirrored in
slough water?

Seedlings

The plum thicket is
a dark green covert
sheltering the ricked up

fireplace lengths
of alder that blew
down in the storm.

Sprouting underfoot
like spring beauties
are desires for one

day's worth of childhood.
I could make a play-
house here with stones.

Eternal She

Outside the brick tomb that protects
not Placidia's dust but certain mosaics
the art lover may sniff warm clover.

A clarion cackle derides Roman
lawgiver and barbaric invader:

Tut tut tut! Alaric, Justin-
ian was it or Theodoric
got uppity? What of it? Look look
look at it! I did it! Look at it!

There is a new egg in Ravenna.

Fawn

Out of a high meadow where flowers
bloom above cloud, come down;
pursue me with reasons for smiling without malice.

Bring mimic pride like that of the seedling fir,
surprise in the perfect leg-stems
and queries unstirred by recognition or fear
pooled in the deep eyes.

Come down by regions where rocks
lift through the hot haze of pain;
down landscapes darkened, crossed
by the rift of death-shock; place print
of a neat hoof on trampled ground
where not one leaf or root
remains unbitten; but come down
always, accompany me to the morass
of the decaying mind. There
we'll share one rotted stump between us.

Journey

Morning:

      a silent singing (a vibration
over the trickling dawn-music of creek water
as earth tilts ripple and pool eastward)
awakes in air
stirred yet quiet, tense with shadow
stretched through the valley until the sun
rising crumbles the mountain rim in flame.

For joy of it, water sparkles,
fire pales, bridge planks and grass are warm.
Sun up to sun down, sun up to

Afternoon:

      let water weave on some snow slope
an umbrella of cloud, a screen of itself, for
itself, of rain. The sun licking
the stream splashes
scalding light into shade, invades
the under surface of bridge and leaf
and shrivels water at root source and stem.

Heat pants from the rocks while earth
embraced in the sun's tyranny
tilts downward, eastward, away, towards

Evening:

      heat lingers. Air is tepid.
Darkness comes so slowly even in these deep canyons.
But night falls and the water's own breath,
cool, rises now,
rises towards the mountain walls

bare to the hidden moon, white
with moonlight. Far moon, cold light, memory

moving across the mountain's face,
pantomiming dawn-to-twilight
journeys from twilight till dawn.

Letter from Byzantium

If you aren't Green, the Greens
will beat you up; if you aren't Blue,
the Blues will smash your shop.
The Emperor won't put a stop
to it. He belongs to the Greens.

If you don't care who wins, it means
you don't care, whoever kills
you: no doubt they both will.

Men have died bloodily in the past.
It has to happen, Priam said, so that
great poets may have stories to tell.

In the year One Nine Nine Two
a scholarly dissertation on Green and Blue
will be written, not published.
Only the author will care then what the row
was about and nobody will care more
for chariot racing than I do now.

A Picture of the Moon

Photography has laid a waste
of sand over the last outpost.
Mythology is displaced.

No longer will Chinese magicians
swinging in space on silken belts
alight upon the lunar coast

and toast Heng O in elixir.
Her dancers in their rainbow silks
are, with the peach trees, lost.

The snowy Tiger of the West—
oh, where is he? And where
the Cassia tree? the Toad of Time?
All now are lunar dust.

Picture Window

The gulls by day, the moon by night
pass and repass the window, weaving time;
opposite, the clock ticks; I move between.
The mailbox watches by the roadside.

The window trembles in its frame
and hums, tuned by the thundering of jets
concealed in cloud. On the river a tugboat
seems motionless with its slow load.

Rain spatters on the glass and smears
the view; sun drenches the drawn curtains.
I wait and watch. A rabbit in the rosebed
completes a corner of the afternoon.

The Pump

In the painted quiet
of snow ridges
above peacock rivers
and blond grass scant
over ledges of rock

a pump is quietly
companionable, beating
under the hollow ribs
of untenanted canyons,

unseen, working
to what purpose?

The little slingshot
of sound challenges
an invulnerable silence.

Real Estate

In late May the grasses
are so tall their plumy
waving tops conceal
a sign saying FOR SALE

by Whitfield Bros. The fields
that lately pastured mules
have now become "homesites"
with "riverviews" but still

are rich in clover, lupine,
vetch—rank flowering weeds
fragrant and peaceful, rustling
above wires laid underground.

The River Under Different Lights

1. The Gorge

Light has the dull luster of pewter
and the clouds move sidewise clawing the tops of the crags,
resting their soft gray bellies
briefly in high valleys.

Foam, plowing against the rapids
gathers all brightness.

2. The Ship

A ship that passes inland between mountains
moves as though resting from the sea's labor.

Riders in the fogging buses peer
at snatches of river between madrona and fir,
at the prow of a white vessel
dividing reflected forests:
a gesture compact with stillness.

3. The Estuary

Where fresh water meets salt
a single wave shears
the fog with a slow edge
lifted by the tide or current or
hull's pressure.

Nothing is sure, neither
tide, season, nor hour
in this flux of stream and ocean,
daylight and fog,
where only the fish,
a secret presence, move
surely on spring's errand.

Two Visits

1. E.P.: Martinsbrunn, 1961

It is an old old shaman
with his hair long, his face
laid bare to the bone.

The masks have all slipped off
except a death-mask stark
as marble; his hands are warm.

The eyes, alive, look sharply
From the skull but distantly as
if from the moon's deadlands

where he has been, possessed
ghosts, and they him: his jaws
unhinged by death will sing.

2. E.P.: Sant'Ambrogio, 1964

Names make news, and today the name
is the Possum's, the nickname audible
even in the drumroll from overseas.

Drums and trumpets, and all that folly—
or so it seems here on the silent hill,
climbing the wet stones of the *salita*.

The firm old feet, soft-shod, go up before me
as quietly as rain falls on the olive leaves,
the eyes and the sea both distant and still
as if we were standing high, high on Parnassus.

TIME AND THE WHITE TIGRESS (1986)

❧

Fit, fytte *obs.* exc. *arch.* Some regard the word as identical with OHG *fiza* list of cloth, mod. Ger. *fitze* skein of yarn, also explained in the 17th c. as the thread with which weavers mark off a day's work; the sense 'division or canto of a poem' might well be transferred use of this. . . .

O.E.D.

PROLOGUE

No society without customs
and with customs come ceremonies
(come feasting and dancing).
With ceremonies come calendars;
before calendars, sky-watchers.

They watch the sunrises moving along the horizon,
the moon with her arches low and then lofty, waxing
and waning, while both the sun and moon hold fast
to the tilted path of the Zodiac's twelve constellations.

10   The feasts are held at new moon, at full moon,
wherever the sun stands still in the north or south,
and turns, again when night and day are equal.
The watchers determine the day or night for feasting,
but not until time is measured, the beat established:
they split the year into halves and then into quarters.
They find the North and South and East and West.
They draw a cross in the sand. They watch the shadow,
the sun and moon, the rising and setting of stars,
and then they mime their knowledge:
20   two dancers, first,
emerge from left and right, from east and west,
miming the laws that they have read in the skies.

FIRST FYTTE—*The Year into Halves*

I.

In the beginning there were two, and they were Twins,
one dark, one light; horsemen and heroes,
physicians, shamans, and sons of God;
> virtuous
> beneficent
> devoted
> inseparable.

The Twins ranged widely, north far as the Baltic,
south to the Punjab and Burma. Their constellation
10   rose over Greece and set over Italy. Carrying
with them a staff notched with the moon's divisions,
they crossed the steppes, the tundras, rambled through all
the Americas, and invariably they were a pair:
like eyes or hands, like feet or kneecaps or wings.
Wherever they went they carried two jugs,
one blue and one black, light and dark,
that measured the dripping water called time.

They were never sun and moon, but sons of the Sun
and Dripping Water, sons of the Moon as Changing Woman.

20   Sons of Leda and Zeus in the guise of a swan,
they hatched from an egg when day and night were equal.
They marked the birthplace of time, and divided the year.

They marked the crossing of three celestial highways,
the first called Path of the Dead, or Watling Street,
or River of Heaven (the galaxy's outer rim).
The second path is traveled by sun and moon,
passing, repassing, above and below, and finally
meeting squarely, the sun blacked out in eclipse.
The third is the path the stars take night after night,
30   intersecting obliquely the path of sun and moon.

They rose and set with these crossings, whatever the season;
and always one set as the other rose; one died

while his brother lived, and whenever the night sky cleared
one Twin or the other was bound to be visible
    rising due east
    setting due west
one Twin escorting the sun at the equinox
while the moon at its full went hand in hand with his brother.

Their legends are beyond counting.

II.

40   We are following here the spoor
of a White Tigress who prowled
Time's hinterlands once
in the Age of Dragons.

Her teats, dripping a moon-milk,
suckled the Twins. The savor,
still on our tongues, is fading.

Here, a pug-mark in the path.
There, bent grass where she crouched.
From this I construct a tigress?

50   A mythical one?
Perhaps. Why
should we cease to make myths?

III.

The angle of the ecliptic
is like a door standing ajar;
its discovery, Pliny said,
opened the portals of science.

Upon that point, says Dante,
where two circles intersect
God's unanswering gaze is fixed,
60   it so inspires His love.

That angle formed the cleft
through which (at the equinox)
the poet stepped out of time
into timeless hell and heaven.

There, at the hour of sunrise
(the sun rising in that angle)
four circles make three crosses,
and light and dark are equal.

Crosses, crossroads, portals.
70 The stars that mark them guard
Crossroad or gateway, being warriors,
archers, scorpion-men . . .
                            or Twins.

SECOND FYTTE—*The Year into Quarters*

I.

The Fishes flicker, as Dante said—
    i Pesci guizzan su per l'orizzonta,
rising in our day with the sun at the equinox
(the vernal equinox, the birthday of time);
but long ago, when a Twin still guarded the crossing,
the Fishes rose with the sun at the winter solstice.

Then or now, of all the Zodiacal twelve,
Pisces must be the silliest constellation;
we see two fishes swimming, one west, one north;
10   two strings extend from their tails to unite in a knot;
and among the quivering, flickering stars of Pisces,
all of them faint, the brightest one is the knot.

Ridiculous. Preposterous.
                        Or is it?
Here is the calendar-priest with his stake and his string,
the instruments of his art. We have his instructions:
"Level the ground. Erect your post or stake.
Mark the end of the shadow cast by the stake
three times during the day—any three times—
20   and call the three points *a* and *b* and *c.*

"Now take the string and draw an arc on the ground
using *a* as the center. Then, using *b* as the center,
describe a second arc intersecting the first.
The figure described by the pair of arcs intersecting
is known as a *fish*—in Sanskrit, *matsya.*

"Now make a second fish with two additional
arcs drawn on the ground, one with *b* for a center
(again), and one with *c* for a center. Next,
the string is drawn through the fishes' mouths and tails
30   in two straight lines, till they meet; then mark the join
(or knot), and draw a line from the knot or join
to the base of the stake. This line will tell us the where

and the when, the north and south, the hour of noon,
and show us the days when the sun turns back on its tracks.

"In the cross of the four directions, this line extended
becomes two arms, and points to North and South.
This line, joining Pole to Pole, is called the meridian
(the word is from *medi* and *dies*, midday, or noon).
Whenever the finger of shadow cast by the stake
40 crosses this line, whatever the day of the year,
the time of day will be noon. When the shadow at noon
is shortest, the day is the summer solstice, the sun
will turn south and his arches diminish. When the shadow
at noon is longest, the day is the winter solstice;
the sun once again turns north. By means of this line
we divide into equal halves the circle of time
(the year) and the circle of space as well—the horizon."

And here, in this figure described on level earth,
we have a pattern for Pisces: here are two fish
50 whose tails are tied by a cord outlining a V,
the crux of the problem solved by the point of the V,
the join, or knot, corresponding to *alpha Piscium*.

At the vernal equinox, at time's beginning,
when one Twin rose from the eastern hills at dawn
and his brother sank behind the hills in the west,
the Fishes were seen overhead (but south of the zenith).
The Knot in the cord would have marked the meridian. This,
I submit, is what we call Myth. Forget about Ovid.
His story of Venus and Cupid fleeing from Typhon
60 is pretty enough, but lacks both the cord and the knot.
The constellations were named by calendar-priests
whose tools were leveled ground, a stake, and string.

II.

Opposite Pisces, Virgo. Across from the Knot,
Spica, a brilliant star, an ear of barley

held in the hand of Kore, daughter of Ceres
the Barley-mother.

                            Spicifera est Virgo Cereris.
An ear of wheat or barley—or is it instead
a barley *corn*?

70   And what obscure tradition
has made the virgin a mermaid—a lascivious creature
by all accounts, like the Syrian Venus of Ashkelon?
Kore was never a mermaid, nor Astraea either
(Astraea, Goddess of Justice, holding the Scales).

At the autumn equinox, at Time's beginning,
when one of the Twins appeared on either horizon,
the Fish were below the earth, the Knot invisible.
Spica marked the meridian. The mermaid marked it.

We should remember about our calendar-priest
80 that he had two tricks up his sleeve.
                        With his stake and string
he could if he liked describe instead of two fish
a single figure that gave him his north-south line.

Sometimes he called it a fish (*matsya*), at others
a *barley corn*. Far-fetched? We think so, perhaps,
but only because it makes sense when we look for confusion.

THIRD FYTTE—*Time Slips a Cog*

I.

Out of the east the days march in single file,
all without name or number. From dawn to dark
today looks much like yesterday or tomorrow.
The night sky differs, marked by the moon's quick changes
from new to full to dark and back to new.
Nights will be named before days: the night of new moon,
full moon, night of no moon at all. We shall number,
first, the nights rounding out a lunation; later,
the days that make up a year. The moon-god, they say,
10   invented and taught mankind the science of numbers.

It must have happened like this: the lunar phases
marked first, and the round of seasons; a year count next;
then the twelve moons of the year were numbered—numbered
and named, with two full moons singled out from the others
and noted especially—moons that rose with the Twins
(the stars marking east and west, and spring and autumn).
These moons seemed always to linger, held at the full
longer than others—the autumn one rising at sunset
on several successive evenings; the other, opposite,
20   setting at sunrise for two or three nights in a row.
One need not be able to read and write to know this.

Harvest Moon, Easter Moon: one or the other rising
at twilight, setting at dawn, announced the year's end
and a new year's beginning, and through (how many?) milleniums
festivals clung and still cling to these moons shining
all night at the full when day and night are equal.

II.

Nothing persists in the face of time and its flux
Like the cultural off-shoots of time—calendar customs.
Mohammed knew, and trashed the solstitial year,
30   dislodged the sun from his count and exalted the crescent.
But aeons ago (in the age of the Twins) a schedule
once made was adhered to, a cycle of feasts once established

persisted; the lore of moon and stars handed down
from aforetime was sacred; changes were not to be thought of.
Not, at least, until time's own face had changed.

Call them the Gemini People: nomads,
perhaps. When the Harvest Moon was full
each autumn (the time and place of its rising
announced by a Twin on his fleet-footed steed)
40   they danced the Dance of the Dead. They mimed,
they mopped and mowed and painted their faces,
dancing in honor of those who had died
since the Harvest Moon last rose. All this
they did each year as their fathers had taught them.

The centuries passed, and the heavens changed.
The Harvest Moon kept pace with the seasons—
well and good; but the Twin that had risen
before it, announcing its coming, now
followed after the moon and off to the left.
50   The Moon of the Dead was now the full moon.
rising between the horns of the Bull.

Mythology changed. Iconography changed.
The Pleiades, stars of the Bull constellation,
joyously danced the New Year in,
dancing at dawn with the full moon of spring,
dancing at dusk with the full moon of autumn.

Their legends, too, are beyond counting.

III.

They are heard as a choir of seven
shining voices; they descend
60   like a flock of wild swans to the water.

The white wing plumage folds;
they float on the lake—seven
stars reflected among the reeds.

Tonight, the Seven Little Sisters,
daughters of the Moon, will come down
to bathe or wash their summer dresses.

They wear costumes of the seven
rainbow colors, they wear feather
mantles they can lift in sea winds

70   raised by their singing, and so rise
flying, soaring, until they fade
as the moon dawns; their voices dwindle

and die out in the North Woods, over
Australian bush, from Spartan
dancing grounds and African beaches.

They have returned to the sky
for the last time, and even
Electra's weeping over Troy is stilled.

What girl or star sings now
80   like a swan on the Yellow River?

IV.

And how did Taurus, the Bull, get into the heavens?
Is there astronomy here? Or did sky-watchers *see* him
outlined in the stars—the great glowing eye of Aldebaran,
V-shaped face, the Pleiades on his shoulder
(for they saw him head-on?)
                Not very likely.

Is Taurus the snow-white bull that abducted Europa
and bore her to Crete? Aratos and Ovid said so.
And is he that other bull, too, whose golden horns,
90   according to Virgil, open the year—the Taurus
candidus auratis aperit cum cornibus annum?

So it would seem. However, the deified bulls,
as well as deities crowned with the horns of a bull,
are so many: Egypt's Apis and Mnevis and Sumer's
Anu, the Great Bull of Heaven, and Nannar the moon-god.
But ancient sky-watchers were, I surmise, not so much
worshipping cattle as watching the moon and planets
passing along the ecliptic, between the horns.

Sky-watchers, lacking a telescope, sight through rings,
100 or, like the Maya, two crossed sticks; they sight
through a forking twig, notched leaves of the palm or even
the horns of cattle. The horns, in any event,
are the most significant feature of this constellation.
The ecliptic still passes between them, though not the equator.
But back in the days—or nights—when Taurus rose
with the Harvest Moon at its full, the crossroads of heaven
passed through his horns and on to the Seven Sisters.

For two thousand years, from the rise of Egypt's kingdoms,
the earliest cities of Sumer and those of the Indus,
110 down through the building of Troy, and Newgrange in Ireland,
the equinox moved on its way through the Bull constellation
and finally entered the Ram. Then calendars were corrected—
sometimes—by decree of priest or king; but the folk,
still timing their holy days by the moon and stars,
ignored the shift in the heavens; their quarterly festivals,
All Souls and May Day, the Feasts of Imbolc and Lammas,
came down as the cross-quartered calendar. Do you believe this?
No, perhaps not; but the Pleiades say it is true.

FOURTH FYTTE—*The Sun in the Well*

I.

Sun-worship, someone has said, goes with kingship. Rather,
the solar year goes with kingship, with organization,
with agriculture and irrigation and towns.
The folk, wherever they are—whether following game
or herding cattle, on plains, in valleys, on mountains—
can see the moon, its phase, its attendant stars.
But to name the day when the sun turns *ageyneward*—the solstice,
summer or winter—the calendar-priest needs a temple
or simply a gnomon enclosed for its own protection
10   in sacred precincts; and that will turn into a temple.

After the sun-watching priest has found out for certain
the length of his gnomon's shadow at midsummer noon,
and measured the angle between the two solstice points—
if he then moves north or south, his labor is wasted.
His work is all to do over. Reason enough
why calendars pegged to the sun are useless to nomads.

And a calendar pegged to the sun is pegged to the solstice—
northernmost, southernmost points of the spiraling journey
the sun makes twice each year from tropic to tropic,
20   and *that* he does because earth's axis is tilted,
providing the cycle of seasons, inspiring poets
to dream of a cycle of ages, from golden to leaden.

Without the tilt, we should see the sun coming up
due east each day, and shadows cast on a dial
would be identical day after day year-long.
The nights and days would be always equal in length
and the year would be at the spring forever and ever.
Such, we are told, was the case in the Golden Age
(in Saturn's reign) and such was the case in Eden
30   before Eve tasted the apple, and God in anger
commanded the angels to push earth's poles askew.
Then mankind first knew winter and work and illness,

but sages taught that eternal spring would return
(the axis, that is, would revert to its upright stance)
but slowly, slowly, and not for a very long time.

II.

The orientation of temples and tombs
and dancing grounds, of huts and hogans
and stone-age graves is an endless theme.
Some, like the Pyramids, stand foursquare
40   to the cardinal points, but some are skewed
to solstice sunrises: Stonehenge faces
the summer, Newgrange turns to the winter.

We all know all about Stonehenge, and mainly
we know nothing; and having said that,
we all leap in and start guessing. Why not?

Call them the Hyperboreans, like Graves
and Diodorus Siculus. Building in wood,
rebuilding in stone, improving, perfecting—
a process that lasted for hundreds of years—
50   they labored to raise this temple to Time.

And what did they do there? We take it for granted
they watched the sun rise over the hele-stone
(between two hele-stones, if there were two).

But *something* surmounted the giant trilithon,
central of five. A sundisk in bronze?

Let me digress.
                One night a mouse
and a camel laid bets on which would first
see the sun. The confident camel looked east,
60   but the mouse, climbing up on his hump, looked west
and won when he saw the sun's first rays
illumine the highest peaks in the west.

None of us know. I think they faced west
and when the unrisen sun's first ray
lit gilded bronze, they clashed their cymbals
and shouted and danced the dance of the dragon.
I'd like to know, but it's fun not knowing.
Whatever they did, they must have been somehow
Obsessed with *solstice*. Why? Oh why?

III.

70   If you were standing at noon on midsummer's day
on their invisible line called the Tropic of Cancer,
the sun would be straight overhead; you and your gnomon
would cast no shadow at all. The ancients observed
the phenomenon, marking the spot.

                    And there were wells.
The ancients also observed that a well sunk here
would trap the sun in its depths on the longest day.
The sun would reflect from the water—the accurate method
of finding the solstice, and marking the spot on earth
80   above which the sun stood still and turned to the south.
And a well is a permanent fixture. It may last for ages.
The need for water protects it; it may become sacred
and old traditions will gather thickly around it.

There *were* such wells and they did not move. What moved
was the Tropic. This has nothing to do with Precession,
but just as the ancients surely observed Precession,
they must have observed the moving midsummer solstice.

They must have become aware that a well renowned
for trapping the sun on the longest day of the year
90   held nothing but shadows now, spring, summer, and winter.

The solstice sunrises marked by stone-age alignments
were also moving, the angle between them (summer
and winter) diminishing ever so slightly as both of them

moved toward East, and each other, and spring . . .
Someone seems to have noticed and wondered about it.
Would seasons of freezing and burning sometime give way
to spring the year round, a return of the Golden Age?
Did the Hyperboreans wonder and watch and measure?
Such engineers as they were, they might have done.

FIFTH FYTTE—*Time Standing Still*

I.

I am asked, "But why don't they come out even?"
(For example, the solar and lunar time-counts.)
An oversight, I explain, on the part of God.
But nothing in all this cosmic clockwork ever
will come out without some fraction remaining.

    It follows, then, that we count, we tinker,
    we count again: after twelve full moons
    the moon catches up with the sun. But no—
    she is falling behind and we count again
10   on fingers, toes or beads or knotted string:
    we score on wood, or bone, and we tinker
    A dozen moons to the year, about—
but once in a while an extra, thirteenth moon.

The horseshoe crab knows well, the Nereids know
whenever the thirteenth moon is about to intrude.
The spawning rhythm responds both to moon and sun,
adjusting their disparate cycles—awaiting their union.

Time as a constant seeping away is at once
indistinct and unbearable, a thin high sound
20 never swelling or breaking, continuous to the world's end,
stretching our nerves like a bowstring.
                    Ebb without flow.

    But time-counts marked by a stamp of the foot
    release the string to be drawn again.
    A rhythm established by moon after moon,
    tide after tide, and year after year
    has formed a framework for all our cultures,
    a pattern of custom that echoes the pattern
    woven by time in the heavens. And so,
30   like the horseshoe crab and nereid worm,
    we marked the thirteenth moon with a pause.

Time was at rest. Behavior altered.
The thirteenth moon was "lost" or unlucky.
It might be a signal for abstinence, or,
in some other culture, the New Year carousal
might be prolonged for another lunation.
The monarch, perhaps, remained in seclusion.

The thirteenth month is the thirteenth hollow log
in which the Moon was found, restored to life.

II.

40   But this was a cumbersome calendar. Sooner or later
the lunar count gave way to the solar year.
The thirteenth moon remained as a handful of days
when time stood still, and the moon caught up with the sun—
a dozen days at the year's end; this was the epact,
an interregnum, when, through a twelve-day chink
in the calendar, beings from outside time slipped in,
when mummers paraded, chain-dancing from door to door,
when Father Liber was king and the servant was master.

Babylon counted eleven days in the epact—
50   five days of abstinence followed by six of feasting:
these occurred in the spring, when the New Year began.
But Christian Europe paused at the winter solstice,
when nights were longer, the season of Rome's Saturnalia.

From Christmas Eve to the night of the Magi's visit,
Epiphany: these were days when time was at rest,
and all the things that turn like time on its axis,
cart wheels, mill wheels, spindles, must also rest.
No courts of justice were held, but during the Zwolfen
the Frauen rode through the night with their train of hounds.
60   This was the Yule, the turning-round of the year.

The stars of the Dipper, the Hindus said, were resting
(the Rishis, the Seven Sages who order the seasons).
Time paused; life paused, and then began again.

III.

In Egypt the counting continued, and number took over.
Their years, cut loose from sun and moon, had an even
one dozen months, their months had thirty days,
The twelve-day epact dwindled to five: five days
outside the months, between one year and the next,
five days lost by the moon in a crap game: holy
70   festival days, birthdays of the five
children of Nut, the sky-goddess. Five days
outside time, which must—

                        apparently it simply must

have a stop.

Across the Atlantic, number became an obsession.
The Maya included among their elaborate time-counts
a year composed of eighteen twenty-day weeks
with five days falling between one year and the next,
an interval ruled by the snub-nosed pole-star god,
80   five days when, we are told, the Maya refrained
from combing or washing, and likewise from heavy labor
lest some evil befall them. Life, brought to a halt,
was held in abeyance until the time-gap was over,
and then began again, all new. All new.

But not in Islam. There the moon
is in the ascendant. The sun is nowhere.
Number is nowhere. There is no epact.
Twelve lunar crescents round out the year
whatever the season. The month of fasting,
90   the days of feasting slide through the solar year,
slipping against the circle described by the Dipper.

However, an infidel may yet wonder
whether the thirteenth moon has survived
in despite of Mohammed, not as a twelve-year epact—
not as a five-day pause—rather,
its somber spirit tinges the ninth

Islamic moon, Ramadan: the difficult month
of dawn-to-dusk fasting that ends in a three-day feast . . .

No time-count ever begins *all* new.

SIXTH FYTTE—*Song for the Northern Quarter*

I.

The sun is a drum
                    the moon is a cymbal
the flow of time is caught in a cup.

Cupful by
            cupful by
                        cupful time
is cut; if not,
                    we should choke.

By night in the northern quarter the Dipper
10   or Northern Ladle or Bushel Measure
turns like the hand of a clock measuring time
although no punctuating tick or tock
notches its arc, sunset to sunrise.

Its handle divides the year into seasons,
pointing towards earth at dusk in autumn,
upward at dusk in spring, in winter
twilight west, in summer east.

And so it is and was and shall be
but not world without end (and neither
20   was it so from the world's beginning).

II.

The stars of the northern sky revolve
in a circle dance, but slowly, slowly
(serpent mating with tortoise). The round
is a carol, revolving counter-clockwise
against the sun's apparent motion, as witches
turn with the left hand in, or withershins.

Instead of a ladle, instead of a dance,
a Bear: a lumbering she-bear nosing

the trunk of the cosmic tree. Or again,
30   the seven sages, the Hindu Rishis,
pace round the cosmic mountain. Instead
of any of these, it may be a plough.
It may be a thigh, or the leg of an ox.

It may be a carriage, a long-tongued cart.
Carol, carolus; it is Charles's Wain,
the cart of Carolus Magnus, Charlemagne.
And in China, a chariot again, a triumphal car
for the pole-star god, Shang-ti, with winged attendants.

III.

Praying, some face Mecca; some face the East,
40   the sunrise, the new day dawning, the future.
The Son of Heaven faced north, saluting the pole-star,
his double: the unchanging, unwobbling Center. Planets,
moon and sun and the stars that partner them
all pass from sight and return, but there at the axis
eternity is unmoved and out of time's reach.

This is a tent-pole of heaven, the shaman's tree
or the ash tree Yggdrasil. Or it may be a deity,
K'uei, for instance, the one-legged dancing master
who twirls on his single foot at the center of space
50   to set the stars in motion, and time's wheel turning.
Or Siva, dancing the dance of creation.

                            North
is more than cold. Wherever winter nights
are long and the Dipper wheels high in the sky,
too high for setting, the sovereignty of time
lies with neither sun nor moon: it dwells
in the mysterious core about which time turns.

SEVENTH FYTTE—*The Mating Serpents*

I.

Time has three distinct movements; the first is easy:
up and over and down from east to west
the sun and moon and stars careen together
as though on a giant wheel, riding its rim.
Darkness succeeds to light, and Yin to Yang.
That is the primary movement, east to west.

The second movement divides one year from another:
the sun moves backward along the rim of the wheel,
backward from spoke to spoke among the stars,
10   and a year has passed when the backward round is complete.
The moon, as well, moves backward along the rim
in the time (almost) of new moon to next new moon,
twelve times (about) to the sun's one backward round.
Some see the opposing movements as "good" or "bad,"
or the sun as willful, fighting against the stars,
or the sun as simply slow, and the moon still slower.

And then the third—a movement from north to south:
the heavens are seen as tilted, circling *their* pole
(hub of the wheel), as the stars go round and round;
20   but sun and moon dance round a different May-pole
and make a slanting passage among the stars.
They follow a path long ago y-clept th'ecliptic,
where sun and moon meet now and then in eclipse.

> *Three movements / three causes:*
> *First: earth turns on its axis.*
> *Second: earth orbits the sun.*
> *Third: earth's axis is tilted.*

II.

Let us be clear about this: an eclipse of the sun,
an eclipse of the moon, are two quite contrary things.

30   The moon in eclipse is a full moon shadowed by earth;
     her face is dulled; she is "sick," but visible still.
     The sun and moon are on opposite sides of the earth.

     An eclipse of the sun is much more dramatic and dangerous.
     Month after month the moon overtakes the sun,
     and, unseen in daylight, passes him by
     above or below: but now and then they meet—
     the moon's path crossing the sun's at a trysting place.
     The two embrace, and we see the moon's black disk
     surrounded by flames; but let the voyeur be aware
40   of watching that copulation. Blindness can follow.

     This is a total eclipse; the moon more often
     contents herself with a bite from the rim of the sun.
     These partial eclipses give rise to familiar tales
     of monsters attacking and eating both sun and moon.
     The monsters are various: toads and jaguars and snakes.
     On the north we have Skoll and Hati, two hungry wolves,
     the first pursuing the sun, the other the moon,
     The gods were known to be doomed—the world would end—
     whenever the Fenris wolf escaped from his chains
50   and swallowed both moon and sun. His head was a wolf's,
     his body that of a dragon—serpentine.

III.

         The sky-watchers, tracking a three-fold motion
         (the east-west movement of sun and moon,
         their backward movement among the stars,
         a to-and-fro motion from north to south
         and south to north, solstice to solstice)
         found that the paths formed coils, or spirals—
         were serpentine—and drew two serpents
         holding the sun and moon in their twig-like arms.

60   Eclipses occur on the lunar nodes;
         and "node" is from *nodus,* "knot,"

the point where the sun's path crosses the moon's
and lovers join. The lunar nodes,
which are two, have ancient, significant names.
They are *caput draconis* and *coda draconis.*
Head of the Serpent, Tail of the Serpent
(or dragon). "Snake" in Greek is *drakon.*

An eclipse is then a conjunction of serpents,
70   the sport of a pair of celestrial dragons,
a tryst of lovers, and more than this;
a beat in the longer rhythms of time.

Eclipses, we know, occur at predictable intervals.
Even in ancient times the rhythm was noted;
the watcher perceived, at least, that a cycle existed.
The imminent union of a sun and moon was watched for,
observed as marking the end of a cycle, and feared
as possibly putting a period to time itself.
Warnings were issued and due precautions taken;
prayers were repeated and drums were beaten,
80 horns were sounded and fire-tipped arrows loosed at the sun.

And not in vain, for time has not yet ended.

EIGHTH FYTTE—*The Jars*

I.

The sun by day, the moon and stars by night
display the elapse of time—if skies are clear.
The sundial's finger of shadow, telling the hours
on sunny days, is erased by rain and darkness.
Then what of the sentinel's watch on a foggy night?
How was it timed before the invention of clocks?

To measure the briefer intervals, day or night,
the ancients invented the *clepsydra*, "water holder."
A clepsydra measures time by water descending
10   like sand in an hour glass. Two identical pots,
one filled with water that trickles out of a hole
to fill the other below it, are all we need.
A lawyer's speech was timed by a pair of cups;
amphoras, one for day and one for night,
measured the relative length of night and day,
and—most important—determined when these were equal.
The twin amphoras along with the stake and string
were primary tools for the earliest calendar-priests.

II.

Time, then, was water flowing
20   cupful by brimming cupful . . .

Time was water dripping.
It dripped from a dragon's tongue
in Chinese gardens (a clepsydra
molded in dragon-shape
measuring the night hours—
            plock! plock!).

Time dripped like spaced-out drops
falling in limestone caves,

with infinite slowness
30   building stalactites
like spikes of solidified time,
monuments, as it were,
to the passing milleniums.

Time has many faces
and some are the masks of God.

III.

Time slipped a cog, as I have described.
The sun at the winter solstice, the moon
at her full midsummer, deserted like Fishes
and moved to Aquarius, Water-Carrier
40   or Water-Pourer—a jar being emptied.
Astrologers called it the clock-makers' Sign.
The pot, to them, was half of a clepsydra
brimful of water. Summer or winter,
the longest day or the longest night
had filled it to overflowing. For once,
perhaps the astrologers' judgement was sound.
Or was it tradition? Who knows by now?

Water is life, and water is time,
and human life is a span of time:
50   a cup running over or emptied in death.

IV.

The watering pot of Aquarius, pouring time,
is the only Zodiacal vessel of any description.
Nevertheless, the Gemini, Castor and Pollux,
are known in ancient art by a pair of amphoras
appearing sometimes beside them, sometimes alone:
identical jars, identical twins—twins, who,
in the Gemini period, presided over the equinox,
jars that we know were used to determine the date.

Of the twelve Zodiacal figures, the Scales appeared last,
60 the symbol of balance replacing the Scorpion's Claws
as the equinox moved from the Pleiades to the Ram
and the full moon of spring rose opposite in the Scales.
Time means nothing unless it is measured. The Twins
with their stars and jars were earlier symbols of balance.
They signify the division of time into halves,
for they are the halves of an egg, the halves of the year,
the halves of a circle that runs from sunrise to sunrise.
Twice each year, midway between solstice and solstice,
the earth from pole to pole shares equal dark
70 and light. The Twins have ranged almost as far.

V.

Time and space coalesce, of course. They must.
The organs of time define the quarters of space.
East is the rising-direction, west the setting.
Slow stars creeping around the pole spell north.
The sun at midday, south. Abstractions like these
need handles, a name, a color, a picture to tell us
this direction is east, this north. Let east
be green and south be red as in ancient China,
color north black and color west white. We may,
80 besides, incise a symbol in stone. Let west
be a tiger, south a bird and east a dragon,
the north a tortoise or serpent and tortoise mating.
    White Tiger
    Green Dragon
    Red Bird
    Black Serpent and Tortoise.
Then give the sun to East and the moon to West
(it is there the moon is born each month).
Give spring to East and the Dragon,
90 give autumn to West and the Tiger,
give summer to South and winter to North and at last
the universe is in order. We know where we are.
When we build our hogans and temples, or bury our dead
we know how to place them in space and in time.

And there we are, too, with four graven images
standing alert to gather power to themselves
and spring to life as Chiefs of the Four Directions—
doubled Twins pouring water (or wind or rain?)
from four identical jars. Bacabs, Chacs,
100 personified, deified quarters of space and time.

NINTH FYTTE—*La Donna*

I.

The moon is a woman, because it controls
a woman's flow of blood, or because
the moon is changeable, fickle, *mutabile*
or *mobile*; because its light is weak
compared to the sun's fierce rays (although
in eclipse the moon blacks out the sun).

The moon is a woman—not always, of course—
not in Japan; but let that pass.
For the most part she is a woman.
10   Perhaps because she is female the moon
has womanly skills—she spins and weaves.
Her spindle, potent for witches' spells,
turns, turns, turns in her fingers
spinning the thread of time, for time,
which is trickling sand, is also a thread.

Trivia, Hecate, or Triformis,
the goddess has three phases: crescent,
full and waning, and time three faces,
past, present and future. Whether,
20   in triple form, the spinner be time
or the moon, the thread she spins is life.

> *My thread is spun.*
> *My glass is run.*
> *My life is done.*
> *Go cause the bells to toll.*

II.

La Donna has also the matronly skills
of a midwife. Mayan women in childbirth
cried out to Ixchel, a goddess wearing
a knotted snake in her headdress, weaving

30   her thirteen skeins of colored yarn
into time's intricate patterns. She,
like Peruvian Mamaquilla, like Brigit,
like mighty Diana diva triformis
(and heaven knows how many others)
is cast in the role of midwife for obvious reasons.
Nine lunar cycles will bring the child to birth.
She favors, la Donna, moisture, dew,
the sea whose tides dance to her measures,
and such shellfish and other sea creatures
40   as spawn by her calendar; rabbits are hers,
and night birds like the owl companion her.

III.

Or, in another epiphany
she may be the Evening Star.

Appearing in early twilight
in the still-gilded western sky
she is the smiling planet
that leads young lovers to bed,
or she is reviled, hated and feared
as the treacherous, lecherous, feminine
50   force that is man's undoing.

Venus, Freya, Ishtar, Astarte;
the planet is never the goddess.
The brilliant, mysterious point of light
appearing and disappearing,
always keeping close to the sun,
is but one epiphany
marking the times of her ascendancy.

TENTH FYTTE—*Song for the Millenium*

I.

If the world exists, it must have begun;
if the world began, it must come to an end. . . .

If time began, must it not end?
But when the beginning, and when the ending?
And may we not hope that when time ends,
it begins again, as a year will end
and a new year begin? We arrive in this fashion
at months of years and years of years
and ages of ages, sometimes likened
10   to reigns of kings: time's dynasties.

Meetings provide the divisions of time:
the coming together of moon and sun,
moon and star, planet and planet—
eclipses and occultation—all these
may serve to begin an age and foretell,
as well, the hour of its ending.

                        Then Ixchel
draws a thread, for the fytte is finished.
She leaves her loom and Aquarius-like
20   empties her painted water-jar.
Her gesture brings the age to an end.

II.

Five lesser lights, companions of moon and sun,
move along the ecliptic, backward (like them)
among the stars, but then (unlike the sun
or moon) reverse their motion, gain on the stars,
and finally, seeming to change their minds, drop back.
Because of these apparently whimsical movements,
the planets play only one role in calendar making.
They help to determine the longer cycles of time.

30 Imagine a primal conjunction of all five planets
  and sun and moon lined up in their starting gates
  at the hour of Creation, and set them all in motion.
  The sun will have circled the course a dozen times
  to Jupiter's once, providing our year of years.
  Saturn, the slow old man, takes thirty years
  to go around once, a "month of years" as they say;
  personified, his image is with us still
  as Father Time or the Old, departing Year.
  But Venus, with her irregular comings and goings
40 takes over in Meso-America. There, her cycles
  (his cycles, rather, for Venus there is a male)
  determined the night when the Bundle of Years was tied,
  when the sacred fire was extinguished, to be lighted again
  in the heart of a human victim. End and beginning.

III.

Time moves in a round.

       The moon and sun
appear to spiral around the earth,
passing among the stars that turn
like a wheel.

50   The year is a ring
(*annus*, annular, annual)
that goes from spring to fall to spring
as the sun, leaving the Fishes,
circles around to the Virgin
and circles on until it returns
at the year's end to the Fishes.
As year is added to year the rings
expand; but always the coiling serpent
will have his tail in his mouth.
60   Cycles are circles.

"The gyres! The gyres!" cried Yeats
of time that moved in a circle

and played the same tune over
and over and over; but others
have held that the cosmic wheel,
reversing itself, will play time backward
whenever the Magnus Annus ends.

Thus the Great Year's seasons,
the ages of gold, of silver, of bronze,
70   of iron (the present) returning
in backward order will bring mankind
again to a Golden Age when winter
and war and pestilence are unknown.

The shepherd will pipe to his sheep
and the lion will lie down beside them.

IV.

But, whether time is believed to proceed or turn back,
the end of any age is marked by *kataklysmos*,
a Deluge. Then Ixchel's painted jug is emptied
and water flows in a stream form the serpent's mouth.
80   But some say the Hero Twins, smashing their jars,
released the water that washed away all of Creation.
Still others blame the Gods of the Four Directions,
the Bacabs (or doubled Twins) who caused the Flood
and later restored the universe to order.

Others elaborate on the theme: successive ages
are ended by earthquake, wind and conflagration;
however many the ages, however many
the forms of destruction, the end is seen in the heavens,
foretold by conjunctions of sun and moon and planets,
90   and, beyond these, by Precession. But even this,
the so-called Platonic Year, is dwarfed by cycles
the Maya imagined, and India's cosmic seasons,
wheels whose rims were measured in millions of years.

Or is time a spiral, circling but never repeating,
a spiral extending without beginning or end?

But endlessness we cannot comprehend.
As the vernal equinox moves to the Water-Pourer,
as another millenium comes to a close, we shiver
as we have always shivered, and hope as always.

100 Life runs on and on, and time runs on
and around, but measured by moons, by daylight and dark,
by tides that rise and fall, and by feet that dance.

CODA—*Song for the New Year*

The Pleiades slide into place
at midnight over the smoke-hole. . . .

A star that was lost in daylight
reappears at dawn (heliacal
rising) glittering in pale sky. . . .

The moon, too, dies in light
and returns at dusk, a crescent
signalling with sun and star
time at its turning point.

10   Sea-kingdoms trumpet the news
through their winding shells,
but shepherds through ram's horns;
bells clang in the steeples.

Time now to empty our houses
of ghosts and the year's rubbish;
chain dancers prance through the streets
and turn into dragons; firecrackers
pop; steam-whistles shriek.

The event is both social and astral,
20   an end, but not final,
a beginning that will end:
a serpent with his tail tucked into his mouth.

NOTES

Description of astronomical phenomena in this poem are not designed to give the reader an explanation of the actual workings of the solar system as we now understand them. With one exception I have limited myself to descriptions of phenomena visible to the naked eye (i.e., to the ancient sky-watchers). My imaginary observers are viewing the heavens from somewhere in the north temperate zone. My account of the apparent movements of sun, moon and planets among the stars marking the ecliptic holds good for all parts of the earth, although the seasons are reversed in the southern hemisphere. The puzzled reader may consult any handbook of astronomy for clarification.

[Figure 4] Figure 1. One thing must be kept in mind by the reader: the movement of the sun and moon among the stars is *backward*. Think of a Ferris wheel with twelve cars, each representing one Zodiacal constellation. The wheel turns steadily from east to west, completing a circuit in twenty-four hours. The sun travels east to west each day with the wheel, but at the same time it moves slowly backward from car to car so that it rides once in each car in the course of a year. The moon also travels from east to west each night with the wheel, but moves backward from car to car so that it rides in each car in the course of a month. When the moon rides in the same car with the sun, she is invisible (dark of the moon). When she is riding opposite the sun, the moon is full. The car (constellation) in which the sun is riding is always invisible, but the moon and the constellation can be seen together. This, combined with the moon's more rapid passage and changing phases, makes the moon more important than the sun in unsophisticated calendars.

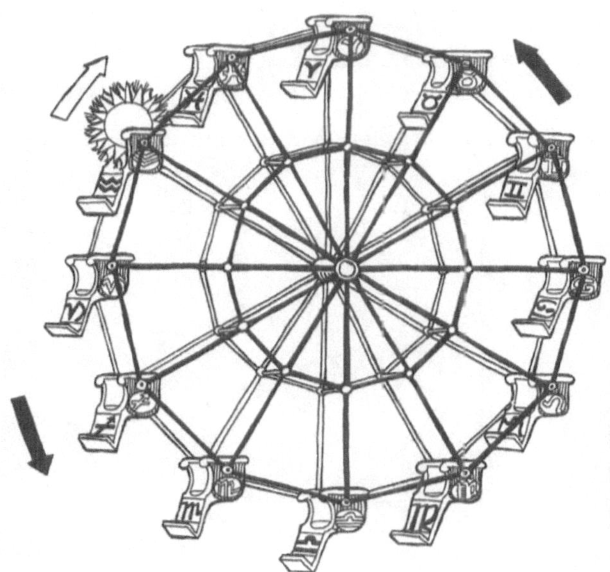

My volume of essays, *The Mythmakers* (1966), available from Breitenbush Books, gives a general background and bibliography for much of the material used in the poem, which is presented not as a work of scholarship, but as a work of the imagination; however, I include a few notes for the reader who might be curious about my sources.

FIRST FYTTE: *The Year into Halves*

For general background information see *The Mythmakers*, chap. 15, and authorities cited.

Lines	11–15	This is a staff described by Alexander Marshack in a lecture at the Smithsonian, 1983. He did not associate it with the Twins.
	22–30	"At Time Zero, the two equinoctial 'hinges' of the world had been Gemini and Sagittarius. . . . The exceptional virtue of the Golden Age was precisely that the crossroads of ecliptic and equator coincided with the crossroads of ecliptic and Galaxy, namely in Gemini and Sagittarius. . . ." Giorgio de Santillana and Martha van Dechend, *Hamlet's Mill* (1969), p. 63. This would have been the case for roughly two millenia, between 6000 and 4000 B.C.
	53	The angle at which the circle of the ecliptic crosses the circle of the equator is approximately 23½°.
	55–56	Pliny, *Natural History*, Book II, vi.
	57–60	Dante, *Paradiso*, X. 7–12.
	67	Dante, *Paradiso*, I. 39.

[Figure 5] Figure 2. Diagram of ecliptic and equator with axis indicated. The broken line indicates the ecliptic.

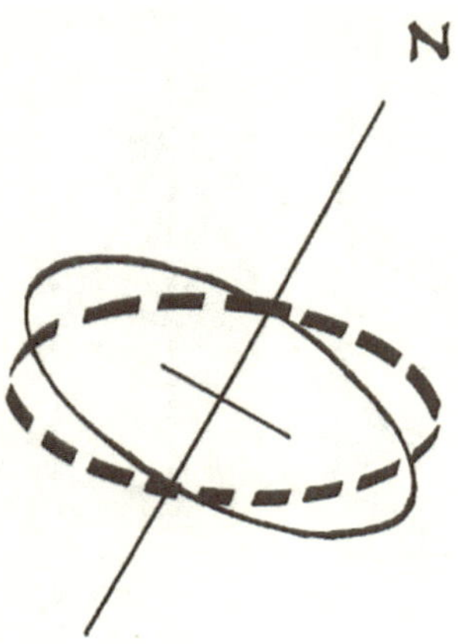

[Figure 6] Figure 3. Diagram of ecliptic and equator with Zodiacal constellations indicated. The constellations are shown in the positions they now occupy.

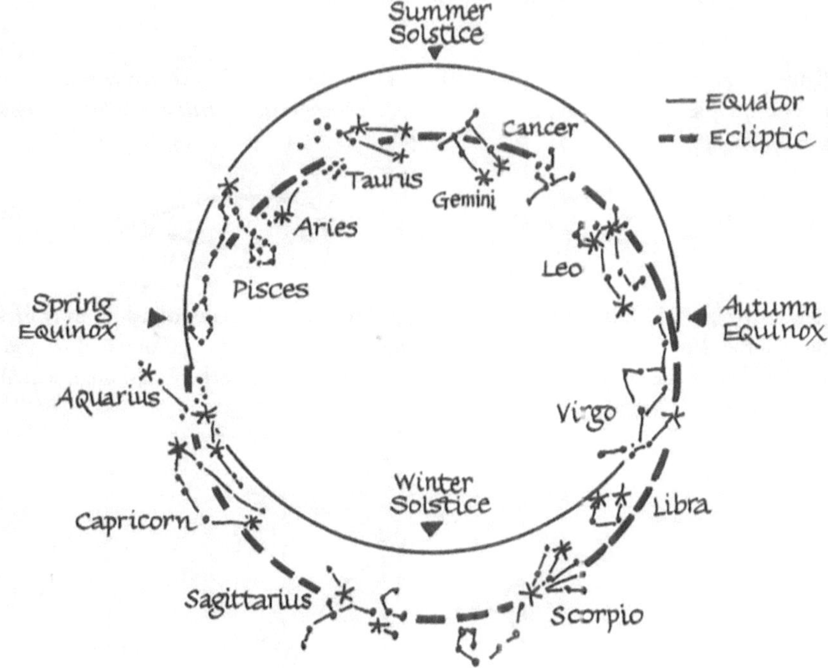

SECOND FYTTE: *The Year into Quarters*

Lines 1–2   Dante, *Inferno*, XI. 113.

15   The promulgation and regulation of a calendar is normally a priestly function, among the Pueblo Indians as among the Egyptians and in most parts of the world. Our present calendar (the Gregorian) was promulgated by Pope Gregory XIII in 1582, and its predecessor, the Julian, by Julius Caesar as Pontifex Maximus of the Roman Republic in 44 B.C. The names, number, length and order of our months are those of the Julian calendar, but incorporating a few changes made under the Empire.

17–47   The text paraphrased in these lines is from *The Panchasiddhantika* by Varahna Mihira (sixth century A.D.), ed. and tr. by G. Thibaut (Lahore, 1930), chap. 14, stanzas 14, 15, and 19. See also G. R. Kaye, *The Astronomical Observatories of Jai Singh* (Calcutta, 1918), p. 78.

59–60   Ovid, *Fasti*, Book II. 458–474.

67   Manilius, *Astronomica*, II. 442.

81–85   Varaha Mihira, *op.cit.*, chap. 4, stanza 19.

[Figure 7] Figure 4. Fish pictograms. The one on the left is North American Indian, the one on the right is Egyptian. From A.C. Moorhouse, *Writing and the Alphabet* (London, 1946), p. 8, fig. 3.

[Figure 8] Figure 5. Diagram showing how to find the meridian according to instructions in the *Panchasiddhantika*. *x* is the gnomon. *h* is the knot. Points *a*, *b*, and *c* were believed to lie on the circumference of a circle, as shown here, although actually they do not.

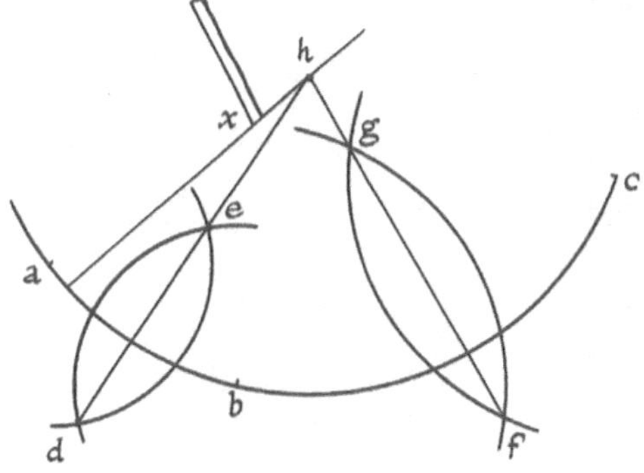

THIRD FYTTE: *Time Slips a Cog*

In this fytte I am dealing with the phenomenon called Precession of the Equinoxes. See any astronomical handbook for the scientific explanation. However, one thing must be stressed: to an astronomer the Zodiac is an abstract circle of 360° divided into twelve segments of 30° each. The segments (called Signs) bear the names of constellations that coincided with them more than two thousand years ago, but not now. This does not confuse astronomers in the least. It need not bother the reader too much because I am referring in this work *always* to the constellations unless I use the word *Sign*. I am writing about a time before the abstract 360° circle had been devised. The same stars remain on the ecliptic, but the vernal equinox moves through the twelve constellations in about 26,000 years. In Cicero's day the cycle was estimated at 30,000 years.

Lines   14–20   For an explanation of the unusual behaviour of the full moon at the equinoxes, see an astronomical handbook. For further background to this fytte, see also chapters 12 and 13 in *The Mythmakers*.

   91   Virgil, *Georgics*, I. 217.

[Figure 9] Figure 6. The Pleiades as depicted by the Babylonians (*a*, *b*), the Navajo (*c*), and Blackfoot Indians (*d*). The Pleiades are always referred to and depicted as seven, although only six are visible to the naked eye, and the placing of the seventh varies. At one time all seven stars were visible and many myths account for the disappearance of the seventh.

[Figure 10] Figure 7. Diagram showing the equinoctial and solstitial holidays and those of the cross-quarters.

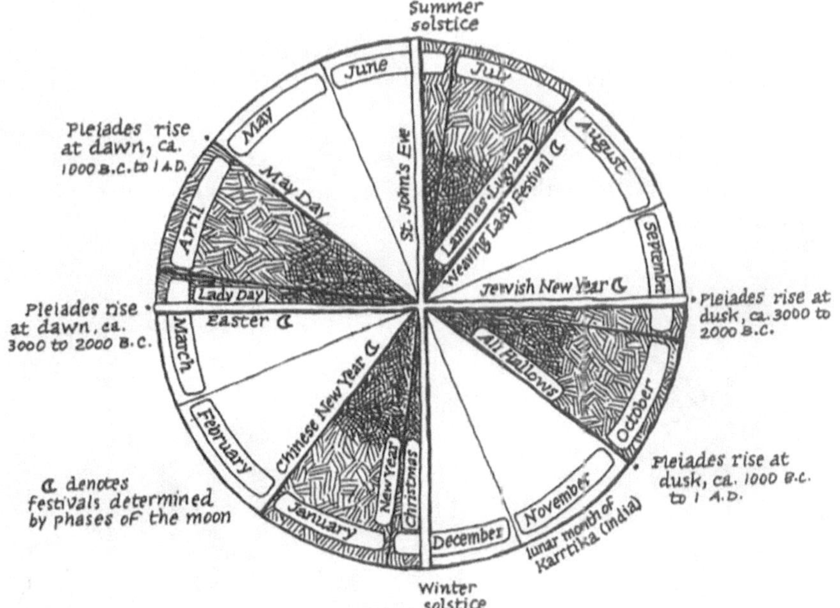

FOURTH FYTTE: *The Sun in the Well*

Lines	1	Mircea Eliade in *Patterns in Comparative Religion*, tr. R. Sheed (New York, 1958), pp. 124 and 150.
	28–29	See, for instance: Hesiod, *Works and Days*, lines 110–120; and Ovid, *Metamorphoses*, I. 89–112.
	29–32	Milton, *Paradise Lost*, X. 668–671.
	42	Newgrange: a large passage-grave in County Meath dated to *ca.* 3100 B.C.
	47	Diodorus Siculus, *History*, II. 47.
	54–55	The lintel of the central trilithon of the inner horseshoe (see Figure 10) has fallen along with one of the uprights. Two man-made depressions, as if for the placement of some superstructure, are visible on what was once the top of the lintel. Their existence is unexplained. See R. J. C. Atkinson, *Stonehenge* (1956).
	57–62	See Uno Holmberg, *Siberian Mythology* (1927), p. 437. In this fable the mouse and the camel were vying for the honor of opening the year, that is, of leading the list of twelve animals in the Asiatic Zodiac.
	84–85	The moving tropics are caused by "a very slight cyclical change in the inclination of the earth's equatorial plane to the plane of the orbit. It has a period of about 40,000 years . . ." Atkinson, *op. cit.*, p. 86.

[Figure 11] Figure 8. The earth with its axis inclined at an angle to the plane of its orbit, which causes summer and winter.

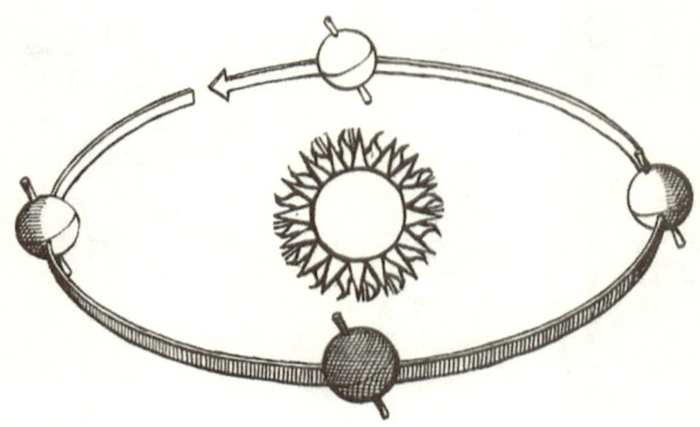

[Figure 12] Figure 9. The earth with its axis upright as Milton realized that it would have been in a Golden Age when spring lasted all year long.

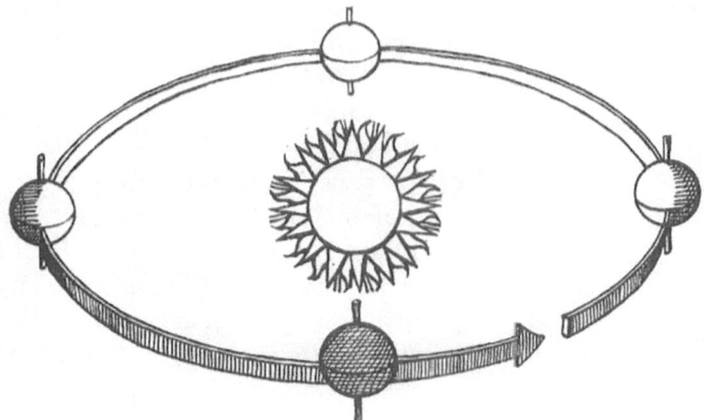

[Figure 13] Figure 10. Diagram showing placement of the upright sarsen stones at Stonehenge. Those in the outside ring were joined by a continuous ring of slightly curved stone lintels. The larger uprights forming the horseshoe were joined in pairs by five lintels to form five "trilithons." The central trilithon was the tallest (24 ft.).

FIFTH FYTTE: *Time Standing Still*

On the lunisolar spawning cycles, see *The Mythmakers*, chap. 10, and authorities cited; also Rachel Carson, *The Edge of the Sea* (1979), pp. 34–36.

Lines 38–39   J. Eric Thompson mentions this tale in his monograph, "The Moon Goddess in Middle America" (1934).

42–53   The actual length of the epact varies slightly from year to year, hence the length of the interregnum varies between eleven days as in Babylon, and twelve days as in western Europe. For examples of the interregnum, see Mircea Eliade, *The Myth of the Eternal Return* (1954). On the Babylon festival, see Stephen H. Langdon, *Babylonian Menologies* (1935), p. 107. The latter cites a tablet of the seventh century B.C. which "states distinctly" that the eleven days of the festival are a supplement to the lunar year. In Brittany, the twelve days of Christmas were known as the *gourdeziou* or supplementary days. For examples of customs and superstitions associated with the twelve days of Christmas, see Hutton Webster, *Rest Days* (1916), and Clement A. Miles, *Christmas in Ritual and Tradition, Christian and Pagan* (1912).

64–98   For the Egyptian, Mayan and Muslim calendars see the article "Calendars" in the *Encyclopedia of Religion and Ethics*.

73–84   Sahagun, quoted by Sylvanus Griswold Morley, *The Ancient Maya*. Revised by G. W. Brainard, 3rd ed. (1956).

SIXTH FYTTE: *Song for the Northern Quarter*

Lines 19–20   Precession also causes the aspect of the northern sky to change during the millenniums.

39–45   On the importance of the north-south axis in Chinese culture, see Ernst Zinner, *The Stars Above Us,* tr. Johnston (New York, 1957).

SEVENTH FYTTE: *The Mating Serpents*

For the mythology of lunar and solar eclipses, see *The Mythmakers*, chap. 11, and authorities cited.

Lines 38–39   Because the moon is much smaller than the sun, if it were any farther from the earth, it would move across the face of the sun without eclipsing it; on the other hand, if it were closer, we should be unable to see the corona. As it happens, the moon is at precisely the right distance to cover the sun without covering the corona.

52–54 Bear in mind I am describing the way the sun and moon *appear* to move. The earth is actually orbiting the sun, while the moon orbits the earth.

58–59 For examples see Richard C. Rudolf, *Han Tomb Art of West China* (1951).

EIGHTH FYTTE: *The Jars*

Lines 13 Martial refers to a long-winded speaker who would have pleased everyone if he had wetted his throat from the clepsydra. *Epigrams*, VI. 36. Caesar's legions, like the Chinese armies, used the clepsydra to regulate the length of night watches.

19 The Romans had a phrase, *aquam perdere*, literally, "to lose water," figuratively, "to waste time."

22 Chinese clepsydras were usually ornamented with a dragon's head which spit water into the lower vessel. A poem by Hueh Feng (ca. 845 A.D.) mentions such a water clock.

34–35 With a bow to Joseph Campbell.

41 Robert Eisler, *The Royal Art of Astrology* (1946), p. 107.

59–64 Virgil (Georgics, I. 208–209) refers to Libra, which brings the hours of day and night into balance, *et medium luci atque umbris iam dividit orbem*—divides the world (*orbem*, sphere) in half between the light and shadow. In ancient China, the autumn equinox was the time when instruments for weighing and measuring were to be adjusted. *The Li Ki*, tr. James Legge (Oxford, 1879–85).

71–100 On the colors of the animals of the four directions and four quarters of the year, see chap. 13 of *The Mythmakers* and authorities cited.

NINTH FYTTE: *La Donna*

See *The Mythmakers*, chap. 3, and authorities cited.

Lines 7–8 The lunar deity is male in Japan, and the sun is female. Several mythologies, including those of Sumer and Egypt, seem to have had both male and female lunar deities.

16–20   For the Triple Goddess, see Robert Graves, *The White Goddess* (1948), *passim.*

27–31   Thompson, *op. cit.,* 133–134.

52   Robert Chadwick in a lecture at the Smithsonian, 1983.

TENTH FYTTE: *Song for the Millennium*

My sources include the article entitled "Ages of the World" in the *Encyclopedia of Religion and Ethics*; Mircea Eliade, *The Myth of the Eternal Return* (1954); W. B. Yeats, *A Vision* (1925) on the Platonic Year or Magnus Annus, which he also mentions in a number of his poems, especially "The Gyres."

Lines   35–38   The planet Saturn was assimilated to the Greek God Kronos. The scythe of Father Time was originally the sickle with which Kronos castrated his father Uranus.

39–44   A good discussion of the Mayan Venus cycles can be found in the new translation of the *Popol Vuh* by Dennis Tedlock (New York, 1985).

50–56   In a sense the year is a prototype of all circles, for in our geometry the 360º of a circle are derived from the 360-plus days of a year.

70   In any system of ages descending from good to bad, the present age is always the worst.

76–84   See *The Mythmakers*, chap. 14, and authorities cited.

All diagrams and line drawings are the work of Anita Bigelow. I am also indebted to Garry Stasiuk for his generous responses and assistance in matters astronomical.

from *NANTUCKET GENESIS:*
THE TALE OF MY TRIBE (1988)

Editor's note: This volume reproduces Barnard's verse essay (comprising three sections, grouped under the title "The Narrative" in the table of contents, which dominate the volume) as it appeared in print in 1988. Where lines are separated in that volume by a page break and there is reason to assume the lines are continuous (rather than divided also by a stanza break), then the lines are reprinted here as continuous.

Nantucket Genesis: The Tale of My Tribe *ran to sixty-five pages in its full publication by Breitenbush Books, prefaced by two additional pages I have included here—"The Ten Generations" (where, inevitably, Barnard notes only her birth date) and "A Note on the Name Barnard"—and closing with a page entitled "Colophon," which references the use of cuts by Anita Bigelow and the calligraphy by Christie Payne for the family tree, which appears on the endpapers.*

The main body of the work—"The Narrative"—takes the form of poetry interspersed with historical prose, such as court records, conveyances, the deed of sale signed by Wanack-Mamack (Chief Sachem of Nantucket), letters home, wills, and inventories. The introduction is reproduced entirely in full as it offers a compelling overview, not least explaining why Barnard found her story could only really be fully told in verse.

The contents page of Nantucket Genesis: The Tale of My Tribe *in full is as follows:*

Introduction

The Narrative
*   I. Before Nantucket*
*   II. Nantucket*
*   III. After Nantucket*

The Begats

The Documents
Reproduction of documents

The Nantucket Muse

A Note on Places and Place Names

Sources

Index of Surnames

There is no reproduction of material beyond these parameters owing to some unusual formats that are difficult to reproduce without access to original source documents. Readers interested in the post-Narrative sections can source a copy of Nantucket Genesis: The Tale of My Tribe *(the original an exquisitely produced book) through libraries, secondhand booksellers, or contact with the literary estate. "The Documents" includes the text of the will of Nathaniel Barnard and text from the settlement of Benjamin Barnard's estate, including the inventory of the estate of Benjamin Barnard, dated February 7, 1734/5 (reproduced at 60 percent of its original size).*

The Ten Generations

Thomas Barnard ca. 1612–1667
Nathaniel Barnard 1642–1718
Benjamin Barnard 1681–1734
Francis Barnard 1718–1800
Francis Barnard 2nd 1747–1805
Reuben Barnard 1786–1865
Jesse Franklin Barnard 1810–1883
Samuel L. Barnard 1835–1889
Samuel M. Barnard 1882–1969
Mary Barnard 1909–

A Note on the Name Barnard

Barnard, the surname, is almost entirely derived from the baptismal name Bernard, probably pronounced in the English fashion, Barnard. (Cf. Berkley/ Barkley, Clerk/Clark, and Derby/Darby.) It was apparently accented on the first syllable. Whenever it is misspelled in early documents, the error occurs in the second syllable. In other words, the name may be spelled "Barnett" or "Barnud" but never "Burnard." The two more famous American Barnards, George Grey Barnard, the sculptor, and Frederick Augustus Porter Barnard, the president of Columbia University for whom Barnard College is named, pronounced the name with the accent on the first syllable. This is the pronunciation I prefer and the one I have used in my narrative: Thómas Bárnard, not Thómas Barnárd.

Introduction

Until a few years ago all I knew of my father's people was that they had come from North Carolina to Indiana, where he was born. I had assumed that they had come to North Carolina from England. I also assumed that they had arrived about 1800, two mistakes I might not have made if I had known more about colonial history. Few emigrants sailed from England directly to North Carolina. The settlers in that region came for the most part from other colonies, squeezed out or thrown out. It was a country described by Virginia's William Byrd II as "Lubberland."

Furthermore, the great wave of English emigration to the New World (as distinct from Irish and Scottish, or Scotch-Irish) took place in a single decade from 1630 to 1640. A few brave spirits came earlier and a good number of stragglers came later, but most Americans of English descent have ancestors who put down their roots along the Atlantic seaboard in the 1630s. In the 1940s, when I was assisting Carl Van Doren in the editing of Benjamin Franklin's papers, he startled me by pointing out that the colonials who rebelled in 1775 were, most of them, *fifth* generation Americans. Neither their fathers, their grandfathers, nor their great-grandfathers had ever seen England. They did not think of themselves as transplanted Englishmen, but as Americans.

When I pieced this line together, I found that Francis Barnard 2nd, at the time of the Revolution a young man with a wife and three children, was indeed a fifth generation American. Both his parents, all four of his grandparents, and all eight of his great-grandparents were born in what is now either New Hampshire or Massachusetts. With two exceptions, the original emigrants in each line arrived in the 1630s. Thomas Gardner came first in 1623, sailing from Weymouth on the *Zouch Phoenix* with his wife and three sons. He came not for religious reasons, but in the hope of establishing a lucrative fishing station on Cape Ann. Tristram Coffin came last, in 1642, bringing with him his wife, several children, two unmarried sisters and his mother, aged fifty-eight.

From time to time someone would ask me whether I was descended from the Nantucket Barnards. One man assured me that Nantucket was covered with Mary Barnard gravestones. That might be, but it seemed to me most unlikely that the family would have moved from Nantucket to North Carolina and then on into Indiana. I persisted in thinking of my ancestry as wholly southern—from Virginia and Kentucky on my mother's side, and North Carolina on my father's.

While I was working with Carl Van Doren on Benjamin Franklin's correspondence with his sister, Jane Mecom, I needed to do some research on their Nantucket connections. Their maternal grandfather was Peter Folger, one of the first Nantucket settlers, and they still had many relatives on the island, including the notorious Kezia Folger Coffin, who had been indicted for treason against the infant Republic. My research turned up the information (irrelevant to the project in hand, but interesting to me) that an exodus of Nantucket families from the island to the mainland had occurred immediately before the Revolution. Many families went to North Carolina and eventually moved on to Indiana and Illinois. My curiosity was piqued, but almost forty years passed before I began my search for the missing links.

My grandfather was born in 1835. There should not, I thought, be more than two generations between 1775 and 1835. Nantucket genealogy, as my Franklin research had shown me, had been comprehensively tabulated down to the time of the Revolution, and the results published. My idea was that I should find out which Nantucket Barnards went to North Carolina and then look for the links. I might find that there were no links and that my family came from elsewhere, but my curiosity would be satisfied.

With a good deal of luck and help from other people I managed to put the story together in a comparatively short time. In many ways it seems to be a typical American story, with more or less typical migrations that took us in nine generations across the continent. In other ways the story may be typical, but is certainly not what I had been led to expect.

Nothing I found in researching my own line surprised me more than the longevity of both men and women and the low infant mortality. I have often heard it said that the men of colonial New England who lived to a ripe old age usually buried at least three wives. This was definitely not the case among my ancestors. Several of the men were widowed and married again, but the same is true of the women, and one woman, Sarah Starbuck, was widowed twice and married three times. The first Mary Barnard, born 1648, was seventy when she died; Judith Gardner Barnard, born on Nantucket in 1693, was seventy-two, and Sarah Hopcott Macy was eighty-nine. Sarah Shattuck Gardner, born about 1624, bore ten children and lived to be ninety-two; Mary Severance Coffin, born at Salisbury, Massachusetts, in 1645, brought fourteen children into the world and died at ninety-six. Among the men, Nathaniel Barnard, Tristram Coffin, Thomas Macy 1st and 2nd, Reuben Barnard and Jesse Franklin Barnard died in their seventies. Francis Barnard 1st, Edward Starbuck and James Coffin were octogenarians.

Apparently long life and a vigorous old age were not uncommon among the islanders in general. W. O. Stevens, in *Nantucket: The Far-Away Island*, has this to say on the subject:

One outstanding characteristic of the Nantucketers from the beginning is their amazing longevity. There must be something about the air that keeps the old cardiac pump going longer than it does on the mainland. "Three score years and ten" never meant anything more than callow youth in Nantucket. Crèvecoeur speaks of the remarkable number of "green old men" whom he saw. As one reads the life stories of various people born here, it is astonishing how many lived to be over ninety. And this is true of those who were born in Nantucket but moved away in their youth. . . . Men in their eighties used to take their dories out deep-sea fishing and think nothing of the hard, physical labor. Benjamin Hussey, for example, was over eighty when he was killed, while standing at the wheel of his ship, by falling ice from an iceberg in Greenland waters.

I have often heard it said also that back of the bad old days parents had to have ten or twelve children in order to have four who reached maturity. This, again, was not the case in my family. Of Nathaniel and Mary Barnard's eleven children ten (at least) reached maturity and married. All were born on Nantucket Island. Their son Benjamin and his wife Judith had eight children, all of whom lived to maturity. One died unmarried at age twenty-two, but the rest married. Francis and Catherine Barnard had had ten children, some born on Nantucket, some in North Carolina. One died in childhood. In the early nineteenth century Reuben and Jane Barnard had thirteen children born in North Carolina, all of whom who lived to maturity. Jane lived to eighty-three and perhaps longer—her death date is uncertain.

Statistics, which tell a different story, include the city slums where malnutrition, contagious diseases, neglect and abuse must have taken a heavier toll. Statistics also include the privileged classes where infants might be handed over to a wet nurse of questionable health and habits. We can be fairly sure that the mothers in these Nantucket families nursed their own children and continued to do so until they were at least a year old. This was a way of postponing the next pregnancy, and accounts for the fact that most of the children are spaced about two years apart. Typically the men were twenty to twenty-three when they married, the women eighteen to twenty-one. Ten to eleven children in the ensuing twenty years was the norm, though the number could run as high as fourteen or as low as eight. In this respect my family seems to have been typical.

What staggers me about all these sturdy children and durable old people is the thought of their diet: salt beef, pork and cod, with occasionally fowl and fresh fish, cabbage, pumpkins, a few tubers from the cellar, Indian pudding, bread and cheese, and for the well-to-do some lemons that came from the West Indies along with the rum. They also drank cider and home-brewed ale or beer. They had no refrigeration and no antibiotics. In the early days there was not even a doctor on the island, but considering the state of medicine in the seventeenth and eighteenth centuries, that may have been an advantage. The women were not only midwives, but herbalists. Obed Macy, the first Nantucket historian (1835), says of these women: "They were always ready, with soothing appliances, to leave their homes to visit the sick, to whom they administered both in the capacity of nurses and physicians. Many were skilled in the use of roots and herbs, the medical properties of which they had learned from the natives. For many years the healing art was practised almost exclusively by females, and more confidence placed in their skill than in the knowledge of men professionally educated."

Another interesting discovery relates to women. In New England, at least, they seem to have been treated as legally competent creatures. Elinor Barnard was executrix of her husband's will probated in 1677. In two of the oldest wills recorded on Nantucket, the testator named women as executrices, in one case the widow, in the other two married daughters. Judith Barnard was made administratix of her husband's estate in 1735. She was also appointed legal guardian of her three younger children, all under age fourteen. An uncle was appointed guardian of sons aged fifteen and seventeen. Rather more surprisingly, Dorcas Starbuck, an unmarried young woman, was one of three witnesses to the deed of Wanack-Mamack (1671).

It is clear that husbands were expected either to control their wives or pay the penalty for their misbehaviour: as for instance in the case of Richard Gardner, who was excommunicated (and thereby lost his voting privileges) because his wife refused to keep her mouth shut. But that was in Salem. On Nantucket Island women exerted considerable influence. Mary Coffin Starbuck could be counted upon to speak her mind in town meetings, although she invariably prefaced her statement with: "My husband and I think—" One of the earliest Quaker preachers to visit Nantucket said of her that "the islanders esteemed her as a Judge among them, for little of moment was done there without her." Kezia Coffin, whose life has inspired more than one novel, owned and operated in her own right a fleet of whaling vessels in the eighteenth century.

The fact that many husbands were seafarers undoubtedly contributed to the self-reliance of wives and mothers. Crèvecoeur, in his *Letters from an American Farmer* (1782), mentioned this aspect of Nantucket domestic life:

As the sea excursions are often very long, the wives are necessarily obliged to transact business, to settle accounts, and, in short, to rule and provide for their families. These circumstances being oft repeated give women the ability, as well as the taste for that kind of superintendency to which, by their prudence and good management, they seem to be in general very equal. This ripens their judgement and justly entitles them to a rank superior to other wives. To this

> dexterity in managing their husband's business whilst he is absent,
> the Nantucket women unite a great deal of industry. They spin
> or cause to be spun, abundance of wool and flax, and would be
> forever disgraced and looked upon as idlers, if all the family were
> not clad in good, neat and sufficient homespun cloth.

Two nineteenth-century women who inherited this Nantucket tradition of feminine self-reliance and even aggressiveness were Maria Mitchell, the first American woman astronomer, and Lucretia Coffin Mott, the abolitionist and perhaps the earliest champion of women's suffrage, a tireless worker for humanitarian causes. Both these women were descended from Tristram Coffin, Thomas Macy, Edward Starbuck and Richard Gardner, not once, but two, three or four times each.

The inbreeding characteristic of Nantucket is probably typical of islands everywhere, as of all isolated communities. Francis Barnard 2nd, belonging to the third generation born on the island, was descended twice from Richard and Sarah Gardner. However, after the marriage between Nathaniel Barnard and Mary Barnard in 1662 I found no first-cousin marriages among my Nantucket forebears, although they are plentiful in my Virginia-Kentucky line. Also, the Nantucketers seem to have come together first in the Merrimack Valley or on the island. Tristram Coffin came from Devonshire, Thomas Macy from Wiltshire, and Thomas Gardner from Dorsetshire. The inbreeding began, therefore, with a fresh pool, in contrast to that of some close-knit American communities whose founders emigrated in a body from a common home in the Old World.

As time went on the inbreeding continued both on the island and off. Typically, again, families do not migrate individually but in clans. Quakers prohibited marriages of a certain degree of consanguinity but, on the other hand, they disowned any member of the sect who married outside the fold. Accordingly, we find Starbucks still marrying Macys and Folgers still marrying Barnards in Indiana in the mid-nineteenth century. So far as I can find out, no genetic problems have arisen, but then it is possible that no geneticist has yet investigated the Nantucket inheritance.

Once I had the Barnard line pieced together and began to write my narrative, I found myself sprawling all over colonial history. Finally in desperation I began to put the story into verse. The constriction of the metric disciplined my narrative and, I hope, has made it more readable. However, the decision to limit myself to the experiences of my forebears meant that I had reluctantly to omit related episodes that lay just outside the scope of my narrative. For instance, I should like to have introduced Samuel Shattuck

(Sarah's brother), who, after being flogged and thrown into jail, took his grievances directly to Charles II; and Robert Pyke, who defended Thomas Macy at considerable expense to himself, refused to order the flogging of Quaker women, and, late in life, effectively denounced the witchcraft trials. Pyke was one of the First Purchasers of Nantucket, but never lived on the island. He has a modest monument in Salisbury. The doughty, sea-going wives of Nantucket ship captains belong to a period after my family left the island. There are a number of popular histories of Nantucket for those who are interested in reading more widely.

This compilation is obviously not intended as a work of historical scholarship, nor yet a genealogy. Specific information such as the month and day of birth, the dates of marriages, the spouses of the siblings and the siblings' birth and death dates have all been omitted. If this history should fall unto the hands of a genealogist who wants that kind of information, I can supply photocopies of my charts. Primarily it is intended for my Barnard cousins, their children and grandchildren and, further, for all the Nantucket kin: descendants of Tristram Coffin, Thomas Macy, Richard Gardner and Edward Starbuck, as many as are interested.

I am indebted to too many people to mention of them individually, but especially to the following:

John Stephenson, who suggested my first move—a query in the *Tri-State Trader* that paid off handsomely by putting me in touch with Bill and Fran Barnard of Seattle just before they began the publication of *Barnard Lines*.

Bill and Fran, whose publication in turn put me in touch with Charles D. Barnard of Los Angeles and Thomas Allen Barnard of Hickory, North Carolina. They were both most generous, and their assistance was invaluable.

Mary Ann Seymour of San Francisco, whose expert search of the census records helped me to piece the line together.

Jane Ruby, who took me twice to Nantucket for research.

The very obliging staff of the Nantucket probate court.

Other correspondents, friends and researchers who especially deserve my thanks are: Betty Montoye, Larry Suits, Gene Swain Kuechman, William J. Taylor, Jr., Osmer Wells, and Martha Mae Frost.

I. Before Nantucket

FIRST, a roll-call of seven emigrant ancestors:
THOMAS GARDNER, THOMAS MACY,
THOMAS BARNARD, ROBERT BARNARD,
JOHN SEVERANCE, EDWARD STARBUCK,
and TRISTRAM COFFIN, Esquire.

A roll-call of wives, also in order:
ELINOR BARNARD, wife of THOMAS
(the only one whose maiden name
is unknown), MARGARET FRIER GARDNER,
10   SARAH HOPCOTT MACY, KATHERINE
REYNOLDS STARBUCK, JOANNE HARVEY
BARNARD (wife of ROBERT), ABIGAIL
KIMBALL SEVERANCE, DIONIS STEVENS
COFFIN ("Dionis" from Dionysia).

These women had sixty children among them.
The children married each other, the grandchildren
married each other, and *their* children married each other.
By now their descendants are counted in tens of thousands.

There are two more shadowy men to add to this list
20   and one wife, not at all shadowy. JOSEPH AUSTIN,
who settled in Dover and married a STARBUCK daughter,
fathered six children and died. The other,
a man named Shattuck, Christian name unrecorded,
place and date and manner of death unknown;
he left a widow, DAMARIS, a son and a daughter.

The first great tidal wave of English migration
washed them into New England's estuaries:
the Merrimack and the Piscataqua, for two.
What set them in motion? Hunger for land, or greed?
30   A migratory contagion? Desire for freedom
combined with a thirst for power—God-given power
to curb the freedom of others? Six of our seven
emigrant ancestors seem to have been "the others."

As new arrivals they settled well north of Boston
outside the limits of Puritan jurisdiction,
but after a score of years in the Merrimack Valley
or farther north, in Dover, their lives were changing.
THOMAS and Goodwife BARNARD, SEVERANCE, MACY
and TRISTRAM COFFIN, all with children all ages,
40   were living in Salisbury, some in deep discontent,
as the 1650s began to draw to a close.

A name and two dates carved on a headstone,
a birth and a death inscribed in a family Bible:
these are us, once we are gone. Without letters
(usually lacking) only the legal records
help us to flesh out our forebears. The wills, for instance,
the inventories, the judgements, the summons to court.
Respectable men held office, but that tells little.
We know much more about people who got into trouble.

50   DIONIS COFFIN steps into the light for a moment
to answer complaints that she overcharged for her beer.
Her beer, she claimed, was better than common beer
and well worth the price. She won her case in court.

But, as the Boston theocracy flung out its tentacles,
giving the classic reason—its riffraffish neighbors
were quite unable to govern themselves—the chances
of finding oneself in trouble increased tenfold.
With Oliver Cromwell securely in power in England
the colonists passed repressive religious laws
60   exceeding anything known before or since.

TRISTRAM COFFIN, never a man to forget
his aristocratic connections, left England, he claimed,
because the Roundheads had ruined him. He was not happy.

THOMAS MACY, though not ordained as a preacher,
made bold to exhort his neighbors on Sundays, thereby
infringing the law. He must have been discontented

even before he was charged with harbouring Quakers.
Here is his written reply to a summons from Boston:

On a rainy morning there came to my house Edward Wharton and
three men more, the said Wharton spoke to me saying that they
were traveling eastward and desired me to direct them in the way
to Hampton, and asked me how far it was to Casco Bay.

I never saw any of the men afore except Wharton, neither
did I require their names, or who they were, but by their carriage
I thought they might be Quakers and told them so, and therefore
desired them to pass on their way, saying to them I might possibly
give offence in entertaining them, and as soone as the violence
of the rain ceased (for it rained very hard) they went away and I
never saw them since.

The time that they stayed in the house was about three quar-
ters of an hour, but I can safely affirm that it was not an houre.

They spake not many words in the time, neither was I at leisure
to talke with them, for I came home wet to ye skin, immediately
afore they came to the house, and I found my wife sick in bed. If
this satisfie not the honoured Court I shall subject to their sentence.

I have not willingly offended, I am ready to serve and obey
you in the Lord.

THOS. MACY

*MACY was fined thirty shillings. (Two shillings at this time was a day's wage
for common labor.) Two of the Quakers, William Robinson, merchant of London,
and Marmaduke Stephenson, of Yorkshire, England, were hanged in Boston on
the 27th of October, 1659.*

∽

EDWARD STARBUCK, a prosperous Dover citizen,
70   must have been walking around with a chip on his shoulder:
      first he spoke of the minister sent from Boston
      with insufficient respect; rebuked for that,
      he professed the Baptist heresy. Action was taken:

The Court being informed of great misdemeanour Committed by
EDWARD STARBUCK of Dover with profession of Anabaptism

for which he is to be proceeded against at the next Court of
assistants if evidence be prepared by that time & it being very
farre for witnesses to travill to Boston at that season of the year,
it is therefore ordered by this Court that the Secretary shall give
Commission to Capt. Thomas Wiggan & Mr. Edw. Smyth to send
for such persons as they shall have notice of which are able to
testify in the sd. cause & to take their testimony uppon oath and
certifie the same to the secretary so soon as may be, that further
proceedings may be therein, if the cause shall so require.

    Was STARBUCK fined? If so, the record is lost.
    However, fines were plentiful: absence from church,
    defending the actions of others, letting one's hair
    grow over one's collar—we know that STARBUCK paid that one.

    We can't be surprised that under these irritations
    STARBUCK, MACY and COFFIN moved to an island
80   thirty miles out at sea and south of Cape Cod.
    Nantucket, a few sand dunes surrounded by ocean,
    had little to recommend it except its location
    outside the hated Puritan jurisdiction.

    They took no minister with them and built no church.
    Not that they fled in the night, as Whittier has it.
    They formed a company (COFFIN being prime mover)
    with THOMAS BARNARD, one son and a son-in-law
    of TRISTRAM COFFIN, COFFIN himself, and MACY,
    and four more men of Salisbury and Hampton.
90   They bought the right to settle one fourth of the island,
    that fourth heretofore owned by Thomas Mayhew
    a second owner after the resident Indians.

Be it known unto all men by these Presents that I Thomas May-
hew of Martin's Vineyard, Merchant do hereby acknowledge
that I have sold unto TRISTRAM COFFIN THOMAS MACY
Christopher Hussy Richard Swain THOMAS BARNARD Peter Coffin
Stephen Greenleaf John Swain & William Pile all that Right and
Interest that I have in the Island of Nantucket by pattent the which
Right I bought of James Forret Gentleman, Steward unto the Lord
Sterling. . . . as by Conveyance under their hands and seals for Ever

with all the privilidges thereunto belonging for and in Consideration
of the sum of Thirty Pounds of Currant pay unto whomsoever I the
sd Thomas Mayhew mine heirs or assigns shall appoint and also two
bever hats one for myself and one for my wife and further to this
to Declare that I the sd Thomas Mayhew have reserved to myself
that Neck upon Nantucket called Masquetuck. . . .

Mayhew reserved for himself one share in the company.

Each man of the original ten took a partner:
THOMAS BARNARD, his brother ROBERT of Andover;
THOMAS MACY, his good friend EDWARD STARBUCK;
and Peter Coffin, his younger brother JAMES.

Not all the twenty First Purchasers moved to the island.
NATHANIEL BARNARD, the second son of THOMAS,
100 received his father's share and married his cousin
MARY, daughter of ROBERT. NATHANIEL and MARY,
JOANNA and ROBERT moved to Nantucket Island,
but THOMAS died "abroad"—that is, on the mainland.
Peter Coffin, too, remained on the mainland,
but JAMES and his brother JOHN with TRISTRAM, SR.
moved out to Nantucket, and so did MACY and STARBUCK.

JOHN SEVERANCE had no part in the island venture.
However, his daughter MARY came to Nantucket
as wife to JOHN COFFIN. JAMES married DEBORAH AUSTIN
110 daughter of JOSEPH and grandchild of EDWARD STARBUCK.
STARBUCK, AUSTIN, MACY, BARNARD and COFFIN:
the rope is almost ready to twine, but two strands
are still missing: the GARDNERS and SHATTUCKS of Salem.

THOMAS GARDNER, planter and merchant adventurer,
failed with his first attempt at a Cape Ann colony.
Later, the settlement, moved to a new location,
was renamed Salem, and here the founders prospered.
Forty years later THOMAS GARDNER was wealthy,
a land-owner, office-holder, head of a clan

120 (he had nine children). Widowed, he married a second time—
DAMARIS SHATTUCK, a widow, a Puritan-baiter.
The widow's daughter SARAH took after her mother,
and RICHARD, the seaman son of old THOMAS GARDNER,
married this SARAH SHATTUCK, his step-mother's daughter.
Both father and son had repeatedly to pay fines
incurred by wives who defied as a matter of principle
laws against (for instance) consorting with Quakers.
Finally RICHARD himself was hailed into court
for failing to put a curb on his spouse's tongue.

130 (She spoke derisively of a magistrate
in her husband's presence, and he didn't stop her.)
RICHARD'S friends in Nantucket, watching this drama,
extended an invitation. They needed a seaman.
Would RICHARD join them? All things—and wives—considered,
we can't be surprised that RICHARD accepted the offer.

A grant was made to RICHARD GARDNER, halfe Accomedacons,
According to the Grants made to Seamen and Tradesmen, upon
condition that hee exercise himself as a Sea-man, and the come to
inhabit here before the end of May, 1668, and after his entrance
here, not to depart the Island in Point of dwelling for the space of
three years, upon the Forefeiture of the Grant aforesaid.

Later his brother Captain John Gardner would join him.
From that time forward Gardners would marry Coffins,
Macys, Starbucks and Barnards; Coffins would marry
Barnards, Starbucks, Macys and Gardners. Also

140 they might marry Folgers, Colemans, Husseys or Swains,
but few people married "off-island" for decades to come.

II. Nantucket

"Nantucket! Take out your map and look at it. See what a real
corner of the world it occupies; how it stands there away off
shore, more lonely than the Eddystone lighthouse. Look at it—
a mere hillock and elbow of sand; all beach, without a background."

So says Melville, or Ishmael says it for him.

Fourteen miles in length, with a harbour, swamps
and fresh-water ponds, the vegetation scrubby:
that was Nantucket Island, its only inhabitants
peaceable, well-disposed Indians. Peter Folger
10   had already lived among them, learning their language
and preaching the gospel. When asked to join the settlers
he came with his wife and children, a man much-needed
when trouble arose, as it did now and then arise.

The settlers had bought their land from Thomas Mayhew,
and he, in turn, had bought from the Nantucket Indians.
Nevertheless, to confirm their rights to the land
the settlers bought again from the natives: the right
to own and settle one fourth of Nantucket Island.
The deed was signed by Wanack-Mamack, head Sachem.

These Presents Wittness yt I Wanackmamack Head Sachem of ye
Island of Nantuckett, have Bargained and sold, and doe by these
Presents Bargaine and Sell unto TRISTRAM COFFIN, THOMAS
MACY, Richard Swayne, THOMAS BERNARD, John Swain, Mr.
Thomas Mayhew, EDWARD STARBUCK, Peter Coffin, JAMES
COFFIN, Stephen Greenleafe, Tristram Coffin Junior, Thomas
Coleman, ROBERT BERNARD, Christopher Hussey, Robert Pyke,
John Smyth, and John Bishop these Islands of Nantucket, namely
all ye west end of ye aforesaid Island unto ye Pond comonly called
Waquittaquay and from ye head of that Pond to ye North side of
ye Island Manamoy; Bounded by a Path from ye Head of ye Pond
aforesaid to Manamoy; as also a Neck at ye East End of ye Island
called Poquomock, with the Property thereof, and all ye Royaltyes,
Priviledges and Immunityes thereto belonging or whatsoever Right
I ye aforesaid Wanackmak have, or have had in ye same: That is, all

ye Lands afore menconed and likewise ye Winter seed of ye whole
island from ye End of an Indyan Harvest untill Planting Time,
or ye first of May, from Yeare to Yeare forever, as likewise Liberty
to make use of Wood and Timber on all Parts of ye Island; and
likewise Halfe of ye Meadows and Marshes, as long as ye aforesaid
English their Heyres or Assignes live on ye Island; And likewise I
the aforesaid Wanackmamack doe sell until ye English afore men-
coned ye Propriety of ye rest of ye Island belonging unto mee, for
and in consideration of fforty Pounds already received by mee or
other by my Consent or Ord.

To Have and to hold, ye aforesaid Tracts of Land with ye
P'riety, Royaltyies, Immunityes, Priviledges, and all Appertenances
thereunto belonging to the ye aforesaid Purchasers their Heyres
and Assignes forever.

In witness Whereof I the aforesaid Wanackmamack have
hereunto sett my Hand and Seale ye Daye and Yeare above written.
The Sign of Wanack-Mamack

Signed Sealed and Delivered
  in ye presence of
Peter Foulger
Eleazer Foulger
Dorcas Starbuck

20   The usual trouble ensued. The peaceable natives,
       knowing nothing of fences or property not held in common,
       went over the fences—sharing, as they supposed;
       by English law, stealing. But thanks to Folger, explaining
       one to the other, and STARBUCK, a steady man,
       counselling patience, all went reasonably well.
       No blood was shed, not even when Indian wars
       raged on the mainland during Philip's rebellion.

       As for the island's economy, TRISTRAM COFFIN
       envisioned hummocky meadows covered with sheep.
30   The wool sold in mainland markets would bring a good profit.
       Englishmen should have known better. Island-dwellers,
       whether they like it or not, become seamen and ship-owners.
       fishermen, boat-builders, and, in Nantucket, whalers.
       Instead of wool their principal products were oil,

candles and whale-bone; their harbour reeked of oil.
Their port was the whaling capital of the world.

Besides seamen, however, the island had coopers,
carpenters, chandlers and sailmakers, boatbuilders, tradesmen,
smiths and shoemakers; also, they did raise sheep.

40   But first things first: they had to lay out the town
and build it. The BARNARD house-lots (each twenty acres)
lay on the high ground near the Indian boundary line.
In all there were twenty-one lots; of these, one third
were owned by COFFIN, his sons, or his sons-in-law.

And when the town was built and had people in it,
they needed a governing body: a chief magistrate
and seven selectmen. They needed a code of laws
to deal with the usual matters: weights and measures
and civil suits, but also trade with the Indians,
50   use of profanity, drunken behaviour, and so on.
They passed regulations relating to ships and shipping
and proper securing of "Rack'd goods found on the shore"
(to be held one year, in case the owner turned up.)

Having no church and therefore no meeting-house
they met at Nathaniel Starbuck's, and dubbed his home
the Parliament House. In elections they voted "yes"
with a kernel of corn, and voted "no" with a bean.

They had to determine the number of sheep and horses,
hogs and geese a man was allowed on the commonage.
60   They had to determine fair prices, for instance: wheat
four shillings per bushel, barley two shillings and sixpence,
and Indian corn two shillings and eightpence per bushel.

Bread is the staff of life. They needed a gristmill.
First they approved a horse mill. Two weeks later
they changed their minds and voted in favour of water.

They needed roads. Surveyors of roads were appointed
and told to agree with owners on damage due
for land infringed on (the Town to have the last word).
Much of it sounds familiar, including the laws
70   protecting their few and fast-disappearing trees.

They needed a pound for livestock. The minutes tell us:

a bargain was made with NATHAN'L BARNARD and JOHN
COFFIN to set up a pound for the use of the Town which two
men aforementioned do engage to make strong and sufficient good
strong posts and five rales ten feet long and a Cap on the top
and to be finished before the end of June next, and the Town do
engage to pay them three pounds either in Corn, butter or Cheese
at or before the last of September next and this to be paid by a
rate according to the proportion of Every man's Estate in land and
Stock—the pound to be four rod Square. . . .

∾

Early days on the island were sometimes stormy,
and not because of the weather. The Gardners, for instance,
rose in revolt against TRISTRAM COFFIN. They thought him
(with reason) high-handed and he thought them insubordinate—
all as one might expect. But feuds were forgotten;
the clans intermarried and peace prevailed for the most part.

NATHANIEL BARNARD sided with TRISTRAM COFFIN
during the Gardner revolt. He served as selectman.
80   He prospered and fathered a brood of children.
Court records show he was fined in 1709
for selling rum to the Indians; nevertheless,
(like the Byrds, who were doing likewise down in Virginia
and both the Gardners, for that matter, here on Nantucket)
he always remained a highly respected citizen
and held important office a number of times.

We know that NATHANIEL'S death followed soon after MARY'S.
At seventy-six "he departed life in great peace"
town records inform us. Out of eleven children

90   one son had been lost at sea, off the Scilly Rocks;
one daughter, Hannah, had died, leaving a child.
NATHANIEL named in his will the surviving children,
five sons, four daughters, all of them born on Nantucket.
BENJAMIN BARNARD, the fourth of NATHANIEL'S sons,
received his share of the common land and livestock.
That spring his wife was pregnant again; a fourth child,
FRANCIS, was born in August. The couple were Quakers,
among the first on the island, and JUDITH BARNARD,
BENJAMINS'S wife, may well have brought this about.
100 JUDITH, descended from old THOMAS GARDNER of Salem
and, on her mother's side, from TRISTRAM COFFIN
(a great-granddaughter to both these redoubtable men)
was also related to women who entertained Quakers,
listened to their discourse and embraced their faith.

The island's inhabitants, mind you, were pious people
who worshipped God but distrusted and feared the clergy.
Also, they favoured different persuasions: hence,
for fifty years—including the infamous years
when wretched "witches" were being hanged on the mainland—
110 Nantucket carried on without a church or pastor.

Proselytizing Friends who came to the island
around the turn of the century had an advantage:
assembling in private homes, without clergy as such,
and giving leave to both men and women to preach,
they appealed to those notoriously strong-minded women,
SARAH GARDNER, DAMARIS' SHATTUCK'S daughter,
and Mary Coffin Starbuck, daughter of TRISTRAM.
The Monthly Meetings began in 1708
and three years later the sect admitted to membership
120 BENJAMIN BARNARD and JUDITH GARDNER, his bride,
granddaughter of SARAH, grandniece of Mary Starbuck.
For one hundred years and three generations to come
ours was a Quaker family, first on Nantucket,
"the Quaker Island," and later in North Carolina.
Francis, the son of JUDITH and BENJAMIN BARNARD,
married ELIZABETH MACY, who was, like himself,
descended from TRISTRAM COFFIN. Of their ten children,

three were sons, among them a second FRANCIS.

A number of Barnards were captains of Nantucket whalers,
130 but whether any of these were men in our line—
BENJAMIN, FRANCIS the 1st or FRANCIS the 2nd—
Nantucket records have so far not revealed.

We know that BENJAMIN BARNARD owned, at his death,
the type of whaleboat used for off-shore whaling,
harpoons, and nearly one half of a sloop—the *Ranger*.
However, he also owned sheep, and shares in a wharf
and shares in a mill (this may have been one of two windmills
recently built on the island) as well as land—
pasture and other—worth more than a thousand pounds.
140 Whaling captain or not, he lived very well.

FRANCIS, BENJAMIN'S son, lived eighty-two years,
but whether he ever went whaling or sailed in the sloop
or captained a ship, we do not know. We do know
his father-in-law, having helped in killing a whale,
either took or sent his share of the whalebone to England
and bought with the proceeds a clock that became an heirloom,
a history book, and a bolt of Irish linen.

If guilt for our ancestors' sins descends with their genes
I fear we must have the blood of whales on our hands.
150 Nantucket folk, said Melville, were firmly opposed
to the shedding of blood, excepting the blood of whales.
In *that* they excelled.

              So much for husbands and fathers.
We have no need to ask what their wives were doing.
They bore, in three generations, twenty-nine Barnards.
Of these, more than twenty survived and married, most of them
into Nantucket clans—the Coffins, Folgers,
Colemans, Macys, Starbucks, Gardners and Swains—
but FRANCIS BARNARD 2nd, son of FRANCIS,
160 married a girl from New Jersey, CATHERINE OSBORN.

JAMES OSBORN called his daughter after his mother.
The elder KATHARINE, daughter to JACQUES POILLON,
was wife to SAMUEL OSBORN, a New Jersey planter.
JAMES, the son of SAMUEL and KATHARINE OSBORN,
married a woman named ANNE. surname unknown.
When, in 1759, JAMES OSBORN
dictated his will, he mentioned a married daughter,
Rebecca Swain, her brother John, and CATHERINE,
nine years old at the time. The son and the widow
170 each received half the land and the household goods.
Each daughter received a cash bequest—and CATHERINE
fifty-five pounds in addition to be invested—
"put out at interest"—until she should come of age.

ANNE, dying five years later, bequeathed to this daughter,
CATHERINE: bed and bedding, a silver tankard,
a warming pan, two pewter platters, a trunk,
two silver spoons, a looking glass, and clothing.
After a public sale of her other possessions
(household goods, some farm equipment and cattle),
180 and after her funeral costs and debts were paid,
such funds as remained she ordered set aside
"to pay for my daughter CATHERINE to have schooling."
CATHERINE, then fifteen, was to travel far:
a bride on Nantucket, a housewife, mother and widow
in North Carolina, she died at last in Ohio.

Five years after her mother's death we find her
a resident of Nantucket. Why? With whom?
She must have been with relations. Grandparents? Coffins?
Folgers? Swains? (Her sister had married a Swain.)
190 However it was, she there married FRANCIS BARNARD,
the great-grandson of THOMAS and ROBERT BARNARD.
There was a Quaker wedding that seems somehow
to have got out of hand; we read in the record book:

The members appointed to attend FRANCIS BARNARD'S mar-
riage make return that it was pretty well conducted excepting that

some of the young people were very disorderly; whereupon William
Coffin & Samuel Starbuck are appointed to inquire into the
case. . . .

> What *can* they have done? Proposed a toast to the pair,
> or thrown a handful of rice, or kissed the bride?
> Perhaps they simply giggled and shuffled their feet;
> Quaker decorum could be excessively fragile.

> After five years of marriage, FRANCIS and CATHERINE
> now with three small children, "removed from the island,"
> 200 part of an exodus taking place at the time.
> CATHERINE, having grown up on a mainland plantation,
> may well have taken the oily town in aversion.
> Her feelings aside, there were several excellent reasons
> for leaving Nantucket in 1774.
> The island was overcrowded and so inbred
> that finding a panel of jurors in no way related
> to plaintiffs, defendants, or both, was almost impossible.

> Worse, a war with England now appeared certain.
> The tea had been dumped. The port of Boston was closed.
> 210 The shot heard round the world hadn't yet been fired
> but would be in April. The colonies had no navy.
> Nantucket had no defense. She had, however,
> more than a hundred ships and two thousand seamen,
> all fair prey to the British navy at war.
> The Coffin family tended to side with the crown.
> Quakers tried hard to be neutral. Even the patriots
> saw that Nantucket's prosperous times were over
> at least for the present. Great days were still to come
> for those who stayed behind and survived the war,
> 220 but FRANCIS and CATHERINE had no share in that future.

III. After Nantucket

During the early 1770s Macys,
Gardners, Coffins, Barnards, Starbucks and Folgers
deserted Nantucket in droves, but where they went
they clustered; for instance, they clustered in North Carolina.

Now North Carolina was (like the Merrimack Valley)
settled by riffraff, at least so said its neighbours
to north and south, Virginia and South Carolina.
"Riffraff" referred to Quakers and other outcasts.
A Quaker settlement flourished in North Carolina
10   in Guilford County, in what is known as the Piedmont.
For twenty-five years New Garden Quakers had visited
Friends on Nantucket. Now families began leaving the island
moved to New Garden, among them, FRANCIS and CATHERINE.

Migrating from ocean beaches to pine-covered hills,
from sand to red earth, they turned from the sea-trades to farming.
One wonders what sort of success the new planters had
on land not known for fertility even at best.
FRANCIS and CATHERINE lived there for thirty years
until FRANCIS died, intestate, at age fifty-eight.
20   The little we know about them, as usual, emerges
from deeds and inventories and Quaker records.
Besides his land, he seems to have owned a smithy,
a gristmill and sawmill; he also had sheep and hogs,
a number of horses and sixteen head of cattle.
Indoors, aside from tables and chairs and beds,
the pots and the pewter, almost everything listed
speaks of domestic industry: candlemolds
and boxes to follow, for instance; a brewing tub,
a churn, a loom and two small spinning wheels
30   with baskets of wool and cotton. A looking glass
and a clock are almost the only amenities mentioned,
fewer than CATHERINE knew as a girl in New Jersey
(and FRANCIS'S grandparents lived as well, or better).
There were, on the other hand, more books in the house:
John Woolman's *Journal*, for one, and Barclay's *Apology*.

Ten children in all were born to FRANCIS and CATHERINE,
three in Nantucket, seven in North Carolina.
The war with England was over, the Constitution
not yet framed when the ninth child, REUBEN, was born.
40   His was the first generation born off-island,
and first to rebel: the Deep Creek Monthly Meeting
disowned him in 1808 for attending a wedding.
Not long afterward he himself took a wife
called JANE or Jinny, of whom we know very little—
enough, however, to be quite sure she was Indian.

The young couple named their first-born child, a son,
for Jesse Franklin, a North Carolinian hero
who served in the Revolution, fighting at King's Mountain.

Later REUBEN himself would carry arms
50   in the War of 1812. His great-grandparents
had led us into the fold, and REUBEN BARNARD,
three generations later, broke away.
From that time forward, we were Quakers no more.

Of six sons born to FRANCIS and CATHERINE BARNARD,
one died young. The five surviving sons
were Christopher, REUBEN, Samuel, James and Francis.
Four of them, one by one, joined a new migration:
Nantucket families, loosely rooted as yet
in southern soil, began to move northward again
60   in search of a better life beyond the Ohio.
For forty years the migration continued, as uncles,
brothers, nephews and cousins pulled up stakes,
sold out and left. Of FRANCIS and CATHERINE'S sons
only Christopher stayed behind, a widower
living with one of his children, surviving the war.

Their father departed this life in 1805
and three years later Samuel moved to Ohio
taking his mother with him. Francis the 3rd
tried Tennessee first, then settled in Illinois.

70   James went to Indiana, to Henry County,
and REUBEN went to Ohio to look things over.
In April of '39 another Francis,
Samuel's son, wrote urgently to his cousin,
also Francis, this one Christopher's son:

I can inform thee that Father and myself intends to go to the Illinois again as soon as we can get our harvest in and would be very glad to have thy company and as many of the rest of the relations as wishes to see the beautiful country of plains and valleys and great advantages that there is having the land all ready cleared without a stump, stone, or stick in the way of the plough and as black and rich soil as any of the river bottoms. How can you forbear taking a glimpse of such a scene as this? . . .

Tell Uncle REUBEN that this land I have been speaking about [in Ohio] is some of that that he could have had one quarter section of when he was here for $700.00 and Father bought it a short time afterwards for $1000.00. Father is still very anxious for all my uncles and aunts and cousins to move to the west, for he believes that there is the same encouragement to move as there was thirty years ago and surely if they had moved when he did it would have been better for them and all their families, though he says that a contented mind is a continued feast, and a little is enough with contentment, but a great deal gives more. . . .

Please to answer this pretty soon. I wish for Uncle REUBEN's family to see this letter.

Whether or not REUBEN BARNARD saw the letter,
he moved in the 1840s to Indiana—
not to country open and rolling, but flat—
so flat it was swampy; new settlers suffered from ague.
Drainage ditches were dug; the land was cleared
80   of dense deciduous forests. The trees were burned.
Once ready for ploughing the soil was rich beyond dreaming.
Here, as his nephew had prophesied, he prospered.
His land, worth twelve hundred dollars in 1850,
had almost tripled in value a decade later.
REUBEN'S household included JINNY, his wife,
their six unmarried daughters (two died unwed),
as well as the third and youngest son, named Samuel.

Two older sons remained in North Carolina,
at least for a time. The eldest, JESSE FRANKLIN
90 (always called Franklin), had married ELIZABETH HAYES.
His brother Francis (another!) married her sister.
The parents of these two girls were GREENBERRY HAYES
and LEAH THARPE. As GREENBERRY'S will makes clear,
he owned besides a plantation some Negro slaves.

Excerpt from the last will and testament of GREENBERRY HAYES *of the County of Iredell and the State of North Carolina.*

Item. I will that just debts I have unpaid be paid. 2nd, I will that Home Plantation be equally divided between my two sons Asbury Hayes and Greenberry Hayes. 3rd. I will that the large wagon be sold and also my stock of sheep, cattle, horses and hogs. . . . I will to be divided between my five children now living with me . . . each a bed and suitable furniture [bedding], the balance of all the bed clothing to belong to my two daughters Polly and Cynthia. 5thly I will negro boy Wilson to son Asbury Hayes to him and his heirs forever and negro woman Quincy I will to my daughter Polly provided said negro is obedient and behaves well. If she does not I will that my executor herafter to be named make sale of said negro and pay over the money to my daughter above named, to wit, Polly. . . . To my son Samuel I give one tract of land wherein he now lives, also fifty dollars in money. To my daughter ELIZABETH BARNARD two hundred dollars; to my daughter Rachel Barnard one hundred ninety dollars; to my son William I give one tract in which he now lives, one horse and one cow, which horse and cow he has in possession, and fifty dollars in money, and to my little grandson Thomas Gaither I give a suckling colt from my gray mare and my other wagon not before named. . . .

The gray mare went to another son, and a negro girl Nancy to another, except that Nancy's first child should be Cynthia's. The will was probated in 1845.

Rachel Barnard, named in Greenberry's will,
was wife to John, a son of Christopher Barnard:
REUBEN'S Francis would marry Cynthia Hayes;
another Barnard, Elizabeth, Christopher's daughter,
would marry Samuel Hayes. There is no indication,

100 however, that REUBEN or any of REUBEN'S sons
forgot their Quaker inheritance so far
as to own a human being—"Nancy's first child,"
for instance. They, too, were about to leave the South
much as their grandfather FRANCIS had left Nantucket
before the sound of cannon shattered the peace.

FRANKLIN and Francis were settled in Indiana
before Fort Sumter. Of FRANKLIN'S three sons, the eldest,
SAMUEL, married a MARY MELISSA MARSHALL
and farmed like his father and brothers, uncles and cousins
110 in Hancock County. MARY MELISSA and SAMUEL
named their first son Reuben, the second Franklin.
The fourth was named for his father, my father SAMUEL.

When REUBEN the patriarch died in the 1860s
he lay in a land of plenty: his sons, and even
his grandsons, each on his own farm, clustered around him
with daughters and sons-in-law—for Hancock County
was full of his kinfolk, and yet there is somehow a sense
of REUBEN as one apart, looking on from a distance,
not answering letters, and not at home when looked for.
120 A rebel gone sour? Was war a rude disappointment?
Or had his marriage to JINNY been a mistake?
Or was it all those daughters? Life in a house
with seven chattering females can make a man crusty
(Elizabeth Bennet's father only had six.)

His JINNY survived him—lived on with the spinster daughters.
A letter to North Carolina reported as follows:

*Excerpt from a letter written to James Andrew Barnard, Christopher Barnard's
grandson, by William E. Current, a North Carolina neighbour and friend of the
Barnard family, who had gone to Buck Grove, Rush County, Indiana. The letter
is dated October 1871. The "Wash Hayes" mentioned in the letter was Solomon
Washington Hayes, son of Samuel Hayes and Elizabeth Barnard, a grandson of
GREENBERRY HAYES and Christopher Barnard, and therefore doubly related
to the FRANKLIN-BARNARD family.*

There has been great destruction by fire in the western States
this fall. The Great City of Chicago, Ill, was laid in ruins a few
weeks ago, thousands of families left homeless. . . . So far your
acquaintances are all well so far as I know. I have not seen Wash
Hayes since April, but I heard from him about a month ago. He
was well then. He lives about 25 miles from where I stay. He is
the same Wash yet—can laugh as big as ever. He is living with
old Aunt JINNIE BARNARD. He has a good place and is doing
well. I was at FRANKLIN, Francis and Sam'l Barnard's. . . . They
are all getting along finely.

"Sam'l" could be either REUBEN'S *son Samuel, brother of Francis and* FRANKLIN,
or SAMUEL, L. FRANKLIN'S *son, who was now married and living nearby.*

> And so it went: sometimes they were doing finely,
> sometimes not. Occasionally fortune smiled
> and then again misfortune descended. In sum,
> 130 ours was a tribe of no especial distinction.
> None of them got himself hanged, but then not one
> was a general, a senator, saint, or even professor.
> Like Adam they ate their bread in the sweat of their faces.
> They knew their duty was set down in Holy Writ—
> to be fruitful and multiply and replenish the earth,
> and so they did, and behold! we are here to prove it.
> Together they form one almost invisible strand
> in three hundred years of history. Nevertheless,
> each one when living was as alive as you.

UNCOLLECTED

"I found my grief . . ."

I found my grief
In fragrance of a dead geranium leaf
Crumpled between my fingers;
The living breath
Of summer, after summer's death.

Thirst

The cloudy curtains of the rain sweep round
And in my heart the cloudy dust of drouth
Spirals in yellow wind.
The thirst for green salt water drys my mouth,
Nor will my thirst be slackened
By sweet white water from the mountain gorges,
Or river water bursting dykes and flooding
Hollow pastures. Here in a drenched,
Rain-darkened country I sit brooding,
Seeking between the stiff white pages what sea-words
Will turn the rain to brine,
Will cause the rain to mass up green and mountainous
And burst again on rock.

The river lifts and laps the end of the street.
It rubs the creaking piles of the gravel dock
And turns northwest to the ocean.

Thinking of Yeats

What he wished to do, he has done with a bold hand.
He set his friends on nobly moving poems
that they might companion him to his fame's end.
We'll see him, not lonely, riding as one
central in Chaucerian company,
till all are but tracks of their mounts in sea sand.

The Carver

O the night's a carver, carving worlds of ivory;
Carving towns and villages with a silver spoon,
Carving gleaming landscapes of the world of Faery,
With the hard bright chisel of the thin edged moon.

Impassioned Sonnet

If I should ever write a noble verse
To be remembered after I am dead,
This is my wish, that it shall not be read
From textbooks or for school; for there's no curse,
No fate for poetry that could be worse
Than being stuffed in an unwilling head,
Dissected, analyzed, and beauty-bled,
And hurried graveward by a textbook hearse.
Oh, let it not be read except from choice
By beauty lovers who will never groan
And read because they must, but will rejoice
In singing lines, or read and let alone
At least. Let it be thus or let my voice
Sing ever these small tunes, unheard, unknown.

The Pathetic Fallacy

Feeling the serene reflective mood
Of mountain lakes that lie
Face upward in impregnable valleys, I,
Amazed, look upon the ocean's great unease.
Inconsolable still? Oh, sleep on your sorrow.

The water is rich in foam, in desolation.
I, devoid of answering emotion,
Listen (it seems indelicate) to these unburdenings.
Spare me this too incessant gesticulation,
This excess of grief, O Ocean!

Thetis with a surge of anguish turns
From the proffered handkerchief, spurns consolation.

An Evening by the Sea

The sea is green-silver at sunset,
    And a pathway of gold lies straight
Across the waves to the Orient
    And China's dragon gate.

The flash of an arm in the surges,
    Dark brown of the bather's head.
And the gold of the magic pathway
    Deepens to coppery red.

Waist-deep in the foaming waters
    A fisherman moveless stands;
A wee bird follows the ripples
    And pecks at the shining sands.

Silhouettes on the bright horizon
    The ships go by afar,
And the mast of the Alice leans seaward
    Though sunk in the prisoning bar.

Against Lethe

When all of movement
Is a little rocking movement,
And stiffened fingers find no better thing to do
Than pluck at a fringed shawl,
Being too bent and numb with the earth's cold
To sense the surface of carnelian
Or follow outline of intaglio,
Is it better then to hold
A stone, or an unmonumented memory
Dissolving cloudily in a dark glass?

Aquarelle

The hearts that hang
On the alder tree
Beat in their anguish
Perceptibly.

The horse's hooves
On the marshy ground
Strike heavily
With a sobbing sound.

The knight rides by,
But he never heeds
The long hair tangled
Among the reeds.

The floating fingers
Of a king's daughter
Are pallid as lily roots
Seen through the water.

Her wavering face
Struck the moon with terror,
Rising at twilight
To look in her mirror.

She saw her own ghost
Through the alder tree,
Whose leaves were quivering
Dolorously.

Bay Beach

The bay beach is narrow, and the thin tide goes
out without a whisper. It drops back from the little
islands of grass and the pooled mud flats; and when
it turns again, the ripples make a small waking sound.
Wavelets propelled by the imperceptible pale hand of
the moon wash against the flat beach, break in the
heart.

Ripple—"remember?" Ripple—flicker of light
on the water—"remember?" The bay breathes again,
rises lightly against the barnacled piling, rounds
the upturned bottoms of little boats, wavers from
peninsula to island and from island to mainland.
There are light gaps in the abandoned wharf, and the
piling marches out into the bay, bearing tumbled
shack at the head of its column.

Ripple—"remember?" Remember what? Sad things,
sad because for all their beauty they were slight
enough to be forgotten. Moments like songs that we
thought to remember always. After the long silence
of the ebb-tide, and the forgetfulness which is real
death, comes the faint and startling—ripple—"re-
member?" All the poor forgotten things are washed
up on bay beaches, left there wreathed with mist,
blown across with rain, and cracked with the salt sun.

But out beyond the inlet the sea turns and moans
and will never forget. The sea beach is wide with-
out end, and the dunes are heaped against the cold
sky. Let us walk there in a high wind, remembering.

Cream

The furred ear
And the faun's eyes appearing
Over the churn,
Staccato hoof clicking
Against a milk pail
In butter-fragrant shadows—
These could not fail
To give a dairymaid a turn;
But the voice purring,
Guttural like dropping water,
Reassuring,
The tongue flicking
The smooth cream from the lips,
From these
A farmer's wench might learn
To be at ease
With a wood-deity.
And though a farm girl be thick
To a faun's taste,
And though she laugh loud
In the powdered dusk,
He must not be too proud
To be discovered by her scream,
To smother petulance and his own mockery together
If he love cream.

Cupbearer

I shall bear
Scarlet and yellow cups on a crystal tray,
With no drop spilled;
Translucent pottery sun-shot
And filled
With wine no cellarer knows,
Clearer than clear air.

"Fire, snow, and the night . . ."

Fire, snow, and the night
Create a world
Where two may come together.
But violet, gold, and white
Are one gray
With the rain, the light,
And the thawing snow.
In the common day
We walk again remote
With alien gray faces.

Knight-Errant

It was a sad plight
The young witch was in that night,
With her long hair caught in a thorn bush.

Already her small silk shoe
Was blackened with dew
That fell on the feathery grass.

I told her that sober maids
Wear their hair in two smooth braids
And never get hung on a thorn bush.

Of course, I untangled her hair.
Could I have gone and left her there?
I might have drawn out my dagger
And cut it off close to her head.
Instead,
I untangled it lock by lock.

All of the twigs on the thorn bush
Were spindles of fine gold thread.

I asked her what she was doing
Out so late,
She guessed that I was wooing—
But I told her, that could wait.

I didn't follow
When she went off, slow,
Through the hollow.
I thought I would rather not know.

But see how my hands are pricked!

Moonstone

The beach is strewn
With jasper, agate, and carnelian,
And among these the clear
Stone tears of the moon.

Let this song be for you a clouded tear
Found on deserted sands, by a broken boat—
A pitiable thing.
A pale emblem of sorrow to set
In a dull ring.

Shriek of Defiance

(In the manner of Ezra Pound)

Come, my songs,
Let us be unforgivably simple-minded.
Let us gape all afternoon at a johnny-jump-up
And suck our thumbs in round eyed astonishment at a young calf.
Let us prefer skunk cabbages in a swamp to Picasso
And not consider it necessary to say so.
Let us sleep, oh! a very great deal,
And drink milk with our dinner.

". . . Without whose untender criticism this book . . ."

It is so small a flame,
And the towers falling
All about—
With the rush of the stones falling,
The earth slipping,
The slight wind of your breath
Might put it out.
Lo! the hot wax
Dripping
Into the chipped saucer.
I pray you in God's name
Be careful!
It is so small a flame
In this dark wind.

Gourmand Before an Oyster Can

Being sent to the store to buy bread
We observe a commonplace can of Willapa oysters.

It causes us to brood on the hungry dead
Who no longer eat oysters, or any other food,
And upon the sadness it would be to have died
Before eating all the oysters one wanted
Either sauced, souped, or fried.
And how very sad to never any more
Buy them from the Japanese girl at the bay
With her black hair boxing a face
Like yellow caramel, her eyes glossy as black soap,
Her voice small in that listening place
Of mud-flat and sea-pasture; never to revisit
The house on pegs in the half-liquid landscape
That burns with a blue salt flame,
Where boats full of shells are poled with a slow grace
And a seal plays beyond the end of the wharf.

How very sad to have died
Having eaten a great deal of bread
And having too long denied
Oneself oysters.

"My mind is a hall where walk . . ."

My mind is a hall where walk
Straight, beautiful thoughts,
Splendidly clothed.
But I am no artist of speech
And my talk
Is not even a sketch of these;
My words—
Meaningless scribbles and scrawls
Of brown chalk.

Sonnet for Dorothy

You are the palace that is my heart's home.
Its shining walls uplifted on a height
Bear balconies that lean above the foam
Of unsailed oceans; there are courtyards bright
With sun and blowing fountains. I may pace
Cool cloisters, join the great hall's mirth, or jest
With motley on the stairs; and there is grace
Of love in a tower chamber facing west.

But things of which my glad heart never tires
Are those long corridors that always turn
Me back unsatisfied; the cloud-wrapt spires;
The curtained niches where tall candles burn
Unflickering; those seats of mystery,
Sealed rooms to which you offer me no key.

Estuary

Gray light breaks on the water, listless
Water widening. The shores turn each from the other,
Drifting into the sea-haze to the north and south.
In the river mouth
The sharpness of sea-water is softened to long swells.
With the expanding water and diminished hills
Distance flattens, the world circles to a horizon
Opening towards the low-lying insatiable ocean.
The silent pencil of a bare mast tethered
Inscribes the cloud with curving characters
Forboding separation.

Alms

Your words, so freely thrown, I catch
In my cupped palms
And being a mendicant accept
With gratitude these alms.
Theirs is so opulent a shine
I never try
To test them with my teeth,
Or buy
From merchants either fruit or wine
In change for them.
Rather, I laugh to hear them clink—
And do not dine.

Bay Road

There was no sign
Either of blackened bush
Or of scorched pine.
The fragmentary
Agate, the crushed shell
Were unmixed with ash.
Paintbrush and salmonberry
Were mist wet;
Nor was there flash
Of resinous torches snapping against the sky.
Of bright fire and of desolation
Earth bore no trace.
Others walking there will
Not know the place.

Inspiration

It is as if a seed once cast
In some dark corner of my brain
Had found deep soil at last;
Had taken root, and grown,
And in a moment had become full-blown
With golden petals bursting,
Dropping, running molten
Through flesh and bone.
Can you, then, look into my eyes
And not be blinded?
Can you stand talking, and I seem to you
Polite, and only slightly absent-minded?

Raimon the Singer

After a thousand years of wandering
Raimon the singer found
At twilight the grilled ivory gates
That closed behind him with a delicate sound
As if wings brushed.
His horse's hooves tapped lightly the white stone.
He saw peaks,
Were silver-veined of snow;
Below,
Argentine streams clashed, hushed
The dusk-drenched valleys.
At moonrise Raimon the singer knelt
Before the High Queen's throne.
There in humbleness he
Made his need known.
"The songs of earth," he said, "all
Are grown old.
There are no tales but have been
Ten thousand times told.
That I may please my king,
And her I have given to hold
My heart in her hand,
Let my harp be re-strung.
Let me learn the songs that are sung
In Fairyland."

The great Queen honoured him.
He rode that night
In high fields flowering with pale asphodel
The while he heard her tell
The legends that are told in her land.
He saw the sea break white
On dark, glistening cliffs
Of chrysolite.
Watching a ship steal
Between island and mainland,
In prow pinioned with foam,

The Queen said,
"Speak to mariners who
Now return home.
Their wet prows have kissed
Song-bounded shores that lie
Low,
Beyond the sea-mist.
Theirs are the legends that you wish to know."

At dawn from Fairyland Raimon returned.
Nor has he aught spoken
Of any legends he that night learned.
Always he rides in his dark cloak,
His silence unbroken
By songs, the like of which are
Not for our hearing.

Reverdie

Remembering, I weave
A song of May colors.
Wishing so to retrieve
A spring that with the passing of a spell
Passed also from me.

Lilac, laburnum,
And wild blossoming plum
Whose clinging petals fell
Into the long grass,
Down a ravine—

These trees are seen
Dimly as though in colored glass.
There hawthorne spreads
Branches of white coral and red
Under the water in dark crevices.

Under the shadowed green
Pool of days since,
Where no moon-rays
Seek out quince
Trees in flower, leaf becomes legend.

Passing my own belief
Poet and princess
I walk there,
Wearing strange costume, seeming
My own dream.

Uninspired to the Uninspiring

I suppose that nobody could
build a fire with such green wood,
Sodden, spitting water into the struggling flames.
With the sea mist rolling in about sunset
And the sustained bellowing of Ocean
It strains genius, taxes the utmost devotion
To get a fire going; and yet
Were I not so convincingly green,
So reluctantly wet—
In short, with pitchy pine
Kindling and cedar knots
We could put poems to cook in so many pots
And have dinner in no time.

"A cloud comes down . . ."

A cloud comes down
Like the purple lid of a box
Clasping over. No rain
Although the soft air is expectant.
A flock of small birds in the holly
Put up their bitter-sweet clamour,
Jostle the red clusters.
Dark, wet color outside;
In the room yellow roses stand
Luminous in the shadows.

For a Collection of Suburbiana

A primitive goddess has moved in next door
With seventeen seedling fruit trees and some chickens.
Nothing like her ever
Occurred on our street before.
A primitive goddess of fertility she must be.
Who else could have inspired with a very fever
Of growing the pansies and cabbages, friendly companions
To irises, primroses, turnips and onions
Crowding the doorstep?
(Also potatoes thrive in the parking strip.)

She has no lawn—beets, to be sure,
Bridal wreath and forget-me-not—
But no uncivilized, unproductive,
Carefully watered and barbered grass plot.
She turned the grass under and now on one city lot
She has peas, beans, lettuce and bleeding hearts,
Even a grape arbor. And day after day
We see her come home with another tree in her hand
And another basket of plants.

She has twelve children either grown up or dead
Growing things all go the same way
Out of the ground and into the ground.
She digs barefoot in the warm rain. Each morning
I awake to the symbolic sound
Of a shovel cutting the earth.

She is expansive,
Oh lord, she is extensive!
She looks like a picture I once found
Of Gertrude Stein. And her clothes,
As to color and shape, pass any description.

Her accent smells of Astoria wharves
And her language of a logging camp kitchen.
The nice clean ears of neighbouring housewives
Are amazed at blue pinwheels frying the air,

But the humming birds that whir in her honeyed flowers
Never reproach her; her little plum trees bear
The whitest of blossoms. Nothing like her,
Absolutely nothing to approach her
Has occurred on our street before.

Letter from the Country

The wooded cones of the hills stand close
On all sides of my valley.
I could be content here in my own meadows
And my own towers, washed south and west by the river.
Days pacing the low arch of winter from east to west
Go over my head, and I am a young man still,
Reading at the top of the stairs, and riding at early sunset
Between the hedges of holly and wild rose haws.

In my loneliness I have you, my lords, with me.
You kick the table trestles, crying out the old names
And the old jests, that I, at least, have not forgotten.
At such times I think I love your ghosts
More than I ever loved you in the flesh.

Fable

Buttercup, she hashed and learned
What college and what commons taught.
Butterfly, she overturned
The pedagogic juggernaut.

But lamp her now, the brazen child.
She wrote to Ezra and he fell.
Light into the Parnassian wild
Leaps the timorous gazelle.

Drama

Tom, who wanted to write, was accustomed to sit
Hour after hour scouring the floor by the mail-box,
Searching in newspapers after a possible plot,
A situation, a likely dramatic bit
From a village weekly.

                    And I ask him,
What of fingers scooping cold tea-leaves out of a pot,
The chill of night, of a sleeping house, and silence
After a statement of no consequence.
The evening journal does not
Record such events.

                    Looking for plots, for drama,
I find snow falling thick and gray, a curtain
Between me and the light;
Laughter after a jest, and certain
Snowcrowned battlements
Collapse at the sound like the walls of Jericho
At a trumpet blast.

                    Or a clogged evening:
Clouds like gray lint over the sky; the steady flow
Of talk that reaches no climax, impending rain
Unfalling; we sweat with heat and the strain
Of the unsaid thing.

Beyond Medusa

Medusa's clotted snakes had power to lock
My muscles rigid in rock,
Nor had I ever thought to ask
What bruised features bore the hollow mask
Until I stared beyond the stiff grotesque
Into the living eyes that woke my own.

I felt my blood released from the cold stone
And sensed in flesh fragility of bone,
Sensed hair moving. I recognised
The shape of the eyes. The lips concealed
Behind a writhed mouth were not unknown.

I who stood sister to the caryatids
Found under carven lids
Eyes that made me also vulnerable.

Cat

Words always curdled
When she handled them.
Her ivory fingers
Twisted out wax images.
One squeeze beheaded them.
Venom was under her nails.

Had I her skill in malice
I would, for my own delectation
And that of her victims,
Model her drooping figure
In white parrafin
And allow for each laceration
One pin, and the right of insertion.

Dormitory

The dull, drugged afternoons,
The silent Sunday afternoons
With a lulling of small rain drumming on the balconies
And a tenuous gray web between the trees,
Blurring the dark turret-tops of the firs.
The very gables purr
And drowse; a door closes somewhere
But a long way off, in a hall I never knew.
If a step sounded upon the stair
Coming to my door,
It would ease the spell, and a light tap shear
The cocoon from the dry curled
Leaves that my eyes seem . . .
A thick, pale web between my eyes and my brain
And the trembling moth wings of a dream
Tentatively unfurled
Joinville—

Joinville is trying to tell me of Count Peter of Brittany,
How he said, spitting the blood from his mouth,
"Ha! by God's head!
Have you ever seen such riff-raff?"
Meaning the Saracen host.
And how in the night Queen Margaret leaped from her bed,
Naked to the deck of the ship
And cast the flaming scarf in the sea.
They saw it float backwards, burning up the still water
And so were saved.
Joinville, were you writing for me,
Lonely, sleepy, stifling a yawn
In stuffy pillows, dropping a tear of sleepiness
Into the indefinite pink and tan of faded cretonne?
Were you, Joinville?
I think it were better we both slept.

Lament from the Shores of the Boorzh-wah Zee

Nobody here draws purple deer
Nobody here eats lemon rind
Nobody here piles books on the floor
Or irons on Sunday morning.

Nobody here wears towels or less
Nobody here serves stew in kettles
Nobody here sings
"I'm lonesome since my monkey died"
I only am bereaved.

A little more of this life and I shall be writing
Bassinet-verse about a blue moon in a pink cloud
When the sun had set behind the western hills.
I did see it and what I want
Is to see a black moon in a brassy sky
And all the housetops strumming telephone wires.

Lyonesse Sub Mare

It seemed there
As if all grit were strained
Out of our days, all the cloudiness
Allowed to settle, and the clear
Liquid drained into clear crystal.

And I, bathing during those days
In fountains of Lyonesse,
Found there no taint
Of disinfectant or dust
But warm light swimming in cold air,
And azure water in continual movement.

Sun shone on rose-gray
Logs of the south wall.
Foam blowing like snow white scarves
Knotted on bright helmets
Swept forward in sunlight.

An ivory lighthouse on a slab of opal
And winds of that April
I regret still.
Now that the cliff has crumbled into the sea
And the house headlong,
Soiled gray water gulps under oily wharves.

Study

Watching her cross the floor
One knows all about her, seeing
The swaying hips, discreet eye-lids,
The sweep of her brown hair
Over a low forehead.
The heavy hands hanging.

Or seeing her broad shoulders
sunk in cretonne pillows,
Her limbs modelled in lead,
Careful that no movement
Spill the profound gaze
Of a blond man in the doorway.

The moon revolves in a white hoop,
Marking frosty hours.
Stravinsky, Ravel—
From the closed cabinet music
Glides into smoke-barred air
Among scattered tea cups.

The creamy wax of her candles
Drips into ash tray holders.
Silken pajamas pour over her
Like brown water, stirring no more
than do her oval lips murmuring
Veiled obscenities.

Trefoil

When three were swept aside
On the bent straw of a dream
To lie between tide and tide
In Time's eddy;

When three once found
The setting of the stars to be
The measure of music,
And on the narrow ground
Between the sucking bay and the wide-gushing sea
Heard the drum's coercive beat diminished,
Triumphant the flute's melody;

When three found timelessness
This side infinity
And wholeness in trinity,
Should not the weight
Of strata upon strata impending
Mark in granite
A flower trifoliate?

"Waiting for a waning moon to rise . . ."

Waiting for a waning moon to rise,
One watched drowned dreams file past.
And each wore casque of bronze or golden hood,
And each one as it stood
Was laid across with bar of narrow light,
And quenched with shadow-water.
They rose up in our sight
As pallid as pearls that dropped against their cheeks,
Weighted by velvet cloth that stank of water
And dribbled ooze upon the hollow steps.
From these depths
They rose and to them they again descended.
And the moon rose late with half its fullness spent.

Of Possession

Watching another's eyes, I remain
Intact, observant, the look of his eyes
Being nothing to him—unlike
His hat which is a part of himself.

I am on guard against hats
Laid on the knees or the desk.
I may in a freak of vision
See one of them as my own:
I have lifted it from the nail
How many mornings? No. No.
Rebellion follows the illusion.
I won't wear his hat.

These are the tricks of the eyes by which
The convex reverses, the strange
Becomes familiar. But through imagined
Memory to enter this man's life
Is unendurable except to God only
Who, living at once within and without,
Wears such a sorrowful face.

The privileges of possession
Common to deity are rejected by us,
Fearful of discomfort as we split
Into two persons, of helplessness
As the two thereby become one
And all transactions become as impossible
As prayer is, through this merging.

The Colored Stone

A ball of wind, small enough
To lie in the palm of the hand,
A breath curled like a kitten:
So, light this life.
And not hollow, but at its center
Holds an iridescence, a colored stone
Suspended in the moving close-knit air.
A stone, an opal floating
Mid-way of the sphere.

How should I think heavily of the pit
In such imponderable fruit?
For I much doubt its contour,
Its true weight, impalpable as it is
Except for the slight movement
Of air dusting my hand.

I doubt all but its color,
Doubt all but that it is indeed
My self's center.

Cold Heaven

The rain falls in the river
And on the gravelly bars where
Gulls light fitfully.
A fatherless family is reported
To be living on raw fish.

Snow and the clear air
Are higher. Above the dark palisades
Of the forest there are white-shadowed
And immaculate mountains.
Fire appears malicious and rain careless,
But snow falls guiltlessly, being
So cold: is that how you reason,
Withdrawing among the snowfields
In search of numbness? The peace
Of the frost-bitten gods
Be with you, the remote cold
That is insensible to heat of cities.
Passive on swept horizons, the mountains
Never look down.

Curly Locks

Who was it walled me in with cushions,
Pink taffeta cushions frilled with white lace?
My prison-fortress—a puffy masonry
Of pillows embroidered with silk thread
And mortared with a sticky mortar
The troubadours I believe
Are held responsible for.

Somewhere there are
Very high rocks,
Very cold rain,
Even there delicate flowers grow,
Cerise, the color of baked pie-cherries,
And rosy mushrooms big as dinner plates.

I wanna pick *wild* strawberries.

Eavesdropper

The room is full of a sour foliage.
Big dark leaves quivering in corners
Until the fire dies. Arbor of suspicion.

These vines have put their roots through me without
Marring the silence where the nerves
Twitch at the indistinct small sounds of the fire,
The stirring sibilant answers heard
Through an open doorway.

              Coals whisper together; do
Coals also kiss?

Epicure

This wife nourished her husband,
Not with bread, the fine crumbs
Rough on his tongue.
Not with the creamy flesh of nut or fish,
But with the tender meat of petals,
The moist white body of a flower.

She thrust a finger tip into the closed bud,
Exploring the nature of its delicacies,
Then offered it to him like a flaking cup
Of some smooth custard.
Watching his teeth bite on the petal tips
Above the succulent gold heart,
Saliva filled her mouth. She ate.

Mechanism

Out of the late afternoon, this sound.
The dull sunlight on leaves outside the window
Diminishes in an even flow,
But sawing across it, severing
Moment from moment, its monotony
Reaching a crescendo in the mind,
This sound. Words fall in a pattern against it;
We balance carefully. And again,
Hacking the links of thought, the intervals
Of an afternoon, the idiot breathes harshly.

North Window

A book with a green binding
And snow dropping out of a shallow sky:
The falling away of light and blood,
Of all yellow and rose
Leaves only

Forced passage to another country
To a beach without wharf, quiet
Like a lake beach.
          Green cloth and polished horn,
          Stairways of unstained wood.
We sit among grasses,
Among bloodless stones
Or lie at night upon white fur
Watching mist gather under the rafters,
Speaking of the queen's emeralds.

Point of Departure

Apricots cooking in a dark kitchen,
The summer fragrance thick between log walls;
White welter of the sea in winter moonlight
And the rustle of rats in unused
Bedrooms overhead: these combined to make a setting
For our character of her.

We approved the picturesqueness of her poverty.
You loaned her a dollar.
I wrote a poem about her.
She, however,
Deserted in favour of a
Studio couch and the life of one of the thousands of identical drops
In the sea of Manhattan.

Whoosh! go the wind and the waves on vacant beaches.

The Silk Leaf

The silly foliage dandled in light winds
Has made my head light.

But I remember the height of a sand bluff
Where matted boughs were blown back
And furrowed by sea wind;
Where black trunks and the tough
Wet roots of salal gripped the salt earth
And a gull
Coasted with taut wings in a cloven sky.

Lamplight through yellow silk, dry
Breathing through dusty silk,
And no remembrance of cold winds flowing.
Tea cups and talk of taffetas . . .

Tourist

She enjoys poetry, and likewise music.
To her they are resorts which lend prestige
And offer to the holiday traveller
A salutary change of air.

She writes ahead for her reservation,
Packs her bags, closes her house.
She settles her baskets, kittens, canaries, and bonnet
In her fussy mind; anticipates with pleasure
The Vistas of Unequalled Beauty
So often mentioned.

She frequently does not arrive,
And never stays as long as she planned to,
But she adores those quaint little villages.

Without Benefit of Tragedy

Your visages are duller than cotton wadding;
Your stairway smells of last night's cabbages,
But beauty flowering from your dusty carpets
Brought down catastrophe worthy of Greek princes.

The Eumenides honored you with their presences
For a short time, but fled from your table.
Unbruised and savorless you will wear to an end.
No one, dizzied by sudden depth, falls out of swampland.

Ursus Parnassius

<u>To the Critics</u>

All night upon the face of the mountain
The warring armies of the moon,
The warring armies of the wind
Struggled for possession of the mountain.
No one fell and no one held his sword.

A bear came up the mountain.
The bear was bulky and warm,
Well-furred and well-fed
Upon the wild fruit of the mountain.
The warriors took no notice,
Eager, as they were, to die
In the name of the mountain
(Until dawn dismissed them).

The bear, who is a friend of mine
Walked through the wind and moonlight
With a carelessness equal to theirs,
Looking for huckleberries.

"The slenderly poised clean shaft of your fir . . ."

The slenderly poised clean shaft of your fir,
Arrowy and yet still, might have stood in the station,
Beside the Great Northern rails and the wilful water
Of my life, flowing so contrarily eastward.

You remember how the trees at Wind River have that air
Of protecting the water without leaning above it.
No branch droops willow-fashion, trailing leaves
Bubbled with silver, making the water murmur around it.
Without shading the stream, they let fall reflected color.

All time flows down from the same source in the hills.
The current following these rails as if in hollowed rock
Overtakes me, hour by hour. Tomorrow is lying
Now by your drinking roots, green with your love.

Altitude

I stop at the highest turn of the road
To set my feet on the ground
And feel as tall as the mountains.
I stand at the guard rail and look down.

The perpendicular rock
And the river rustling in its gorge
Give to us crawling upon the summits
An illusion of stature that increases
In proportion to vision.

Barely discernible, a houseboat floats downstream,
The launch that tows it lost
In the indistinct floor pattern of evening.
The brave little household gods preside,
We suppose, over kerosene lamp and congoleum.
The big gods do not notice and the mountains
Remain unshaken by laughter.

I crawl again. Not a thousand feet tall,
Not even six feet tall,
I cling at the guard rail. River lights,
Headlights, airplane beacons appear now.

Road to Xanadu

The pea pods are cool, firm,
And easily popped under the thumb;
The naked peas roll into the pan.

On the backsteps, the sun
Comes crimson through low branches.
Tap of clothespins back of the lilacs.
Crunch of gravel at the garage door. Evening.

(And it happens - - the sudden
Freshening of spring water over
Dry stones from a source in shadow
The bright-tongued water spilling
Its syllables, I chosen, hushed channel to
Its extravagance --)

                Peas dropping
Make a small evening sound.
The clouds flush slowly.

Fire

The sea breaking flat
Where smoke makes a bitter darkness—
Cold, finishes with a fine sound

The beach and its rock benches.
A cougar pads on the sand.
A child cries, and the deer
Are near them under dropping ash.

All other smells are blotted in nostrils
Burned by hell's black noon wind.

They shall lie down together.

Convalescence

Like a tooth shocked with heat
The patient is assured he is
Not yet dead while nerves
Bunch and jangle at a soft touch.
He knows that, and knows
Outrage, that this is consolation.

You won't die of it. But what
Of the world's death? Water
That was once rain or hillside spring
Tastes now of your own tongue.
Escape to books—they are as clocks
Are to the heartbeat, the wound
Mechanism ticking in crystal.
False. False. We know infection
Crawls in the bloodstream.

The knife was perilous, but glands
Offer their jot of courage,
Ether for the soul's crisis.
The organ out, the job done, they
Will tell you it is all over now.

All over except the long lying
In a pit of weakness, except
Visits from the sceptical who speak
Lightly of health, while you on pillows
Far withdrawn from them talk
Always with Pain, and talk with him
Of those who did not die. They woke
Years after, in his clasp, at daybreak.

The Accounting

Go underground, not for the preserves stored there,
Which you ate; for the cistern taste of the dark
That kept them against winter. Are you afraid?

Bankruptcy: the smell of the cellar stairs
And the dusty smell of empty potato sacks
And of earth years out of sunlight.

Overhead, a dandelion Sacremento
Blooms around the doorsill, the bees burring,
Promising honey, the sun, its rays
Laddered with yellow dust, promising
Tomorrow. The eyes mint counterfeit.

Take inventory. Set them to study
The shape of the stair, scarred riser and tread.
Turn up the mouldy board. Is there treasure?
Is there nothing to trade? No? Then study the worm.

The questions drop and fear outlines the silence.
Until, white as a root underground, a bare hand
Stretches with the strength of spring: touches, and blood
Throbs softly between the thought and the wood.
I had forgotten. From these fingertips, the flowering:
Craft, the fruit, runs like sap in the hand.

Crossroads

Rotting in the wet gray air
The railroad depot stands deserted under
Still green trees. In the fields
Cold begins an end.

There were other too-long-postponed departures.
They left, finally, because of well water
Gone rank, the smell of fungus, the chill
Of rain in chimneys.

The place is abandoned even in memory.
They knew, locking doors upon empty houses,
To leave without regret is to lose
Title to one home forever.

Preacher

The voice of the mad old man
        preaching reason (down there
        at the end of the garden path)
        carries conviction—I don't
        know how it is, but to my mind,
        hungry for reason, it carries conviction.

Travel Notes

for John Montague at Carron

Here, as always when I awake
in a strange room in a strange country,
the dislocated directions
reel round the bed and settle, so:

they point to window, to door,
to sea, to hill, to bog.
This is the West of Ireland.
But I have been here before

not in Ireland, in Greece.
Why, as I walk along damp lanes
and step over Irish cowpats,
is Hellas so mixed up with Eire?

There are humble, white-washed houses
set among rocks and heather;
stony hills of the Burren and Attica
and light reflected from water,
        dazzling in Greece,
        misty in Ireland;

masonry like that of Mycenae;
small chapels set in the fields;
the presence, strongly felt,
of archaic gods on the hilltops . . .

But there is much more:
a poison sown in the soil
by the Turk and the Briton,
a wasteland created in time.

One senses it always, there and here:
the hatred and rage and shame.
One glimpses a shimmer of gold,

distant—oh, very far back—
        gold mask of the king
        gold torque of the hero,
a lost glory to feed on.

On Arriving

A poem for Poetry *on Its 75th Anniversary*

The first of countless printed rejections
from *Poetry* came sixty-one years ago.
(I was sixteen. You were fourteen.)

The scribbled "promising" on the margin
anaesthetized the pain somewhat.

Eight years and God only knows how many
rejections later, Morton Zabel
(Harriet being then in China)
accepted "Shoreline" and at last
I thought I had arrived. And when
the next year I was awarded the Levinson
I thought surely I had arrived,
being much too young to understand
how a poet can travel for sixty years
and still be always almost arriving.

Arrival implies a journey completed,
and that never happens. Not on this road.

A Dedication

To those two knowing owls,
Mockers of our comings and goings,
Fat Nox and Lux smug in their stone cowls
Under the entrance light, under the sun dial
That told despite the invading vine
Passage of hours until our honorable exile.

POEMS INSPIRED BY SAPPHO

The Fool's Serenade

When there were no more any lights at all
I climbed between the poplars till I came
Where you may see beyond the terrace wall
The foam upon the beach, the little flame
Of moonfire creating every wave; and there
I lifted up my hands and sang to her.
I told her all the love and the despair
That only fools can know. There was a blur
Of tears across my eyes; and then I felt
A rose that fell between my hands and lay
Upon the grass. In reverence I knelt
And kissed its petals.—Every poet knows
The moon is queen, and mighty is her sway,
But would you think the moon could throw a rose?

"In the bridal . . ." (four fragments)

In the bridal
hour of white
lilac we swore
to holly that we'd
love her later

X X X

If only I'd been
poet when the Muse
puckered her innocent
lips on pan-pipes
at Thetis's wedding

X X X

The short-stemmed rose
is red, is perfect; it rests
in a glass vase hardly
larger than one's thumb,
its heart slowly unfolding

X X X

Six out of seven stars
sail high overhead on
cold clear nights. Listen!
Their captured sister is
weeping for her lost wings

Love Poem

Oh plaguing Aphrodite, hear my prayer!
Give back my sane mind which you stole from me,
Or make me madder, not to be aware
How laughable is my insanity.

Blanchefleur

We come in the colorless dusk
Along river marges
Where rain falls in the weeds and the water,
Bringing to you our piled
White flowers in sliding barges—
For a troubled child
Our wax-white flowers half-closed,
Cupping the shadows.

Past the outposts of night
We bring to your side
These blossoms, each petal a white
Polished flake,
As if cut from bone.
We come with mist-white flowers,
As you were a bride
Forsaken,
A goddess singing alone
Without understanding.

Before the tide,
Come, let us make
Sorrowful landing.

Fatigue

Bronze hair glances under the trees with steady precision
Gold in light, dulled in the fleeting shadow—
It is as though
My heart had learned to beat to no other rhythm.

The fractional periods of my days
Are marked by the incessant drumming of one phrase.
The stupid fingers have learned no other.
And through the humming summer air
I catch, almost, the stern
"Repeat. Repeat.
Ah, clumsy-fingered, will you never learn?
Mark well the beat—
Bronze hair,
Laced shadow moving upon
The red and gold of her hair."

Over and over and over and over
Rhythmically moving
Benumbing the tired brain
Percussion of sun and metal at last becoming
A tawdry refrain.

"Tranquil and shallow, spread across the flat stones . . ."

Tranquil and shallow, spread across the flat stones
Like a wide, thin road-bed of water, each creek
Flows upon twilight level toward the earth's edge,
        Quietly drops down.

Soft arrows sharpened by the swift departure
Stir a wind feathered with a misty plumage,
Plumb the night-shadowed pit of air to find no
        Pools, but are lost there.

Commerce

We who dwell apart in our island cities
Stay our lives on commerce that brings us timbers,
Dyes and wool and fruit, the unblemished marble
    Sought by the sculptors.

All my wealth comes here to the harbour wharves, and
I am rich, but ominous days appear when
Unseen cargoes darken the streets with anguish;
    Dearly I bargain.

Ships I send forth find in the storm disaster.
Alien vessels notching the bright horizon
Wake the fear that lurking in cask and bale is
    Deathly contagion.

White-walled cities guarded by reef and headland
Bow to plague, itself, as a lesser woe than
Wharves decayed and sand in the harbor mouth:
    starvation and strangling.

Departure

No one saw her rise from the natal surges
Clear as they are, pierced with an amber light or
Shouldered, overwhelmed by the ravelled breakers
       Crumbling in blossom.

Storm of light and motion on the sea's face
When in flowered terraces flesh of clabbered
Foam arose, a goddess, a lace of froth still
       Rough on her shoulders.

We that saw no white Cytherean maiden
Wading shoreward, see that a single wave spread
Out of night and fog-hooded sound will melt sledge
       Tracks drawing under.

Mask

She who scorned her innocent mouth and longed for
Lips that looked hard, skin that was scarred and dusty,
Longed for cloaked eyes, hiding their depth of knowing,
    Wears a new beauty.

Swift the changes. Working in plastic flesh the
Hands of grief oppressing her cheek and forehead
Gave her beauty such as the child had not, but
    Smiling, she breaks us.

Eyes opaque and polished will not be hers now.
Hurt but still untracked her desirous mouth lost
All it learned. Her face being cleared and calm lies
    Passive to sorrow.

A Defense of the Poet's Method

Where the unfractured water at the cliff's verge
Bent a lucid shoulder above the canyon,
Where the mist arose in a plume above the
    Stream's disappearing—

Even in the act of abandoning its
High ravines it grasped at a lyric instant,
Caught it in the white cannonade, spun it half-
    Obliterated

In shattered pools, not yet aware of its form
Nor of its full significance, till in still
Pools below, a smoky image split into
    Mist; a remembrance.

Later: Four Fragments

1.
Tired we watch
a low sun shaping
hillock and hollow
in what were
noon's flat meadows.

2.
Don't let them tell you
it will all come right
in the end. It won't.
It won't. It won't. Never.
Death is always the end.

3.
Once the sea flowed before us
as far as the Four Quarters,
to ten thousand unknown ports.
See how it narrows
to a ribbon track behind.

4.
The dams have drowned
the rapids and white water
curls in memory with eyes
and voices that come clear
only between sleeping and waking.

Ceremony

The cups were polished
coconut shells cut
lengthwise; they were

never placed upon
the floor itself,
but on bark cloth

laid before priest
or server; never
where one might by

stepping over
desecrate them.
The ceremony

being ended they
were placed in nets
hanging from rafters,

for they were sacred
like the drink they
held
     or like the god.

I like to think of these cups,
mornings, picking up
the beer cans on the lawn.

Chronos

Days equal
years, years
days: the scales

of the easy-
does-it old
calculator

(as they tried
to tell Elec-
tra) hold level.

Late Roman

I shall be
an historic
figure also,
Mr. Achilles.

One digit in
one of Gibbon's
many footnotes
will denote ME!

Now

I never wanted to kill
myself, never wanted
to die: but now, looking
ahead, thinking of thought
some day going awry
and trickling to a stop,
leaving a smelly shell
high on a dry beach

I think—
                    almost
I think—
                    but
No. Not yet.

The Rock of Levkas

You with the salt blue eyes
and a storm quivering under young ribs
sea-marked for coral:

You shrieked Fool! when she leapt,
her rigid feet taking the depth of the green
kelp-cloaked surge under the rocks.

The sea wallows in valleys deeper than these;
between remote continents it spins and knots
webs that will snare its rabbit in desert canyons.

Leave the seacoast, leave the river
hollowing its way to the sea.
Find your way into the pines and
higher than they grow, out upon glaciers—
you will not have escaped. Snow
will be whiter than foam between your lips,
tasteless, more quiet, and colder.

Soft Chains

Soft chains are most
difficult to break:
affection, ease.

The spirit, wide-eyed,
limp-muscled, nestles
on its side
        and waits

Static

I wanted to hear
Sappho's laughter
and the speech of
her stringed shell.

What I heard was
whiskered mumble-
ment of grammarians:

Greek pterodactyls
and Victorian dodos.

II.
TRANSLATIONS

from *SAPPHO: A NEW TRANSLATION* (1958)

1   Tell everyone

    Now, today, I shall
    sing beautifully for
    my friends' pleasure

37   You know the place: then

Leave Crete and come to us
waiting where the grove is
pleasantest, by precincts

sacred to you; incense
smokes on the altar, cold
streams murmur through the

apple branches, a young
rose thicket shades the ground
and quivering leaves pour

down deep sleep; in meadows
where horses have grown sleek
among spring flowers, dill

scents the air. Queen! Cyprian!
Fill our gold cups with love
stirred into clear nectar

53   With his venom

Irresistible
and bittersweet

that loosener
of limbs, Love

reptile-like
strikes me down

61   Pain penetrates

Me drop
by drop

100 I have no complaint

Prosperity that
the golden Muses
gave me was no
delusion: dead, I
won't be forgotten

OTHER TRANSLATIONS

Adonis Dying

I shall miss light
most: sunlight then
star and moonlight

ripe cucumbers and
after pears,
          apples

Book 1 from Homer, *The Iliad*

Sing for us, goddess, Achilles' death-dealing anger
that brought disaster upon the Greeks and dispatched
into Hades a host of heroes' mighty spirits,
leaving their bodies a prey to dogs and a feast
for ravens; this was the working-out of God's will.

We begin when first they started apart in hatred—
Agamemnon, leader of men, and godlike Achilles.

What god was it first caused the clash between them?
Apollo, it was. Enraged with the king for insulting
10   Chryses, his priest, he sent a plague through the army,
killing the soldiers. This is the way it happened:
Chryses came to the Greek ships bringing a ransom
and holding the symbols of priesthood, Apollo's fillets
and golden staff; he entreated all the Achaeans,
but especially Atreus's sons, both Menelaos and
King Agamemnon, to give up his daughter Chryseis:
"O sons of Atreus, and all other well-greaved Achaeans,
may the great gods, who have their home on Olympus
grant that you sack Priam's city and reach your homes safely.
20   Accept this ransom; give back my dear child, and so doing
honor the son of Zeus, far-striking Apollo."

Almost all the Achaeans, approving the speech,
would have honored the priest and accepted his glittering ransom—
all except Agamemnon. The king was not pleased,
but sent him away and threatened him harshly, saying
"Never, oldster, allow me to find you here
among our ships, either languishing now or returning.
For if I do, neither scepter nor fillets will save you.
I'll not give her up; instead, old age will find her
30   in my house in Argos, far from her native country,
moving before the loom and sleeping beside me.
But go. Take care not to vex me if you would go safely."

That was his answer; the old man, frightened, obeyed him.
In silence he passed by the shore of the many-voiced sea

apart from the ships, and earnestly prayed to Apollo,
his king and protector, whom fair-haired Leto bore:
"Hear me, Lord of the Silver Bow, who bestridest
Chrysa, protector of Cilla, the mighty ruler
of Tenedos, slayer of mice—if I ever pleased thee
40   with roof or temple or sacrifice of fat thighs,
goat or bull, on thine altars—now, Lord, grant my prayer:
Let the Greeks pay for my tears under thine arrows."

This was his prayer and Phoebus Apollo heard him.
Angry, the god sprang down from the crests of Olympus.
Hanging upon his shoulders were bow and quiver;
the arrows clanged on his shoulder as he in anger
sped down: he came like night, and knelt at a distance
away from the ships, and sent his arrows among them.
Fearful, the clanging sound of the silver bow!
50   At first he struck the mules and the swift dogs only,
next the men themselves were pieced by the arrows;
thick on the beach the pyres of the dead burned always.

Nine days and nights the arrows rained on the camp;
at last, on the tenth, Achilles summoned a council.
(The white-armed Hera put the thought in his mind,
for she pitied the Greeks when she saw how many were dying.)
When all the men of the council were gathered together,
Achilles, the swift of foot, stood up and addressed them:
"Lord Agamemnon, I think we shall surely be driven back
60   home again, if indeed we escape from death,
for war and pestilence both are threatening conquest.
But come, let us ask some seer, or perhaps some priest
or diviner of dreams, since the dream is also from God;
he may let us know in what way we have angered Apollo.
Are we to blame for a broken vow or hecatomb
Scanted? Or does he require the savor of yearlings,
fat sheep and goats, in order to ward off this evil?"

He finished his speech and sat down; whereupon Calchas
stood up before them, the best of seers, one knowing
70   all things that were, or once had been, or would be;
it was he who by divination, the gift of Phoebus

Apollo, had led the Achaean vessels to Troy.
The seer, a man of good will, addressed them and said:
"Achilles, beloved of Zeus, you command me to speak
and account for the wrath of Apollo, the far-striking king.
I shall obey you, but you must hear me and, speak this:
that you willingly bade me up by deed
and by word, for I foresee I shall anger a man
ruling the Argives, a man the Achaeans obey;
80   and a king when angry is stronger than common men;
for although on a given day he may swallow his anger,
yet he will store it away in his heart for another,
and settle accounts. Promise me now you will save me."

At that, fleet-footed Achilles, answering, said:
"Speak freely and tell us whatever you know of God's will.
I swear by Apollo, beloved of Zeus, to whom you,
Calchas, pray—whose oracles you interpret—
no man among the Greeks shall lay hands upon you
so long as I live and have the sight of my eyes,
90   though you should anger King Agamemnon himself
who boasts that he is the greatest of all the Achaeans."

The seer, when he heard these words, took courage and said:
"It is neither for vows nor hecatombs we are blamed,
but because of his priest, whom Agamemnon insulted,
rejecting his gifts, and not releasing his daughter;
for this, Apollo senses grief and will send more.
He will not protect the Greeks from this pitiless plague
until, without ransom, we give up the bright-eyed girl
and send her home to her own dear father in Chrysa
100   and send a hecatomb with her. Then he may hear us."

With this, the seer sat down, and up rose the hero,
the son of Atreus, wide-ruling King Agamemnon.
He was displeased, his mighty heart brimming over
with black anger. His eyes were sparkling like fire.
With an ominous glance at Calchas the king began:
"Doom-sayer, for me you have never had one good word;
always you love to foretell whatever is evil;
you have never said anything noble, or done it, either.

And now in council you prophesy to the Greeks
110 and say that Apollo visits misfortune upon them
on my account, because I rejected the ransom
offered for this girl from Chrysa, whom, truly, I want
to take home. Indeed, I prefer her to Queen Clytemnestra,
my own lawful wife, for she is in no way inferior,
either in form or grace, either in wit or skill.
But since it is best, I agree to send her away;
I would rather the men were living than dead of the plague;
however, let someone provide at once a prize
to replace her, or I alone shall sit here without one.
120 That wouldn't be fitting. Look—I am losing my prize!"

At that, the swift-footed, godlike Achilles replied:
"Most glorious king, most greedy of all mankind,
how shall the great-hearted Greeks award you a prize?
From what common store heaped up shall we give it? Whenever
some city was plundered, the spoils were properly divided.
We cannot collect them again; it wouldn't be fitting.
For now, send back the girl to the god; the Achaeans
will render you three times or four times her worth if ever
Zeus grant that we sack that high-walled city of Troy."

130   King Agamemnon, answering him, retorted:
"Brave you may be, Achilles, and godlike, but don't try
devious ways; you won't circumvent or persuade me.
Do you desire, while yourself have a prize,
that I do without? Do you tell me to send her away?
But let the good-hearted Greeks bestow some gift,
something I like, and something equal in value—
if not, I shall come, myself, and take away yours,
or that of Ajax, or possibly that of Odysseus;
whichever one I come to—*he* will be furious!
140 But we can talk of all this at some other time.
Come now, let us drag the black ship down to the sea,
and assemble the oarsmen we need, and a hecatomb also;
next, let fair-cheeked Chryseis enter the ship;
and one of the council-members shall go in command—
Ajax, or Idomeneus, or godlike Odysseus,

or you, Achilles, most frightening of all fighting men,
that you may perform the rites and petition the god."

      Then, scowling at him, swift-footed Achilles replied:
      "O King Craftiness, cloaked as you are in shamelessness,
150   how does it happen that even one man will obey you,
      willingly taking the road, or taking the field?
      For I, myself, did not come here as a fighter
      because of the Trojan spearmen; they never harmed me;
      they never drove off my cattle, nor yet my horses,
      not came to my own land, rich-loamed, man-breeding Phthia,
      despoiling the crops, for a great distance lies between,
      some of it shadowy mountain, and some the loud sea;
      but you, O shameless one, we all came to please you,
      to win back honor for both Menelaos and you
160   by fighting the Trojans. To all this you pay no attention,
      threatening instead to come and carry away
      the prize I toiled for, the one the Achaeans gave me.
      Whenever the Greeks have pillaged some well-built city,
      the prizes I win are never the equal of yours;
      although these hands of mine have borne the whole brunt
      of the war, when we come to divide the plunder, your part
      is always the larger, while I, coming back to the ships
      exhausted with fighting, have something small but precious.
      Now I shall go back to Phthia; it seems to me wiser
170   to set sail for home in my ships; I think I'll not stay
      to pile up wealth for you while I am unhonoured."

      To this, Agamemnon, leader of armies, replied:
      "That's right—run away if you like; I shall never implore you
      to stay behind for my sake. There are others about me
      who pay me great honor, among them councillor Zeus.
      You are most hateful to me of the god-nourished kings;
      you are always wanting to argue, and quarrel, and fight.
      If you are stronger than most, your strength is a gift.
      Sail homeward now with your ships; rule over your comrades,
180   your Myrmidons. I shall pay you no heed, nor care
      one whit for your anger; however, I warn you of this:
      since Phoebus Apollo is taking Chryseis from me

I shall send her in my own ship, in the care of my men,
and I shall go to your tent, myself, for your prize,
fair-cheeked Briseis; then you will know by how much
I am the stronger; then no other Achaean
will try to strive or measure himself against me."

He spoke in this vein; Achilles was angered to hear it;
the heart in his shaggy breast pulled this way and that;
190 should he, drawing the sharp-edged sword by his thigh,
arouse the assembled council and kill Agamemnon,
or was it wiser to hold his anger in check?
While Achilles, pausing, pondered these things in his heart,
half-drawing his heavy sword from the sheath, Athena
hurried from heaven, dispatched by white-armed Hera,
who loved and pitied them both, in equal measure.
Athena, standing behind him, took hold of his long,
yellow hair; she appeared to him only; no one else saw her.
Achilles, astonished, turning half-way around and at once
200 recognized Pallas Athena; his eyes flashed fire.
He addressed winged words to her, asking, "Why,
O daughter of Zeus Aegis-bearer—why have you come?
Is it to see Agamemnon's insolent pride?
I tell you this, and I think it will happen, too—
his arrogant acts before long will bring on his death."

The goddess, grey-eyed Athena, addressed him and said,
"I have come from heaven to put an end to your anger
if you will obey me; white-armed Hera sent me,
who loves and pities you both, in equal measure.
210 But come now, bridle your anger; don't draw out your sword;
abuse him as much as you like; tell him what to expect.
For I can speak plainly, and this is what I tell you will happen:
because of his insolence, you will one day have gifts
three times as precious; hold back, and do as we say."

Then, answering her, swift-footed Achilles replied:
"I must obey your commands since you both agree,
rage as I may in my heart; because it is wiser—

the gods are more likely to listen to him who obeys them."
He rested his heavy hand on the silver hilt
220 and pushed the great sword into its sheath, obeying
the words of Athena. And she went straight to Olympus,
home of Zeus Aegis-bearer and all of the gods.

When Athena had gone Achilles berated the king
in a bitter speech, not trying to bridle his anger:
"Sot, with the eyes of a cur and the heart of a deer,
you can never endure to arm and go into battle
along with the men, or go with the best of the Greeks
into ambush—that, to you, would be looking for death.
You find it much cheaper to stay here in camp
230 and seize the prize of the man who speaks out against you.
Ravening king, you rule over worthless louts—
if this were not true, you would surely be insolent now
for the last time. I tell you, and I shall swear a great oath
by this scepter which never again will put forth leaves
and branches, not since it first was cut from its stump
in the mountains—will never flower again since the axe
stripped off its leaves and bark, but now the Greeks
as judges carry it in their hands, as they guard
the law before God—by this I swear my great oath:
240 truly a need for Achilles will one day come
to all the Achaeans; grieved as you then will be,
you will not be able to help the many who fall
before Hector, but, raging, you will gnaw at your heart
because you neglected to honor the noblest Achaean."

When Achilles had ended his speech, he threw on the ground
the scepter studded with golden nails, and sat down.
Opposite him Agamemnon continued to fume.
Then Nestor arose, the clear-voice speaker of Pylos;
words that were sweeter than honey flowed from his tongue.
250 Before him, two generations of mortal men
had been born and reared and had already passed away
in sacred Pylos; he reigned now over the third.
The old king, a man of good will, addressed them and said:

"God help us, this is truly a grief for Achaea,
a thing to make Priam and Priam's children rejoice,
and one that would gladden the hearts of the other Trojans
if they were to learn how the two of you are at odds
who are leaders of all the Greeks in council and battle.
But listen to me; for you are both younger than I.
260 I was companion long since to men stronger than you
and they never slighted me. I've never seen such men
as they were, and never shall see their equal again—
like Peirithoos and Dryas, shepherds of men,
or Kaineus, Exadios, Polyphemus the Lapith
or Theseus son of Aegeus, like the immortals.
Those were the mightiest men ever bred on earth;
strongest themselves, they also fought with the strongest—
wild men of the mountains—and horribly put them to death.
And I myself come from Pylos, a distant country,
270 as comrade in arms, because I was summoned by them,
and I fought on my own as a champion side by side
with men whom no man now living on earth could fight.
And they always listened to me and respected my counsel.

Now be persuaded by me, since that will be better.
Brave as you are, Agamemnon, don't seize the girl,
but leave her alone; the Achaeans first gave her to him.
And you, Achilles, do not contend with the king,
force against force; for yours is not a like honor
with sceptered kings, since they are ennobled by Zeus.
280 It is true you are stronger, but you had a goddess for mother,
and he has the greater power since he rules more widely.
You stifle your rage, Agamemnon; and I shall entreat
Achilles to leave off his anger, for he is a bulwark
To all the Achaeans against the evils of war."

King Agamemnon, answering, said: "My lord,
you do, indeed, speak justly regarding these things.
But this man wants to maintain himself over all,
to rule over all, to hold sway over all, and in short
to give orders to all, but one, I think, won't obey him.
290 Although the immortal gods have made him a warrior,
did they also grant him permission to utter abuse?"

Then, interrupting, godlike Achilles retorted:
"I should be called a coward indeed, and worthless,
if I knuckled under to you in all that you say;
give your commands to the others, give no more orders
to me. For I think that I shall no longer obey you.
I tell you this—you had much better take it to heart;
although I shall not fight either you or another
because of a girl—whoever gives may take—
300 I shall see that you don't carry off against my will
anything else I keep by my swift black ship.
Come try it, in order that these men also may know;
dark blood will stream at once from the point of my spear."

So these two duelled with words and then arose,
dismissing the council among the Achaean ships.
Achilles went with Patroclus and other companions
down to the well-balanced ships and tents. Agamemnon,
launching a boat, chose a score of oarsmen to man it;
he put aboard it a hecatomb for the god,
310 then led to the vessel the fair-cheeked girl from Chrysa;
the prudent Odysseus embarked in the ship as commander.

They sailed away then over the watery ways.
At the camp the king ordered rites of purification;
these the men duly performed and washed the soil
from their limbs in the sea; then they sacrificed to Apollo,
both cattle and goats, at the edge of the restless water.
The savor rose up to heaven on wreathing smoke.

While they were busy in camp, Agamemnon by no means
abated the rage that had made him threaten Achilles;
320 he called upon two nimble squires, Talythybios one,
and Eurybates the other, both of them heralds:
"Go to the tent of Achilles, Peleus's son.
Take fair-cheeked Briseis from him and bring her here.
If he should attempt to forestall you, I myself
shall come with my men, and take her; that will be worse."

So he sent them, laying his stern injunctions upon them.
Reluctant, they passed by the edge of the restless sea

till they came to the Myrmidon camp with its tents and ships.
They discovered Achilles sitting outside his tent,
330 by his black ship, not at all pleased to see them approaching.
The two, being nervous and standing in awe of the prince,
stood still; they neither asked nor told him a word,
but he knew well what their errand must be, and he spoke:

"Greeting, heralds, servants of God and men.
Come nearer; I blame, not you, but King Agamemnon;
because of Briseis he has sent you to me.
Come then, Zeus-born Patroclus, bring out the girl
and give her to them. I call on these men to bear witness
in the sight of the blessed gods and mortal men
340 and before the cruel king, if ever again
I shall be needed to ward off deadly destruction
from all the host. Indeed he is mad with rage
and does not think to look before or behind him
to see how the Greeks may safely fight by their ships."

Patroclus obeyed his good friend, and leading Briseis
out of the tent he handed her to the heralds.
The two returned again by the ships, and the woman,
unwilling, went with them. Achilles, in tears, at once
went aside from his comrades; he knelt at the edge of the gray sea
350 and looked out over the deep; with his arms extended
he earnestly prayed to his own dear mother, saying,
"Mother, because you bore me to live only briefly,
the thunderer on the heights, Olympian Zeus,
was to grant me honor, but now I receive none at all,
for the son of Atreus, wide-ruling King Agamemnon,
insults me; he himself has taken my prize."

As he spoke these words he wept, and his mother heard
as she sat in the depths of the sea by her ancient father.
Quickly she rose up out of the sea like a mist,
360 and she sat down close by the side of her weeping son;
with her hand she caressed him, and spoke, and called him by name.
"Son, tell me, why are you crying? What sorrow is this?
Speak out and hide nothing, so that we both may know."

Swift-footed Achilles, groaning heavily, answered:
"You already know, then why should I tell the whole story
to you who know all that happens? We went to Theba,
Eëtion's sacred city, and sacked it, and brought back
much plunder, shared out among the Achaeans. Fair-cheeked
Chryseis fell to the lot of King Agamemnon.
370 Then Chryses, her father, the priest of far-striking Apollo,
came to the tents and ships of the bronze-clad Achaeans;
he carried a ransom, and asked the release of his daughter,
in his hands the symbols of priesthood, Apollo's fillets
and golden staff; he entreated all the Achaeans
but especially Atreus's sons, the two commanders.
The other Achaeans expressed their approval and said
they should honor the priest and accept his glittering ransom—
all except Agamemnon. The king was not pleased,
but harshly sent him away, with a stern admonition.
380 Although the old man obeyed, he was angry, and prayed
to Apollo, who loved the priest and listening to him.
The god now turned his wicked shafts on the Argives.
Our men were dying, one close after another,
as arrows fell like rain on the camp. Then a seer
who knew our fault made it clear as he spoke in council.
At once I urged that we should appease the god;
then anger seized Agamemnon; he rose up quickly
and threatened me, and now has done as he threatened.
The bright-eyed Achaeans have sent back the girl by ship
390 into Chrysa, with gifts for the gods; Agamemnon's heralds
have just now come to my tent and have taken away
my girl, Briseis, whom the Achaeans gave me.
But do protect your valiant son if you can;
go to Olympus and ask great Zeus to assist you
if ever you pleased him either by word or by deed,
for many a time I have heard you in father's house
when you boasted that you alone among the immortals
once warded off ruin and threatened cloud-gathering Zeus.
That was the time when the others—Hera, Poseidon
400 and Pallas-Athena—plotted to bind him in chains.
But you came to save him, goddess, from shameful fetters;
quickly you summoned the Hundred-armed to Olympus,
him who the gods call Briareos, called by men

Aigaion—one who is stronger than his own father,
Poseidon; he sat beside Zeus and rejoiced in his glory;
and so the gods were afraid and refrained from binding.
Go now, and sit beside Zeus, embracing his knees,
and remind him of this, and ask if he won't help the Trojans
to drive the Achaeans back between ships and sea
410 and kill them; then all may relish their king, and the son
of Atreus, the wide-ruling monarch, may know his madness,
he who neglected to honor the noblest Achaean."

Thetis, with tears pouring down, replied to him, saying:
"Why, my child, did I bear and rear you in sorrow?
Would that you sat dry-eyed and unharmed by your ships
since your span of life is so short, not long at all.
As it is, your life is at once more brief and more wretched
than others. I bore you, I see, for an evil fate.
I shall go, myself, to snowy Olympus and speak there
420 with Zeus, the thunder-bolt wielder, and try to persuade him.
You, however, must sit by your ships; you may rage,
if you will, against the Achaeans, but cease from fighting.
Yesterday Zeus left his home for the Ocean Stream
where he feasts with the proud Ethiopians, all the gods with him.
After twelve days they return once more to Olympus;
then I shall go to his home with its bronze-bound threshold,
and clasp his knees, and I think that I shall persuade him."

With this reassurance she went on her way and left him
still angry at heart because of the trim-waisted girl
430 who was taken from him by force, against his will.
Meanwhile Odysseus, bringing his boatload of offerings,
came into Chrysa. The crew, as they neared the deep harbour,
furled the sails and stowed them away in the ship;
they lowered the forestays and placed the mast in its crutch,
all very quickly, and rowed the ship to its moorings.
Out went the anchor-stones; hawsers secured the stern;
out came the men on the sea-beach, out came the beasts
intended for sacrifice to far-striking Apollo;
out came Chryséis last from the sea-going vessel.

440 Then prudent Odysseus leading her up to the altar
surrendered her to the hands of her father and said,
"Chryses, King Agamemnon has sent me to you
to bring back your daughter and offer on our behalf
a sacrifice to Apollo, that we may appease the god
who now afflicts the Argives with bitter sorrow."

He gave her into her father's hands, and the priest
received his dear daughter with joy. The animals next
were quickly arranged in order around the altar.
The man washed their hands and took up the grains of barley.
450 The priest prayed aloud for them with his hands uplifted:
"Hear me, Lord of the Silver Bow, who bestridest
Chrysa, protector of Cilla, the mighty ruler
of Tenedos, thou hast heard my prayer in the past
and, honouring me, hast scourged the Achaean host,
now, once more, I implore thee to grant my desire:
ward off from the Greeks the loathsome plague that afflicts them."

He prayed in these words and Phoebus Apollo heard him.
Then after praying they scattered the barley about,
drew back the heads of the beasts, and cut their throats
460 and flayed them; they cut out the thighs and wrapped them in fat,
making a double layer, with meat laid on them.
The priest then burned them on sticks of wood and drenched them
with sparkling wine; young men with forks stood beside him.
So he burned the thighs, and next they tasted the vitals.
The rest was chopped in pieces and placed in spits.
They carefully roasted the meat, then drew it all off.
And then, when the work was ended, they made the feast ready,
and dined, and no one there lacked his share of the banquet.
When finally eating and drinking had cast out hunger,
470 the youths, having filled the wine bowls, moved about
and poured out drops in each cup, then filled them all.
And all day long the youth of Achaea appeased
the god with song, singing paeans, and praising Apollo,
the far-worker; he, on his part, was delighted to hear.
When the sun had set and darkness came on, the Achaeans

stretched themselves out to rest by the stern of the ship.
But when Dawn appeared, the rose-fingered child of morning,
they once more put out to sea and sailed for their camp;
Far-working Apollo sent them a following wind.
480 They set up the mast, and on it they spread the white sail;
the sail came taut in the breeze, and around the stem
the dark purple wave gave a shriek as the ship leapt forward.
It cut through the swells, traversing its watery path.
The travellers came at last to the camp of the Greeks,
and there they drew the black ship on the mainland,
high on the sand, and set up the shores, along it.
Then the men dispersed, each one his tent and his ship.

Fleet-footed Achilles, the son of Zeus-born Peleus,
sitting beside his swift-sailing ships, still raged.
490 He did not go to the man-ennobling council,
nor did he go into combat, but ate out his heart
waiting in that place, longing for war-cry and battle.

The days went by at last the twelfth day dawned;
the immortal gods returned in a band to Olympus
with Zeus as their leader. Thetis had not forgotten
the promise made to her son. She rose from the sea-wave
early that morning and went up to highest Olympus.
She found the far-thundered sitting apart from the others
high on the topmost crest of the rugged mountain;
500 she sat close beside him, her left hand clasping his knees;
her right reached up to touch the tip of his chin;
with pleading words she addressed King Zeus, son of Cronos.

"Father, if I, among the immortals, have pleased you
either in word or deed, now grant my prayer.
Honor my son, who is, of all men, to live
but the briefest time; for King Agamemnon insults him;
the king himself has taken his prize and will keep it.
But give my son satisfaction, Olympian Zeus;
for the present, give strength to the Trojans; then the Achaeans
510 will pay back my son for his loss, and exalt him with honor."

This was her plea; cloud-gathering Zeus said nothing,
but sat for a long time silent. Thetis, clinging
against him, still hugged his knees and again entreated:
"Promise me faithfully; nod your head as a sign;
either that, or refuse outright—you have nothing to fear—
and I shall know I am least esteemed of the gods."
Cloud-gathering Zeus, much troubled, at last replied:
"A bad business, this, since you urge me to go against Hera
who is sure to vex me with nagging speeches about it.
520 As it is, she forever rebukes me in front of the gods
And says that I give support to the Trojans in battle.
But now you had much better go, lest Hera observe us;
leave all to me, and I shall see it accomplished.
Come, I shall nod my head, and that will convince you;
this is the surest pledge among the immortals;
when I nod my head, my promise cannot be revoked;
I shall not deceive you, nor shall I leave it undone."
Then Zeus, the son of Cronos, inclined his black brows;
As he nodded to her, ambrosial locks swept forward
530 from the deathless head of the king, and Olympus rocked.

With this understanding they parted. The goddess leapt down
from shining Olympus into the deepest sea.
Zeus went to his home. Then all of the gods together
arose from their seats to greet their father. Not one of them
dared to await his coming, but all went to meet him.
He seated himself on his throne. Now Hera, watching.
was not aware of the plans he had made with Thetis,
the Old Man of the Ocean's silvery-footed daughter.
At once she addressed her husband with mocking words:

540 "With which of the gods are you plotting this time, my schemer?
It is always a pleasure to you, when I am not near you,
to govern with secret counsel; you cannot endure
to tell me freely whatever you have on your mind."

Then the father of gods and men replied to her, "Hera,
you cannot hope to know the whole of my thought;

that would be difficult even though you are my wife;
whatever is fitting for you to hear, no other,
either of gods or men, shall know before you;
whatever I wish to contrive apart from the gods—
550 such things you should not inquire about or pry into."

Then Hera, the ox-eyed queen, at once retorted
"Cronides, terrible one! What a thing to say!
Indeed, I never before inquired or pried,
but left you in peace to plan whatever you wished.
But now I'm afraid that silvery-footed Thetis
has talked to you and brought you around to her thinking;
I know she came early this morning and, sitting beside you,
embraced you. I think you vowed then to avenge Achilles
by letting the Greeks be slaughtered beside their ships."

560   To this, cloud-gathering Zeus replied, "My dear,
you are always thinking something, and watch me always;
by this you accomplish nothing, but turn me against you
so that in the end you will only fare so much the worse.
If it is as you say, it is so because I desire it.
Sit down and be quiet. Do as I tell you—if not,
you will find that all of the gods together can't help you
when once I have laid my invincible hands upon you."

When he had spoken, Hera, the ox-eyed queen,
sat silent and frightened, curbing her strong emotion.
570 The other gods were also disturbed, but Hephaistos,
the glorious artist, began to speak in a vein
that pleased his beloved mother, the white-armed Hera:

"A wretched affair this is—it is not to be borne
that gods should fall out with each other concerning mortals
and carry on quarrels about them. What pleasure is there
in feasting well when ill will has the upper hand?
I can only counsel my mother, who knows I am right,
to give in to the pleasure of dear father Zeus; for if not,
he will surely rebuke her again and ruin our feast.

580 Because, if he wishes, Olympios, god of lightning,
can hurl us all from our seats; he is much the strongest.
However, if you will address him with gentle words,
Olympian Zeus will at once be kind to us all."

These were the words of Hephaistos; he sprang to his feet
and placed the two-handled cup in his mother's hand
and said, "Endure it with patience, Mother, grieved
as you are; if you persist, I fear I shall see you
struck down in front of my eyes, I being helpless
to aid you, for Zeus is a difficult god to contend with.
590 One other time when I was eager to help you,
seizing my foot he hurled me from heaven's threshold.
All though the day I fell, and at last, at sunset
I came down in Lemnos, with little life in my body.
The Sintians took me up and took care of me then."

So he spoke, and the goddess smiled, the white-armed Hera;
smiling she took the cup from the hand of her son.
Next, he poured sweet nectar and passed it around
to all the others in turn, from left to right.
The blessed gods broke out in unquenchable laughter
600 to see Hephaistos bustling about the house.

Then all day long till the sun went down they dined,
and everyone there had his equal share of the feast;
there was music, too, from Apollo's harp,
and the Muses, with charming voices, sang each in turn.
But when at last the shining light of the sun
had set, they parted, and went to their homes to sleep,
for Hephaistos, the famous strong-armed god, had built
for each of them a home by his cunning skill.
Zeus, the lightning-wielder, went to the couch
610 where he usually lay when sweet sleep came upon him;
there he stretched out with the gold-throned Hera beside him.

**The First Chorus from Oedipus King, from Sophocles,
*Oedipus Rex***

Strophe I

Now speaks
The sweet-voiced god.
What shall we hear
In shining Thebes from Delphi rich in gold?
My heart is racked with fear
And terror of all.
I raise the old
Cry of lament. O Paean Delos!
Thee I revere.
10 What must be done I have done
And the new cares come back upon me.
Speak to me then, O golden one!
The child of hope, immortal Voice!

Antistrophe I

First I call upon thee,
Daughter of God, immortal Athena,
And Artemis, sister of thine,
And our own protectress,
Seated on a glorious throne
In the circular market.
20 And far darting Phoebus, Oh
Ye three shine forth upon me
And ward off this death.
If ever, called on by name
To avert my woe,
Thou wert strong to remove the flame
Of destruction.
Come also now!

Strophe II

Oh strange! For I bear
Woes beyond number.

30 All that is mine is diseased
From end unto end,
Nor any spear of thought is there
To defend.
The fruit of our land is not
Increased and the mother
Rises not up from the dire
Labor of childbirth.
Like well-plumed birds
You may see them
40 One hard on another
Rushing wildly like
An irresistible fire
To the coast land of the god of the evening.

Strophe III

Let furious Ares now
Meeting me amid loud cries,
Without the brass of shields enflaming me,
Turn his back in swift
Flight down the wind,
To the great sea
50 Chamber of Amphitrite,
Or to the drift
Of Thracian waters that refuse
Haven to strangers;
For if what night lets loose
Day comes upon,
Him, Father Zeus,
Devour with fire-bearing lightning.

Antistrophe II

From bound to bound
of the city uncounted numbers perish.
60 Death-bringing children lie,
Unpitied, ruthlessly
Stretched out on the ground.
Some here, some there,

The wives and gray-haired mothers found
Before the shore of the altar bear
As suppliants the lamentations
Of baneful burdens.
As the paean shines their voices sound
In mournful concert.
70 For these,
Golden daughter of Zeus,
Send fair defence.

Antistrophe III

O Lycian King,
We celebrate the untamed
Arrows and the bow
With golden string
Stretched in our defence,
And darting radiance
Of Artemis that spills
80 Fire through Lycian hills.
Him I call who wears
The gold head-band,
Who bears the name of this land,
Euios Bacchos of the ruddy face.
O come with flaming bright-eyed torch
And hand in hand
With Maenads,
Against that god unhonoured of the gods.

Odysseus Speaking
(from the *Odyssey,* opening of Book IX)

I am Odysseus, the son of Laertes: men everywhere
tell stories of me, until news of my tricks must,
I think, have reached heaven. Ithaca is my home,
an island of clear skies and a wooded windswept
hill, Mount Neriton—an island that lies
close to its neighbor islands of Samë, Doulíchion
and wooded Zacynthos, yet more to seaward, turned
to the west while they face dawn and sunrise.
It is a hard land, a breeder of men; and I know
no sweeter sight than a man's own country;
the goddess Calypso held me in her rock-walled
cave, wishing to marry me; Circe, the sorceress,
kept me in her high halls, wishing to marry me;
but neither of them could ever persuade my heart,
because this is true: his own country, his own
kindred are what any man loves most, though you find him
settled among foreigners in some richer home.

Three Translations from the Greek

1. Ball Game

Golden haired Love
calls me (tossing
me his bright ball)

to come play at
catch with a young
thing in red sandals.

But she, being off
prosperous Lesbos,
finds fault with my

gray hairs: she hangs
around open-mouthed
after another man.

(*after* Anacreon)

2. Terpander

This poet died
singing in the
village square;

he was not hit
by an arrow,
not by a sword.

Death always has
some excuse: he
choked on a fig.

(*after* Tryphon)

3. Inscription

I was not: I became.
I was: and I am not.
And that is all. If anyone
says otherwise, he lies.
I shall not be.
> (*from the* Anthology)

III.

SELECTED PROSE

Confessional (1932)

Distempre yow noght, ye be my confessour;
Ye been the salt of the earth and the savour.

—Chaucer

Will you, my fathers in learning, be my confessors? My heart is heavy with an accumulation of four years of sin. Let me unburden it to you, and pass to the life beyond this, if God so wills, in peace. It is my desire not to hide anything. May I use this book as the little window of the confessional? I shall shield my face with my cloak, and do you cover yours with your hand. Be merciful to me, my fathers!

I should have written a critical thesis. For the good of my soul, I should have written it, but I swear that I could not. That is a heavy sin for one who has been four years a Novice in the Order. Obviously, I have played wanton with my books. I am devoid of virtue. The council sits in judgement upon me.

I pray you, my fathers, cover your faces with both hands. This is difficult to say. During these four years I have studied under six of you. I have tried to obey your precepts, to walk in your footsteps, to be mindful of the golden sayings that dropped from your lips. What was my fate? To be lost in utter darkness, to find no sure path to heaven, almost, to lose all faith. One of you, I found, would take the green path, and another the purple, and another would climb a golden ladder to paradise. The company of the saints was different for each of you. Even God you could not describe alike. One dwelt on his tone, another on his words, and another on his aspect. Are the Madonna's eyes grey or blue, O you who have seen visions?

I began to make little prayers of my own. I prayed as one of you taught me, but when another heard me pray, he said, "Those words are heresy. I have seen newer visions. The newly-born in bliss teach one to pray otherwise." So, I prayed otherwise, but I was not content. I prayed a little prayer, and one of you said concerning it, "That one word will win a special intercession on the part of Our Blessed Lady." Another said, "That word is anathema. Strike it out." O my fathers, do you wonder at my bewilderment? Weary, and lost utterly, I knelt and tried to learn in humbleness.

When you handed me the writings of the Fathers, the Lives of the Saints, the Books of the Blessed Martyrs, and told me to expound them, what wonder if my limbs became faint and my heart trembled? Who am I to lay impious hands on their sacred garments, stained with the blood of martyrdom? I, too, would suffer martyrdom, in the arena if need be, or at the hands of the soldiery; but ask me not to see clearly where you, masters of so much more of learning than I shall ever have, have failed. You have studied the Scriptures with diligence. You have heard the greatest teachers of the Universities. You have seen visions in your own cells. Each of you treads with confidence his green or purple path. Each of you is attended by a band of neophytes whom my conscience will not permit me to join. Forgive me if I turn aside.

The glory of the City of God binds me as it is fleetingly revealed. I lose myself in adoration and wonder. If I become speechless, do not censure me. I will not describe the City, for I have seen only one tower. I will not deny the visions of others, for their eyes are as clear—and as blind—as mine. If I see a shrine to a sham saint, I will not pull it down. Let the rain and the wind do that. I will pray at the shrine of every saint who was ever known to work a miracle. Yes, I will even propitiate the pagan, the forgotten gods; for I cannot be too sure. For the rest, I will keep the saints' days and the fast days, and I will tell my beads in a walled garden of red and white flowers, saying my prayers as my heart dictates. I shall hope to see the secrets of the City revealed more often and more fully as time goes on. I shall even hope, someday, with the grace of God, to work a small miracle among my red and white flowers.

Creed (1932)

And so many men said many things and every man was
fully persuaded in his own mind

—Jocelin of Brakelond

I BELIEVE in simplicity and sincerity of word and movement and idea.

I BELIEVE that compression and image are central to good poetry, but are not an end in themselves.

I BELIEVE in experimentation and not in cults.

I BELIEVE in the sound of words. By that I mean words that sound as if they grew together, although they may be common and not particularly beautiful in themselves.

I BELIEVE and regret that everyone is caught in the flow of some poetic movement and is greatly influenced by it.

I BELIEVE that the excellence of a poem is to a greater extent measured by whether its meaning increases or decreases with repeated readings.

I BELIEVE that everything good has its place in poetry, but I have a greater weakness for some things than others.

I BELIEVE that perspective is far more important than criteria in judging the worth of poems.

I BELIEVE in Shakespeare and Shelley and Keats and Ezra Pound and Elinor Wylie and Edith Sitwell (though I often have my doubts there) and I should probably mention Homer. I had a passion for Alfred Noyes when I was in eighth grade and may have one for Hart Crane by next year. One can never be sure about things like that.

A Note on Poetry (1940)

Any artist is to me a person who takes nothing for granted; one who, while perceiving the thing's traditional wrappings, sees the thing itself with freshness, as though never encountered before; sees the article as itself, the package as something else, and neither as a reproduction of the picture in the ubiquitous advertisement.

If I have made myself clear, it must also be clear that I could ask nothing more important of poetry just now. Poets, in their particular field, work with words—not only the meanings of words, but the sounds of words, and this to me is extremely important. Beyond these two things, poetry may do different things and be good in different ways; but without freshness of vision, and craftmanship in the building of metrical and melodic patterns, the poetry might as well be journalism.

What I am trying to do in my own work must be apparent in whatever I have accomplished. My approach to almost any experience is, by an accident of life, through a little-known landscape which proves a barrier to some readers. I think of that accident as the luckiest chance of my life, and cannot be sorry for it. Very few of the poems collected here have been written during the past two years, when I have had little opportunity for writing; but I feel that my aims have been sharpened rather than changed, as the world changed.

A Communication on Greek Metric,
Ezra Pound, and *Sappho* (1978/79; 1994)

Editor's note: contains numerous facsimile drafts of Mary Barnard's scansions marks in the supporting examples and printed Greek text as they appeared in her essay "A Communication on Greek Metric, Ezra Pound, and Sappho," Paideuma 23, no. 1 (Spring 1994): 147–52.

When I wrote to Ezra Pound in the fall of 1933, and asked for advice or assistance, he took me on as an apprentice poet. God knows why, but possibly the fact that I had been studying Greek had something to do with it. At any rate, he exhorted me to work with Greek metric. Besides recommending that I try to write quantitative Sapphics in English, he wrote that I should consult *Laurencie et Lavignac's Dictionnaire du Conservatoire, Encyclopédie de la Musique.* The chapter on Greek metric, he said, was "full of good sense."[1] Later he wrote again, urging that I look it up: "I don't know how much real use it wd be . . . but I know *nothing* else of any use. I have never worked on it or with it, but it contains intelligent remarks."[2] Still later, he wrote: "If you have to go to Portland to consult the Lavignac and can't afford it for the home / let me know / and I will send along the Greek section."[3] At this point I confessed that the Lavignac was not available in Portland, and he dispatched his copy.

---

1. Unpublished letter from Ezra Pound, 2 December 1933.

2. Published letter from Ezra Pound, 23 February 1934; *The Letters of Ezra Pound, 1907–1941,* ed. D. D. Paige (London: Faber, 1951) 339.

3. Unpublished letter from Ezra Pound, 28 November 1934.

I don't keep up with all the criticism written on Pound (could anyone?) but so far as I know, no one has pursued this question of the chapter on Greek metric, perhaps because he said in the published letter that he had never worked with it.

While I was waiting for the Lavignac, I had got hold of the only book on Greek metric available to me, and my notebook from those days show that I was looking for examples of Greek meter in *The Cantos*, for instance:

Figure 14. Greek meter in *The Cantos*.

Glyconic: Hear me, Cadmus of Golden Prows!

Aeolian Tripody: Peerless among the pairs

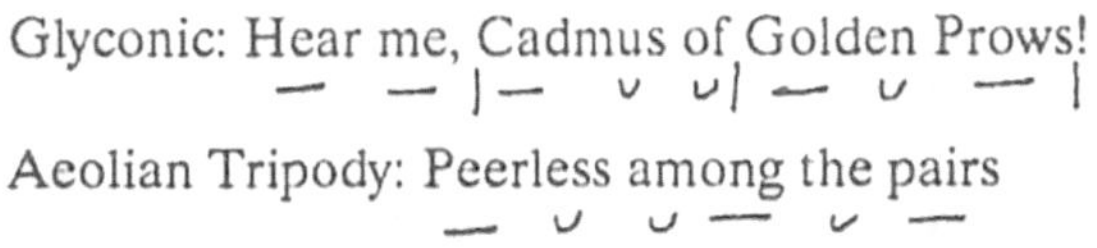

and

Figure 15. Greek meter in *The Cantos*.

Two Epitrites: And the vinestocks lie untended

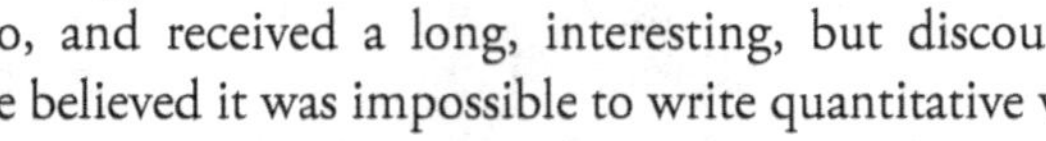

Pound also suggested at this time that I write to W. H. D. Rouse about metric. I did so, and received a long, interesting, but discouraging letter in which he said he believed it was impossible to write quantitative verse in English. Nevertheless, I kept on trying to do Sapphics, but without much success.

Eventually the Greek section of the Lavignac arrived from Rapallo, and I went to work on that. I have not seen the volume since I returned it to him a month or so later, and I shall not attempt to give a resumé of what is in it from my notes taken at the time. I shall discuss only one part of the work, the part that made the deepest impression on me then, and the part I found most useful afterwards.

Now it should be said that I had a pretty good idea of what I wanted. I wanted to write poetry that sounded like poetry, not chopped up prose, but at the same time, I wanted to approximate speech rhythms. I wanted the sound of the speaking voice. I realize that there are other ways of writing poetry, but the sound of speech was what I was after. I obviously had not found it. Pound wrote me in one letter: "I *still* think the best *mechanism* for breaking up the stiffness and literary idiom *is* a different metre, the god damn iambic magnetizes certain verbal sequences."[1]

About this time someone (can it have been T. S. Eliot?) said that most free verse was really iambic pentameter broken into uneven lines. It was held then, and still is held, I believe, that iambic pentameter comes closer than any other meter to approximating English speech rhythms. That may have been true at one time, but I do not think it is true today, or at least, it is not true of American speech rhythms. I wanted to find the sound of the speaking voice that was native to me. I admired the poetry of William Carlos Williams, and approved his endeavor to find an American metric, but I did not feel that he had found the solution, or at any rate, not the solution that would work for me. I did not really expect to find what I was looking for in Greek metric, but I found in the Lavignac something that struck me as a possible answer to my problem.

I was interested in certain lines, dimeters in which the longs and shorts constantly varied in position, but *balanced*. The Greek text was not given, only the analysis of the rhythm. One was headed, *"Air de l'anonyme"* and went like this:

Figure 16. Scansion marks.

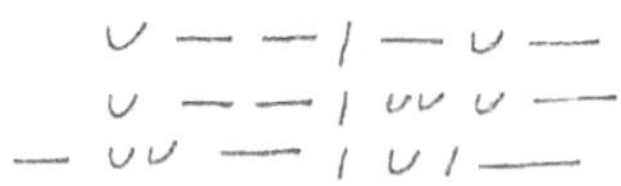

$$\cup \;—\;—\;|\;—\;\cup\;—$$
$$\cup \;—\;—\;|\;\cup\cup\;\cup\;—$$
$$—\;\cup\cup\;—\;|\;\cup\;|\;——$$

Another was described as *"Strophes à rhythmes antagonistes"*; this was from *Helen*:

Figure 17. Scansion marks.

$$\cup\cup\;\cup\;—\cup\;|\;—\;\cup\;\llcorner\!\!—$$
$$\lrcorner\cup\;—\;\cup\;|\;—\;\cup\llcorner\!\!—$$
$$—\;—\;\cup\;—\;|\;\cup\!—\cup\;—$$
$$—\;—\;\cup\;—\;|\;—\;—\;\cup\;—$$

---

1. Letter from Ezra Pound, 13 August 1934, Paige 346.

And finally there were dimeters of Sophocles from *Philoctetes*, including the following:

Figure 18. Scansion marks.

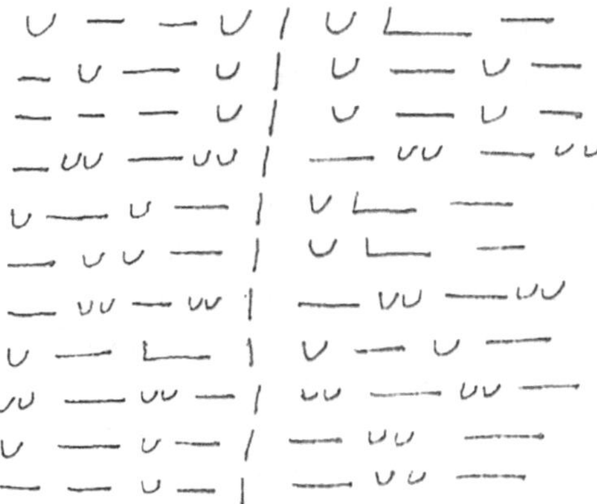

I tried another variation [*Editor's note: see Figure 19 below*] but found it wouldn't work. It turns into two dactyls and a spondee.

Figure 19. Scansion marks.

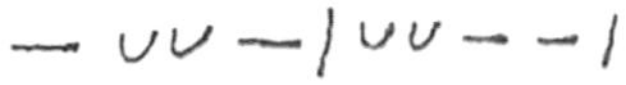

I played with these meters off and on for years. I wrote an ill-fated verse play in dimeters, but failed to introduce enough variation. I found that Pound's line, "Eyes, lips, dreams, and the night goes," scanned by T. S. Eliot as a spondee, a dactyl, and another spondee, really made better sense as a balanced line:

Figure 20. Scansion marks on a line from Pound.

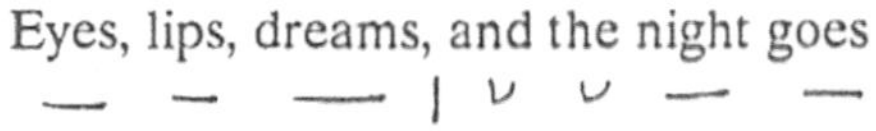

Eyes, lips, dreams, and the night goes

Occasionally, I used balanced dimeters in my own lyrics, and then for a time wrote no verse at all.

The work I had done on the Lavignac volume finally bore fruit when I came to do my translation of Sappho. Here I was faced with two different problems: what to do with the long poems, some of which were in Sapphics, and some not; and what to do with the short fragments, which were almost too short for any meter to establish itself, yet which must, I felt, have a metric if they were to sound like poems when they stood alone on the page. One of the things that attracted me to Sappho's poetry and made me want to translate it was the sound of speaking voice which was audible both in the Sapphics and the fragments: "τεθνάκην δ' ἀδόλως θέλω," ("Frankly I wish I were dead").

The brevity of the fragments reminded me, of course, of haiku, and I told myself that if the Japanese could write a poem in seventeen syllables, I could do the same, but I could see that the convention of the haiku offered no solution. I must work out my own convention. Here I turned to my experiments with the balanced line, but I saw that with poems so short, a foot would have to be a line. Each line would have to balance against the others.

By this time I had given up trying to do strictly quantitative meters, though I took quantity into account. I thought of a long syllable rather as a weighted syllable, weighted with a long vowel, or cluster of consonants, a stress, or an emphasis dependent on a sense, a conversational emphasis. A "long" might be one of these or a combination of two or three.

Following are a few examples[1] as I scan them *[Editor's note: number of examples reduced owing to copyright restrictions]*:

Figures 21 and 22. Various lines of poetry with scansion marks inserted.

59.	I said, Sappho	69.	This way, that way
	∪ — — ∪		— ∪ — ∪
	Enough! Why		I do not know
	∪ — —		∪ — ∪ —
	try to move		what to do: I
	— ∪ —		— ∪ — ∪
	a hard heart?		am of two minds
	∪ — —		∪ ∪ — —

---

1. The following translations are from *Sappho: A New Translation,* University of California Press, 1958.

Some of the longer poems I translated in what I hoped was a free approxima-
tion of the original metric, but those which were in Sapphics in the original
were another problem. Sappho's verses move swiftly, and, as I said, carry a
speech cadence. It seemed to me impossible to get these effects in English,
as I wanted, if I used a Sapphic meter. I used, therefore, a meter similar to
the balanced lines I had used in the fragments. One of the stanzas that best
illustrates my solution to the problem is that beginning καὶ γὰρ αἰ φεύγει
ταχέως διώξει. I translated as follows:

Figures 23 and 24. Various lines of poetry with scansion marks inserted. *[Editor's
note: example's last line omitted owing to copyright restrictions]*

For, let her
— ᴜ ᴜ

run, she will soon run after;
— — ᴜ | — ᴜ — ᴜ

if she won't accept gifts, she
— ᴜ — | ᴜ — — ᴜ

will one day give them; and if
ᴜ — — | — ᴜ ᴜ —

she won't love you – she soon will
ᴜ — — | ᴜ ᴜ — —

Naturally, I did not work out the scansion first, and fit the words to it,
but I worked back and forth, scanning when a line sounded wrong, to see
where it needed adjustment. Every fragment and stanza went through dozens
of versions until I was satisfied that I had done as well with it as I was likely
to do.

Now I am working on Homer, and that is another problem entirely.

Meeting Marianne (1982)

One[1] day in mid-April I came home to my furnished room on West Eleventh Street to find a note from R. L. Latimer of the Alcestis Press. He had called to see me while I was out. The note was an invitation to a party at an apartment in Brooklyn. William Carlos Williams was coming over to sign the colophon sheets of his new book, *Adam & Eve & the City*; Marianne Moore would also be there. Naturally, I went. Following Mr. Latimer's directions, I found my way over to Brooklyn Heights by subway. The party was in a penthouse apartment with a magnificent view of the Manhattan lights. I arrived early (a bad habit I have never been able to break). Dr. Williams and young Mr. Latimer, who had been having dinner together, arrived later, as did Miss Moore. Meanwhile I was in the awkward situation of having to introduce myself to people I had never heard of, who had never heard of me and could not quite imagine what I was doing there. Miss Moore arrived and was introduced, but failed to catch my name until Dr. Williams came in and greeted me. After that we tried to talk, but she was the center of attention, so that we had no private conversation though she promised to come to see me the following week. Only Williams, of the people at the party, had met her before, and he said that he hadn't even seen her for years. I was delighted with her.

> She's a grand person. I'm very enthusiastic about her and not scared
> of her any more. [I had found her letters somewhat intimidating.]
> She talked a blue streak, and Williams said it was because she was
> frightened and was trying to build up a barrier of words to hide

---

1. These reminiscences are excerpted from a work-in-progress entitled *Assault on Mount Helicon*. They are based on letters I wrote home from New York during my first visit there in the spring of 1936. M. B.

behind. I don't know about that, but she did get quite flushed, and she probably did realize that she was the center of the party. Anyway, she was most entertaining.

At this time Miss Moore was a straight and slender middle-aged woman who had not yet assumed her well-known trademark of the tricorne hat. She wore her once-red and still luxuriant hair braided in a coronet around her head, as she continued to do so until the end of her life. At age forty-nine she dressed, not like my mother, but like my grandmother, in almost ankle-length skirts. In other words, she dressed like *her* mother. Her eyes were round and very alert, not sharp, but completely frank, open and observant—so observant that I tended to look instinctively for cover when they turned in my direction. Her voice, as is well-known from recorded readings of her poems, was nasal and unattractive, but listening to her talk I forgot the voice as I tried to keep up with her quick turns of thought. I felt as though I were one half of an unrehearsed flying-trapeze act. In a tête-à-tête conversation she would have been frightening except for her open, almost confiding manner.

When Miss Moore left, Latimer exclaimed that he had been trying to run that woman down for years. A young poet to whom I had already taken a dislike aroused my ire by crying out that she was "just like Emily Dickinson!" Not to my mind. I could not imagine Emily Dickinson as editor of *The Dial*.

Miss Moore kept her word. On the 28th she came to see me and stayed two hours. My report to my family on that visit is unfortunately brief. "I couldn't begin to tell you what she said—" I told them, "she talked too fast." Apparently we talked about the manuscript I had brought with me, and which poems to include or exclude when I submitted it to a publisher. A letter had come that morning from Dr. Williams, who had made a list of poems I should leave out. It is not surprising that their opinions differed. We talked about his criticism, and "she said not to pay any attention to what Dr. Williams told me—as to content. As for technical advice, he might be very good. Then after some more, she said she was a menace, and I oughtn't pay any attention to her either." I believe it was also at this meeting that she cautioned me against Dr. Williams and his friends: "It is NOT necessary to be Bohemian," she said firmly.

Finally: "She said she really knew very few people, but if she could help me at all she would be very glad. She stopped on her way here to leave a note in T. C. Wilson's mailbox to tell him I was in town." She had surmised that I would be diffident about calling people to say, "Here I am!" because she found it almost impossible to do herself. In London she had seen none of the literary people with whom she had corresponded, because she did not know how to go about letting them know that she was there.

When I returned from a visit to Cambridge in May, I wrote again to Marianne Moore and invited her to have lunch with me, but she countered with a proposal that I meet her in the dentist's waiting room. I met her as she suggested, and in a letter I wrote that evening, said:

> I had quite a long and interesting conversation with Miss Moore—all about my poems and my future. I've hardly thought about anything else since. She gave me some advice I thought was very good and some I'm doubtful about. Also found out that keeping up a correspondence with Ezra as long as I have without being insulted is a record. He even insults her. But maybe she would think she was insulted when I wouldn't. She was very pleased when I told her how nicely he always spoke of her in his letters.

Marianne Moore is the only person I have ever known who always said "Mr. Pound." She and "Mr. Pound" had not yet met, but had been corresponding for a long time, I gathered. She discounted the bluster, and emphasized his kindness. Once, she said, she wrote to him, complaining that she was not getting anything published. Shortly thereafter she began to hear from editors not only in the United States and England, but from as far away as India and Australia. All the letters said the same thing: Ezra Pound had informed the writer that she might be willing to let him have some of her work for publication in his magazine.

She also chided me gently for not writing better prose. She had found my letters not very well-written, and impressed upon me her view that a good prose style was very important to poets. I lamely explained that fright had probably helped to make my style a bit stilted; she nodded understandingly and said that she thought that might be part of the trouble.

Sometimes Miss Moore seemed impossibly Victorian, as when she informed me that she never rode the subway alone at night, not because she was frightened (almost no one was, at that time), but because she did not consider it "suitable." However, too much has sometimes been made of her primness. I was once told that when she was editor of *The Dial*, she refused to publish anything by E. E. Cummings, but that was not true. She published several of his poems; and she was the first person to ever tell me to read *The Enormous Room*.

During our conversation I told her about my visits to Concord, Salem and Marblehead, and especially about the cemetery in Marblehead. As I remember, it was on a small promontory overlooking the water. Among the graves there were a number of monuments inscribed with lists of names of men lost at sea, and just behind this green knoll we came upon a little pond where children were sailing toy boats with colored sails. There was a germ of a poem in it, but I never wrote the poem. Instead I told Miss Moore, who never forgot it. Several times in after years she mentioned the Marblehead cemetery, and once she told me that friends had taken her and her mother to Marblehead. She remembered about the cemetery, she said, and would have liked to have seen it, but unfortunately her mother was unable to leave the car, and of course she stayed with her mother. This kind of thing made me want to beat my head against the wall. And in this connection a letter she wrote me the next day after our talk is worth quoting almost in full:

> It strikes me in connection with the Concord group, what ascetics they were; how little they had materially, yet what great givers they were; their writings are lasting and we have to remember that they were the expression of what they—the writers—daily lived. I think young writers naturally feeling the weight of work coming can scarcely believe enough that often the foundation for it is in giving to others and taking care of their interests. Many things in life have been hard and I have often thought how much better it would be for me if circumstances were different, but a remark of Katherine Cornell—in a magazine—about her art stays in my mind since acting is the most obstructed form of expression perhaps that we have—: "Nothing is keeping me back but myself." But even the force in that idea does not enlarge one so much as the above idea, that in giving to others and taking care of their interests one has real self-expansion.
>
> I spoke of hoping that you will read the (Sheed and Ward) Henry W. Wells edition of Piers Ploughman; and perhaps you would care to read too when you can, Kagawa's novel, *A Grain of Wheat*.
>
> I hope you can feel too that opposition and advice are appreciation, not an illegitimate cutworm.
>
> Sincerely yours,
>
> Marianne Moore.

I regretted that she herself found it necessary to give quite so much, but when, a few years later, I came upon her poem, "What Are Years?" in the current issue of *Kenyon Review*, I had to ask myself whether the poem was not worth the price she had paid for it. It seems to me one of the great modern lyrics, and certainly one of the finest ever written by a woman.

Ezra Pound, Sappho, and My Assault
on Mount Helicon (1983)

Fifty years ago, when I first appealed to Ezra Pound for advice and criticism, I told him frankly that I hated translation. The retort came promptly: "You hate translation??? What of it?? Expect to be carried up Mt. Helicon in an easy chair?" Well, yes, I suppose I did. Or perhaps I expected to fly to the summit and thought he could tell me where the wings were kept. He then suggested that for exercise I try to write poems in the metric of Sappho's ode to Aphrodite, keeping to quantitative rather than accented verse. He never actually recommended that I translate Sappho, although he did suggest the *Odyssey*, a thought that appalled me. I dutifully worked away at the English sapphics without much success, but for the next twenty years I continued to give translation a wide berth. I finally turned to it during a crisis in my life brought on by two potentially fatal illnesses, one following on the heels of the other.

After spending weeks in two different hospitals, I was at last at home, where I heard my doctor's voice on the telephone telling me to stay in bed another month. He had been saying, "Stay in bed another week," and I had been patient. When he said, "Stay in bed another month," I protested vehemently, but he remained firm. I went back to bed and thought things over. I could see that it would be not just one month, but many months, before I would be able to live a normal life again. (I was quite right about that; when I was permitted to sit up, it was for fifteen minutes a day for one month, and half an hour a day for the next month.) I felt that I must do something to make this catastrophe *pay*, to move it somehow from the loss column to the profit column, to make it turn out to be, like all the disasters in English history since 1066 and all that, "A Good Thing." I wanted to feel, when at least I was able to be active again, that I had accomplished something; the way to bring about that result, I thought, was to do something I would *not* have done if I had been on my feet. At the same time, it had to be something I could do comfortably while propped up on pillows. There are other ways of dealing with a stone wall besides trying to climb over it or bash a hole in it or dig a tunnel under it. One can follow it to find out where it leads. Mine led me to Greek. I finally remembered that I had thought and said repeatedly that if I ever had time I would like to take up my Greek again. During my summer vacations at home I had occasionally taken my Homer out into the garden and read a bit, but the tools were definitely rusty. This was my chance to do something about it.

Once I had my answer, I went to work immediately. Since I had two beginner's grammars in the house, I began by working my way through both of them. I then read twelve books of the *Iliad*, but because I was unable at that time to get the text of the last twelve books, I switched to the *Odyssey*, which happened to be available, and read twelve books of that. If you have to be in bed for weeks at a time, there is nobody better to be in bed with than Homer—in the original. I wrote to friends in Italy, told them about my illness, and mentioned that I was reading Greek. They sent me in return a copy of Salvatore Quasimodo's little volume, *Lirici Greci*, containing poems by Sappho and other Greek lyricists in the original, with Italian translations. In order to explain what that little book meant to me, I must say something about the problems of translation.

In the first place, it should be said that the perfect translator of poetry would presumably be someone who was completely bilingual, having grown up speaking both languages *in* the countries to which they belong, one who was equally well-read in the literature of both languages, a contemporary of the poet to be translated and a poet of genius in his own right. If he were temperamentally akin to the original poet, that would be a help, too. Whether there have ever been any such translators is doubtful, but obviously there has been no such translator of ancient Greek since Roman times. The translator who does not speak the original language like a native is willy-nilly dependent upon lexicons and cribs, which are, in the case of ancient Greek, compiled and composed by classical scholars, usually late-Victorians. They often erect another barrier, as T. S. Eliot said of Gilbert Murray's translations, between the reader and the original text. I had tried to read Sappho in the original, but I needed a crib, or notes, or a lexicon, and my efforts only left me wondering what all the fuss was about. The first thing Quasimodo's translations did for me was show me the text through the medium of a language that was not English, living or dead, leaving my mind free to balance between the Greek phrase and the Italian phrase while I searched for the truly equivalent phrase in living, not lexicon, English. This little book removed one of the chief obstacles to translations, so far as I was concerned, by showing me how to use a third language as a bridge.

In addition, I found the Italian translations very beautiful and wanted to match them, if I could, in my own language. Most important of all, however, I found here in Sappho's Greek, as revealed to me now through the medium of the Italian, the style I had been groping toward, or perhaps merely hungering for, when I ceased to write poetry a number of years before. It was spare but musical, and had, besides, the sound of the speaking voice making a simple but emotionally loaded statement. It is never "tinkling" as Bill Williams's friend A. P. characterized it. Neither is it "strident" as Rexroth described it: it is resonant although unmistakeably in the female register.

Hesitantly, I tried to put together a few of the fragments and one of the longer poems into English. I sent some of them off to Pound, whose reply was: "Yuz—vurry nize—only grump iz yu didn't git to it 20 years ago."

This was followed by a typewritten letter that accompanied my manuscripts, which he now returned. The letter is dated November 1, 1951.

> AN ADVANCE, so far aZi kno on earlier trans *i* of S / BUTTT yu mix two languages, the LIVE
> > as in first line /
> > and the dead / on delicate neck by me.
> Waal gorrdammit / what is the time lag / 25 years / but better now than never. / no, time lag 16 years. not bad for murka.
> > Now as fer the sittin-on-the-tree bird, that wd / be german order.
>
> Can't perfect simply by deleting useless words and words NOT in the speech of line 1.
>
> BUT there are other good lines. Job not wholly wasted by any means. The circled words can't simply be cut out
>
> merely energy gets lost.

In a postscript he added:

> THE JOB of the writer of verse is to get the LIVE language AND the prosody simultaneously. Prosody: articulation of the total sound of a poem (not bits of certain shapes gummed together.)

A marginal note on the manuscript said:

> crit cannnotttt consist in mere
> excision. ergo this is NOT definite
>   some stickum and / or stitches must replace jaboutz

Obviously, although I knew what I was after, I was not yet achieving the effect I wanted.

I kept on revising and after Christmas sent him new versions. I give the reply (dated January 31, 1952) in full:

>   *Frankly I
> Yes, *it is better. That is to say, my first impression is that it is better.
>
>   NOTE that what grampaw canNOTTT do is come out of wherever, AND concentrate on anything tother whatsoDAM.
>
> I can STILL see rewrite / I do not spose yu want ME to rewrite it.
>
> it is now more homogene / it is purrhapz a bit lax / whether one can emend that occurs wd / lax it still more ??? it still reads a bit like a translation /
>
> what is the maximum abruptness you can get it TO? Fordie: "40 ways to say anything"
>
>   I spose real exercise would consist in trying them ALL.
> for wot good it did / old Sternberg made Antheil do a fugue a week for a year, *on the SAME theme.* One fug / NO exercise.
>
> 52 on SAME theme: some training.
>
> Cleis: bout time "fair" was ousted fr / poetic jarg / utility of syntax? waaal the chink does without a damLot

I kept on trying. Eventually I think most of the fragments and each stanza of the longer poems did go through about forty versions. The fragments, especially, were great pillow-work. I could lie there rolling them around and around in my mind, trying different words and different arrangements of words, asking myself over and over: what did she *mean*? why [sic] did she say gold *sandals*? is [*sic*] she speaking or is someone else speaking? why [*sic*] would peace be difficult to endure? When I sat up for my allotted hour or two, I typed the versions I had been trying in my head; usually the fragment went through many more typed revisions; often I would work in one direction, then backtrack and start off in another. If I had been leading an active life, I would never have had the patience to work so long over each fragment, or if I had, the job would have taken me ten years. As it was, I worked for a year or more on the one hundred poems and fragments, although the last things I did came more easily.

I made no attempt to translate into the original meter. Greek normally has more syllables than English. I have never been able to see any way of rendering a Greek stanza in the equivalent number of English syllables without padding. The padding may take several forms: the embroidering of an image, repetition, or the introduction of unnecessary words ("I really believe"), all of which contribute to make the poem lax, to use Pound's word for the effect. One may also use a great many words of Latin deviation, or follow the Greek syntax slavishly; either of these dodges might work for Pindar—I don't know Pindar well enough to form an opinion, but they are out of place in translations of Homer and Sappho. Underlying the stanzaic form there is, I swear (in the teeth of those who have said otherwise) a cadence that belongs to the speaking voice. That underlying cadence is what I tried to find an equivalent for, because, so far as I knew, no English translation had yet conveyed it.

William Carlos Williams and
the Poetry Archive at Buffalo (1983)

These pages are excerpted from Assault on Mt. Helicon: A Literary Memoir, *to be published in 1983 by the University of California Press.*

The Poetry Collection at the Lockwood Memorial Library was the first of its kind, so far as I know; that is, it was the first archive set up for books, manuscripts and letters of modern and in most cases still living poets. (Chronologically the Collection began with Yeats's first volume, and Yeats was still living when the Collection began to take shape.) It was also the first to solicit working manuscripts that showed the process of composition. It would be difficult to say which of these two aspects of the Collection excited the most ridicule. The English were the first to double up with laughter; there was even a cartoon in *Punch*. To the English the joke was all the better because the manuscripts were to be collected in a city with the barbarous name of Buffalo. They found the whole idea simply hilarious and have not stopped poking fun at the quaint American notion of what constitutes a scholarly archive. While attempting to put myself to sleep last night with an English detective story, I came upon this: "American universities have fallen on hard times. Most of them have stopped buying second-rate authors' cast-off underwear." Honor Tracy has written a whole novel about an impecunious writer who was busy manufacturing a "working manuscript" of his last book. Ah well, yes. We were asking for papers that otherwise would have gone into the trash basket.

The idea that it was part of a university's business to collect materials for research into the work of modern poets was as strange (not to say scandalous) to most American professors, including those on the University of Buffalo campus, as it was to the British. No self-respecting scholar would think of wasting his time on living writers. Charles Abbott himself believed that the

Collection would come into its own "perhaps in a hundred years." The scholars would begin to come when we were long gone, he said, but the time to collect materials was the present. He was collecting for posterity. Living poets would one day be dead, the present would have become the past, the scholars would eventually become interested, and by that time the materials they needed would be much more difficult and expensive to obtain. This was surely true. The fifty dollars we paid for Williams's little pamphlet simply called *Poems* (Rutherford, 1909) seemed fantastic even to me, but thirty-five years later and the same book sold at auction for sixteen thousand.

I began my work as the first curator of the Collection forty-three years ago, on August 8, 1939. Charles Abbott had recently returned from England with a plentiful supply of letters and manuscripts not yet catalogued and filed. The book collection was still in the Librarian's study. Besides cataloguing and filing the accumulation of letters and manuscripts, I was supposed to write letters, and in some cases my personal and professional correspondence over-lapped. It must have been in a Christmas letter to William Carlos Williams, whom I had first met in 1936, that I mentioned the manuscripts we hoped to get from him. He replied cordially on January 8, 1940, saying,

> . . . thank you for a friendly letter and I wish you might be filing away scripts of mine as you should be if I had any to send you. I have a lot of junk lying around which I can bale up and dump on your lap if you want it but I can't imagine that it will be of use to anybody. Anything you want, ask for it. It's yours—with one or two exceptions, such as the script to the second edition of White Mule, now in the writing. I've promised that.

A few months later, in the spring of 1940, Williams arrived in Buffalo to give a lecture and reading. He and Flossie, like other visiting poets, stayed with the Abbotts at Gratwick Highlands, the first of many visits they were to make there over the next twenty years. Visiting poets and household crises, I was to learn, were apt to go hand in hand, but Mrs. Abbott reported that she found the Williamses, following hard on the heels of Wyndham Lewis, "very restful." For a while we had feared they would be there together, a possibility I didn't like to contemplate. In a letter to my parents, I said:

> One new complication is that the Lewises are going to stay until next Tuesday or Wednesday, which means the Abbotts will be entertaining them and the Williamses at the same time. I should

think the Williamses would be very easy to entertain, but how Wyndham and William will hit it off at the same dinner table is another question. They're both friends of Ezra's, but that would give me qualms as quick as aything [*sic*]. I'm pretty sure Williams wouldn't take offense—or at last would have too much respect for his host to take offense—at anything Lewis would say, but Lewis is awfully touchy and likely to fly off the handle at something Williams is most likely to say—because he's impetuous and certainly doesn't weigh well his words before he speaks, though he's willing to laugh almost anything off, himself.

As it turned out, I needn't have worried, since the Lewises left early, but I was also nervous about the lecture. This was the first time I had ever heard Williams perform in public. His coming had been partly my doing, and I was on edge about how the evening would turn out. He had read a few poems one evening when I was at Rutherford, probably when I was there with Fred Miller, and I had not thought he did them justice by any means. Mrs. Williams apparently felt that he did not read well, because she said, "Oh, no!" when he offered to read to us. I knew that he had done very few public lectures or readings up to that time, although on this trip he was appearing at Penn State, Dartmouth and Middlebury. My chief concern, however, was whether anyone would show up. At this time the Buffalo Public Library contained not a single volume of his work, poetry or prose, and interest in modern poetry (by anybody) was almost non-existent on the University of Buffalo campus outside the second floor of the library. All in all, I was afraid the audience would be limited to a handful of people who would wonder why he was there. Again, I need not have worried. My next letter home reported that the evening was a success:

The lecture was good. I was afraid he'd be nervous, which he was, and that that would make him stiff as it does some people, instead of natural, but he very successfully got rid of his own nervousness and the audience's stiffness by being very natural indeed and he had everybody laughing at least half of the time I should think. The crowd was respectable, and seemed to like him. When he mentioned quitting—drawing to a close, some girl behind me whom I didn't know, said "Oh, no, no, no!" very fervently. Most of the time he read from his poems. At the end, instead of asking whether there were any questions, as they usually do, Mr. Abbott said anyone with questions should come up and ask them personally. He won't do it again. A group of students, a large group, and I'm sure not from U.B. (never saw any of them before and I can't imagine where on earth they came from) literally mobbed him and wouldn't leave. Mr. Abbott told me enthusiastically that he thought the lecture was "swell" and Dr. Williams inquired whether he had disgraced me and Mrs. Williams invited me to be sure and come to see them next time I came to N.Y. Which I would like to do, but wonder when I'd squeeze it in.

My trips to New York were not so frequent as I would have liked, but were combined with library business so that I had a little expense money and a longer time to stay. The library business eventually took me to Rutherford again, not just for an afternoon call, but for a visit of several days. One segment of the Collection that had become my own particular domain was composed of little magazines: *The New Freewoman*, and its successor *The Egoist, transition, Broom, The Little Review, Others, Exile, Blast, This Quarter*, and a great many more. Some were intermittent, most were short-lived, and all our runs were gap-toothed. Filling in the gaps became my responsibility. I soon realized that if we attempted to supply the missing items from book catalogues the prices would bankrupt us. I suggested, therefore, that when I went to New York for a week-end, I might take an extra day and see what I could find on Fourth Avenue. My first tour of second-hand bookstores, though brief, was so profitable that from that time on I combined magazine-hunting with pleasure every time I went to New York. It was dirty work, but fun. For the only time in my life I experienced the collector's itch. If we had six issues of a magazine that ran for seven issues, the thought of that missing number 4 or 5, or whatever it was, plagued me until the run was complete.

When I was in search of defunct little magazines, I was haunted by the thought of all that I had seen in the Williams attic the first time I went out to Rutherford. We proposed to the doctor that he sell us the lot, but he said he wanted to go through them and keep any issues in which he had published stories or poems, and he saw no hope of getting round to it soon. With the entry of the United States into World War II and the mobilization of doctors, that hope receded still further. Finally a solution was found: *I* was to do the job. Naturally, I was delighted. I looked forward both to the work and the week-end I would spend at 9 Ridge Road.

One very hot Saturday afternoon in June of 1942 I went to Rutherford, taking my suitcase, and moved into one of the spare bedrooms. (Bill was in the Navy, in California, and Paul was working for Republic Steel in Canton, Ohio.) My next letter home had a full report on the week-end. I wrote that after I had washed off the grime,

> we had a delicious dinner with chicken and trimmings, and sat out in the back yard admiring the roses until the mosquitoes got bad, and then came in to drink iced lemonade with stalks of mint in it until bedtime. It was terribly hot until morning, and I kept tossing around thinking how hot it would be in the attic, but a cool breeze blew up around seven o'clock. There were windows in each end of the attic, with the breeze sweeping through, so I didn't suffer. All day Sunday I worked in the attic.
>
> In the morning I sorted magazines and books. There's an enormous amount of material, and it was all scattered. Vol. 1, No. 1 in a book case, Vol. 1, No. 2 in a trunk, Vol. 1, No. 3 in a desk drawer, another copy of Vol. 1, No. 3 under a table, and so on and so on. I sorted one magazine from the other, books from magazines, and things we were interested in from things we weren't. It was dirty, but I had fun. After lunch the doctor came up with me, and we both sorted, and began to get out letters. By that time I was down to making lists, so I wrote and he read letters to me. If the lists are right, it's a miracle, because I was so interested in the letters. As for giving them to us, first he would, and then he wouldn't, and then he didn't know. I think what finally threw a monkey wrench into the business was Mrs. Williams putting her foot down, with the result I came away with only two letters, but very good ones, one from Pound about 1907, one from H. D. when she was working on the *Egoist* in 1916. We may get others later.
>
> The magazines are less important, but I found a lot of things we need. The duplicates I know he'll let us have. Some of the others we may get, and in any case, I know a lot of magazines I didn't know about before—what's in them, and what we need. That information in itself is so hard to get. Monday I finished my lists and did some more rooting around in the grime, turning up things I had missed the first time.

I worked at a big table by the window, at the front end of the house. From that window I looked down to the sidewalk. On Monday, every time I glanced out I saw the same scene: a baby carriage, empty, was sitting in front of the house; another baby carriage (occupied) was approaching; another was rolling away just out of sight around the bend of the street. It went on all day long. On Monday morning the Williamses suggested that instead of going back to New York, I should remain in Rutherford and commute until time to return to Buffalo. They were so cordial that I gave in easily, and stayed on for several more nights. Monday evening we had a blackout that lasted about twenty minutes. Williams had to rush for the schoolhouse, which served as a first aid station, and Mrs. Williams and I went upstairs and watched for a searchlight display that didn't happen.

At Christmas time that same year I paid a call on Bill and Flossie and, to my surprise, came back to Buffalo with a big carton of letters. Writing of this event, I said:

> I think we now have most of the Williams letters. He said he might as well give them to us, because if he died, well, Flossie would be interested for a while, but then (so-and-so) or (so-and-so) might come around and carry them off, and he'd rather we had them. Besides, I think I've sold him on the idea that having his things in our library is just like having a private secretary. I've looked up and copied several things he couldn't find, have an order to do another one, and he's even thinking of sending us all his magazines, with poems he would like to anthologise checked for me to copy and compile. It seems that's why he's holding them, and he'll *never* get around to it without help.

I believe I was mistaken in thinking that we already had most of the Williams letters at that time. Others came later. Besides giving us manuscripts, letters and magazines, by the time I left Buffalo in 1943 Bill had also filled in two of the worst gaps in our book collection by selling us his copy of Pound's first volume, *A Lume Spento* ("I'll buy a War Bond!" he said), and finding a Rutherford friend who was willing to sell us his copy of Bill's *Poems*, 1909. Of course none of us had any idea of the fantastic prices those books would one day bring.

Further Notes on Metric (1994)

Perhaps Homer's *Iliad* seems at first glance to have little in common with Sappho's lyrics; but one thing is bound to strike the reader of both poets, and that is the way their poems *move*. Perhaps this is characteristic of Greek poetry in general, but I am not qualified to say. I shall play it safe and keep to Homer and Sappho. In both poets there is visual movement and auditory movement.

Take metaphor: Neither poet compares one *thing* to another. Their metaphors are more like equations, in which *a* acts on *x* as *b* acts on *y*, and the *likeness* is in the verb. Sappho does not say that love is like a whirlwind. She says, "As the whirlwind *swoops* on an oak / love *shakes* my heart." She does not say that love is like a serpent. She says that love *strikes* as a serpent *strikes*. In Homer's more extended metaphors he compares one movement with another. On the battlefield, when Paris sees Menelaos approaching, he takes a sudden step backward like a man who has been startled by a snake in his path. Or Diomedes dashes about the field like a river in spate, bursting its banks.

As for the narrative, metaphor aside, of course there are great stretches of hand-to-hand combat described in detail:

With a rush he grabbed the helmet crested with horsehair
and turning about dragged Paris among the Achaeans,
half-choking him as the strap bit into the flesh.
 (author's trans.; III.369–71)

Or:

Now Meges, that famous spearman, coming up close to him,
struck with his sharpened lance at the nape of the neck;
the points came out through his jaws and severed his tongue.
 (author's trans.; V.72–74)

This is the point at which readers of the *Iliad* in translation find the going heavy. Most modern readers, even with the best will in the world, have to make a valiant effort to read the whole epic in translation. But most readers of Greek find it hard to put down, and most of the latter agree that, wonderful as the *Odyssey* is, the ancient Greeks were right; the *Iliad* tops it. Trying to analyse my own fascination with the poem, I finally concluded that the combined effect of the visual movements and the rhythms were carrying me forward as though in spite of myself. When I analyzed the two movements further, I found that a visual movement was begun and completed often in one line, as in the examples given above, although sometimes the movement is begun in one line and completed in a second.

Pope was very much aware of the movement in the original Greek. In the Preface to his translation of the *Iliad* Pope says of Homer, "What he writes is of the most animated nature imaginable; every thing moves, every thing lives, and is put in action." Unfortunately when Pope came to translate, he wrote six lines to three of the Greek. Where Homer says of Athena's favorite, Diomedes (in my translation):

> She kindled upon his helmet and shield a point
> of unwearying fire, like the star of early autumn
> that shines most brightly after its bath in Ocean. (V. 4–6)

Pope translates:

> High on his helm celestial lightnings play,
> His beamy shield emits a living ray;
> The unwearied blaze incessant streams supplies
> Like the red star that fires th'autumnal skies,
> When fresh he rears his radiant orb to sight
> And bath'd in Ocean, shoots a keener light. (V. 5–10)

This is just plain overdoing it, possibly because each couplet had to have an end-rhyme. But doubling the number of verbs in this case simply delays the action.

It seemed to me that if I were to translate Homer, I would want to use a five-beat line that would accommodate the dactylic names and carry approximately the same amount of action as Homer's six-beat line. A six-beat line in English would lead to padding.

A critic writing in the *TLS* some time ago said, "Let us hear no more of Greek having more syllables than English." He went on to argue that if one put into the translation all that was *implied* in the poem, there would be enough syllables in English and to spare. Of course he was right about that, but would he have a poem? I found, when I experimented with a few passages, that a five-beat line in English carried the same sense and completed the same visual movement as the Greek hexameter.

Angela Christy in her paper on my *Sappho* put her finger on one peculiarity of my style, especially when I am translating Homer or Sappho. I tend to use monosyllables more than most poets do, and by the same token, to avoid words of more than three syllables.[1] This is not deliberate, or only partly deliberate. I am not sure where this tendency has its roots—perhaps in the enthusiasm for "Basic English" that coincided with my poetic beginnings, or in a distrust of "such words as 'humanitary' which have a paralysis in their tails," as Thoreau said. Or perhaps it is a mark of infantilism. But that is the way I write, and I found that in this line of five heavy syllables ("stressed" or "long" or "weighted") separated from each other by either one or two light or unstressed syllables, I could do what I wanted to do. I found, however, that certain things had to be avoided. I could take liberties with the beginning and the end of lines. Lines could end with the fifth weighted syllable, but in that case the next line (unless it started a new sentence) needed to begin with either one or two short syllables. A line could end with one light syllable and the next line might begin with another, or a line might end with two light syllables as in "coming up close to him"; but then the next line needed to start with a weighted syllable: "struck with his sharpened lance." Each line had to have at least one foot containing two light syllables, but each line also needed at least one foot with only one light syllable. Spondees could also be introduced where three weighted syllables came together: "and turning about *dragged Par*is among the Achaeans."

Here is Pandarus fitting the arrow's notch to the spring, then:

grasping the notch and bowstring together, he drew back
the string to the nipple, the point of iron to the bow;
he pulled until the great bow rounded into a circle;
the bow sang out, the string gave a mighty yelp
and the sharpened arrow leapt eagerly into the ranks.
  (author's trans.; IV.122–126)

I might never have come even this far with my experiments had I not learned of someone who wanted an original translation of a passage from the

---

1. "The Mary Barnard Translation of Sappho," *Pai* 23.1 (Spring 1994) 50.

Iliad to accompany the publication of some prints inspired by the epic. I said I would like to see what I could do, and went to work. As it turned out, my efforts weren't used, but I kept going through five books. This time, instead of revising and polishing as I went, I worked rapidly, thinking that I would go back and work on the rough spots later. The main thing I was after was to make the thing move, and I think it does move. The metric came more easily as I went along, but there were other problems that I could not solve to my satisfaction, for instance, the epithets: to use them or to drop them? And if they are to be used, how are they to be translated? An even more difficult problem was the dialogue, and there is so much of it. I may be kidding myself, but I am almost certain that I hear the sound of the speaking voices in the bickering of Zeus and Hera, but when I attempt to translate their words, the right tone is almost impossible to find. In the end I never got further than my first draft.

Metric is a very slippery subject. I often wonder whether I am doing what I think I am doing. The irregular five-beat line that I was using for the *Iliad* seemed to me sometimes to have a too-emphatic rhythm. What was my astonishment, then, to find that a college student who read a few pages in typescript had mistaken it for prose. Later I showed a few pages to another poet, who said, "I don't think you can do this without a metric," and I said, "But I have a metric." He looked at me in disbelief, and we let it go at that. I quit worrying, at any rate, about the too-emphatic rhythms.

After a hiatus of about ten years when family responsibilities interfered with writing, I began again with *Assault on Mount Helicon* and intended to continue with a volume of essays using material left out of *The Mythmakers* for one reason or another. In no time at all I was in deep trouble. I realized that the book I was trying to write would have no audience and would find no publisher. If, on the other hand, I could turn it into a poem, Breitenbush would publish it and someone might even read it. But, like the translation of Homer, this was something I couldn't do "without a metric." And what kind of metric would accommodate the instructions for finding the meridian as found in the *Panchasiddhantika?* I remembered then that these instructions were written in verse in the original Sanskrit, and I also remembered that the metric I had used for the *Iliad* had worked perfectly for Homer's detailed descriptions for loosing an arrow, building a boat, or sacrificing animals. I had written so many hundreds of lines while translating that despite the elapse of time I fell easily into the rhythm and wrote fairly rapidly. When I felt it was becoming monotonous I varied it by using a four-beat rhythm or in some cases irregular line lengths, but the five-beat line of the Homeric translation is the backbone of the book. It was gratifying to hear from one of the critics who reviewed the book that she was "still very much taken with the smoothness and vivacity of your five-beat line." Smoothness and vivacity were exactly what I had hoped for. Some may say that it is no different from any free iambic pentameter; but I would dispute that because, while a pentameter, it does not have an underpinning of iambic:

> From Christmas Eve to the night of the Magi's visit,
> Epiphany: these were days when time was at rest,
> and all the things that turn like time on its axis,
> cart wheels, mill wheels, spindles, must also rest.
> No courts of justice were held, but during the Zwolfen
> the Frauen rode through the night with their train of hounds.
> This was the Yule, the turning-round of the year.
> (Fifth Fytte, lines 54–60)

As I said earlier, I often wonder whether I am really doing what I think I am doing. Rhythms should please the ear with both repetition and variety, but I also want them to underline the meaning and carry the cadence of the speaking voice, and I wonder whether other people hear what I want them to hear. Some time ago I watched a PBS program entitled, I believe, "The Human Figure in Early Greek Art." The photographs of art work—vase paintings and sculpture—were accompanied by readings from the Greek poets in translation; and the korai were accompanied by a few of my Sappho translations. I don't know who the reader was, but she could not possibly have heard me read the poems. Yet she read them with exactly the cadence that I wanted. I felt that I was eating the pudding—I had proof that my method worked.

I really wonder, though, what happens to them if they are read aloud by a Briton? A recent royalty report included a payment from the BBC for use of the *Sappho* in a radio broadcast. It would be interesting to know how *that* sounded.

EDITOR'S NOTES ON THE TEXT

Notes for each poem and, in the later stages, each piece of critical prose, follow the same format of (a) title; (b) chronological dating (see next sentence); (c) notes (contextual and textual); (d) abbreviated name of manuscript (MS) or typescript (TS) where applicable, to cross-reference with the list of abbreviations, which gives the full citation (e.g., *LBN* for "Little Brown Notebook") and source; (e) details of where published text can be found, with page numbers (where applicable and, again, to cross-reference with the list of abbreviations); and, in the case of published poems in, (f) textual differences between earlier published version(s) that appeared in *Cool Country* (*CC*) and *A Few Poems* (*AFP*) and the version that appeared in *Collected Poems* (*CP*). Regarding (b), years for *published* poems follow the format of (i) primary year—the year of first publication in journals and magazines; (ii) subsequent year(s) indicating year(s) in which the poem was thereafter published in collections and/or other texts. Years for *unpublished* poems are taken from the final date of the manuscript from which the poem is reprinted, where available—this may be based on either Barnard's own date provided on the manuscript, Elizabeth J. Bell's dating for copyright purposes and/or her dating recorded via *PNC* (poem notecard index created by Elizabeth J. Bell), or educated guesses based on the evidence available, with rationale provided in the notes. Where the note refers to "a copy of the TS," the source is the copy given to the editor from Bell.

I. POEMS

COOL COUNTRY (1940)

The Rapids
1940

Published in *Furioso* 1.3 (Spring 1940): 23—see, also, note to "Road to Xanadu." Subsequently published in *CC* (in November 1940), *CP* and, according to *MB/IC,* in D. Johansen, *Empire of the Columbia* (2nd ed., 1967): 587. Also reprinted in Rich Ives, ed., *Rain in the Forest, Light in the Trees: Contemporary Poetry from the Northwest* (Missoula, MT: Owl Creek Press, 1983): 11 and *Anodyne* 2.9 (June 1998): 36. *BKNB* notes that the poem was "[s]ent to Williams Mar 8. '38," whose suggested edits she acted upon in order to send it to *Furioso* (see *MB/Parents,* 11 June 1939). Barnard said that this poem is about human relations (*KBOO*). Poem discussed in relation to Williams' edits in *AMH* 135–37 and *SB/MBAI,* 33, 52, 79, 82, 106, including the poem's geographical references (e.g., Celilo Falls, prior to its destruction as part of the building of the Dalles dam on the Columbia River in the 1950s, and Beacon Rock, a well-known monolith along the river passed many times by Barnard as a child), as well as its appropriation of Greek metric, enabled by her own system of the "weighted syllable" (see chapter 4.2 of *SB/MBAI,* but also the note to the translation "The First Chorus from Oedipus King").

Published text: *CC* 7 (later *CP* 17) **Differences from *CP*:** *CC* version has initial capitals at the start of run-on lines.

Logging Trestle
1938; 1940
First published as "The Trestle" in *Townsman* (London) 1, no. 4 (October 1938): 7 (where "cross-ties" appears without the hyphen) and subsequently as part of a suite of poems in *NR*. According to *MB/IC,* "Logging Trestle" was reprinted in *The Sunday Oregonian, E. 1* (July 31, 1994) in connection with an interview by P. Pintarich and also in *AP V2* 656–57. *BKNB* notes that the poem was sent to Pound on 10 February 1937 as "The Trestle" but was renamed "Logging Trestle" by the time it was published in *CC.* Poem discussed in *SB/MBAI* 54–55, 136 and, in terms of its metrics, *SB/W.* See, also, the note to "Bay Beach," whose imagery somewhat resonates with that of this poem.

Published text: *CC* 8 (later *CP* 18) **Differences from *CP*:** *CC* version has initial capitals at the start of run-on lines; L4 ends with a comma after "hillside" in *CC,* removed in *CP* version.

Highway Bridge
1940
Poem discussed in *SB/MBAI* 32. See, also, the note to the earlier poem "Bay Beach." The idea of wet ground becoming space for the meditative here was one previously rehearsed in an unpublished poem, "The Saragossa Hour,"

where, in the third stanza, Barnard presents an image of a persona inside a lonely beach house who, as a "you," is shown to "sketch the bi-sections of striated, unrippled water / And the seeking tendrils your thoughts put out from sub-merged rocks" on a "[d]rawing board set up in the window" (*MC*). It's a space returned to, much later, in "The Spring."

Published text: *CC* 9 (later *CP* 19) **Differences from *CP*:** *CC* version has initial capitals at the start of run-on lines.

Cool Country
1940

After first publication in the collection of the same name, according to *MB/IC* "Cool Country" was subsequently reprinted in *Willamette Weekly* in the book section "For the Week ending August 8, 1977," p. 12, and in *The Columbian*, August 4, 1994, Sec B, 1 in connection with an interview by Linda Stewart. The poem was also published as part of a suite of poems in *NR* 17.2–3 (1979): 233–42. "Cool Country" was originally called "This Green," but Barnard revised it, deciding at the same time it would make a suitable title for her debut collection (*MB/Parents*, 29 October 1938). *BKNB* notes that the poem was "[s]ent to Williams Sept. 39." Poem discussed in *SB/MBAI* 46–47, 52 with reference to her sustained focus on her northwestern roots in poems produced in her first years in New York.

Published text: *CC* 10 (later *CP* 10) **Differences from *CP*:** *CC* version has initial capitals at the start of run-on lines.

Shoreline
1935; 1940

One of several poems set on the coast of the Long Beach peninsula (see note for "An Evening by the Sea"). First published by editor Morton Zabel in *Poetry* 45.5 (February 1935): 254–56 (see, also, note to "On Arriving"), with various changes from that of the *CC* version reprinted here. Some of the differences concern punctuation, but some are substantial additions, which Barnard later omitted—all changes involved a cutting-down of kinds (see the full reprint of the *Poetry* version at the end of this note). The poem was subsequently published in *CC, CP, The Poetry Anthology*, ed. Daryl Hine and Joseph Parisi (Boston: Houghton Mifflin Co., 1978): 150–52, and *AP V2* 655–56. An early draft of this poem was called "For Those Who Dwell on the Marches," c. 1934, quoted and discussed *SB/MBAI* 43–44. *BKNB* notes that "Shoreline" was sent to Genevieve Taggard (also contributing editor to *The New Masses*), T. C. Wilson and Yvors Winters on 31 August 1934. Barnard also sent it to Pound in letter of 26 December 1934, saying that she wrote it after she had sent him the manuscript of poems in her letter of 28 July 1934. Poem appears in *MC*. Poem discussed extensively (particularly in comparison with the early Imagist work of H. D.) in *SB/MBAI* 4, 6, 7, 8, 21, 33–34, 42–43, 46, 48, 51–52, 78, 80–82, 136.

"the late sail"—when Barnard was a child, the only way to reach the Long Beach peninsula was by boat; as she wrote in *AMH* 16–17, "[w]e had to go to Portland by ferry and trolley, board a river boat sometime in the evening, and next morning debark at Megler on the Washington shore opposite Astoria"—a journey not too dissimilar to that depicted in "The River Under Different Lights."

"Wild roses [. . .] cover the dune shoulder"—such vegetation was a feature of Ocean Park as Barnard recalled in a letter to her parents recounting a time when staying with friends as part of one of their "Utopia" adventures (see note to "An Evening by the Sea"): "[i]n the afternoon it was sunny most of the time, so we all put on our white pantaloons and went over on the dunes. Jo and I slept behind a rose-covered hillock" (*MB/Parents,* date unknown).

"The cracked ribs of a wreck"—one of the shipwrecks in the vicinity of the mouth of the Columbia overlooked by the Long Beach peninsula, and very possibly the *Peter Iredale* that ran ashore four miles south of the estuary on Clatsop Spit in 1906. Barnard associated this shipwreck, emotionally, with the kind of sorrow depicted in the last two lines of this stanza and, visually, with the fortress of the Casbah in Algiers. In a letter from "L'Abbeye aux Dunes" in "Utopia" of the "5th day of the second week," following on from the dune-sleeping episode cited above, Barnard told her parents:

> Most of the day yesterday I had the grut [*sic*] badly. The day started out gloriously on top of a dune, with me reading [. . .] in my white pantaloons + white hat, and a ship sailing by, very close in. By night I was feeling too grutty [*sic*] for words. I think it is partly or wholly from living at such close quarters with three people + not being able to escape. This morning I was feeling worse than ever so I made my pilgrimage to the Casba [sic] + walked it all out of my system. Its barnacled ribs, dripping + steaming in the sun, are a fit altar for sorrows, which is a more dignified way of expressing "grut." (*MB/Parents,* date unknown)

See, also, note to "Blanchefleur" and 152 ("thick on the beach the pyres of the dead burned always") of Barnard's *TI*. The 1935 *Poetry* version of "Shoreline" is reprinted below for the interested reader:

The sea has made a wall for its defence
Of falling water. Those whose impertinence
Leads them to its moving ledges
It rejects. Those who surrender
It will with the next wave drag under.

Sand is the beginning and the end
Of our dominion.

The way to the dunes is easy and not steep.
The shelving sand is stiffened in the rain
And loosened again in the sun's fingers.
Children, lustful of the glistening hours,
Drink and are insatiate. Wind under the eyelids,
Confusion walling the ears, they bend
And balance, warmed by secure and ordered blood
In the cold wash of the beach.

And after,
They walk with rigid feet the planked street of the town.
They miss the slipping texture of the sand
And a sand pillow under the hollow instep.
They are unmoved by fears
That breed in darkening kitchens at sun-down
Following storm; and they rebel
Against cold waiting in the wind and rain
For the late sail.

The harbor town is backed by its fertile valley.
Seines, drying, scallop the waterfront.
Wharf ladders descend to the green swell.
Did you, as I did, feel
A supple braid that dragged against your hips,
Thick as a ship's cable,

And watch the light that slips
And clings along the moving channel wave?

Did you, as I,
Condemn the coastal fog, and long for islands
Seen from a sail's shadow?

The dunes lie
More passive to the wind than water is.

This, then, the country of our choice.
It is infertile, narrow, prone
Under a dome of choral sound:
Water breaking upon water.

Litter of bare logs in the drift—
The sea has had its sharp word with them. The smudged odor
Of wild roses, wild strawberries on the dune shoulder
Stains as with color the salt stench of the sea.
It is a naked restless garden that descends
From the crouched pine
To shellfish caught in flat reflecting sands.

We lose the childish avarice of horizons. The sea ends
Against another shore. The cracked ribs of a wreck
Project from the washed beach.
Under the shell-encrusted timbers
Dripping brine
Plucks at the silence of slant chambers
Opening seaward. What moving keel remembers
Such things as here are buried under sand?

The transitory ponds and smooth bar slide
Easily under the advancing tide,
Emerging with the moon's
Turning.

Clear lagoons
Behind the shattered hulk, thin
Movements of sea grass on the dune rim

Bending against cloud, these things are ours.
Submissive to the sea and wind,
Resistful of all else, sand
Is the beginning and the end
Of our dominion.

Published text: *CC* 11–12 (later *CP* 8–9) **Differences from *CP*:** *CC* version has initial capitals at the start of run-on lines; L23 is followed by a stanza break in *CP,* with L24 (beginning "Did you, as I") starting a new stanza. L54 in the *CP* version includes a full stop at the end, after "these things are ours"—but this was omitted in the *CC* version, an error that was corrected in the *CP* version. The editor has carried this correction over to the version printed here. See also the corresponding notes for "Remarks on Poetry and the Physical World" and "Note to a Neapolitan," which also flag possible typesetting issues.

Provincial
1936; 1940
First published in *ND* 194, having appeared in draft in *LBN* where, on reverse of this draft, the date of "Nov. 14, 1935," is given in Barnard's hand. Both previous versions concluded the poem with an additional two stanzas:

Some would rather stand
On poet-hallowed ground than follow
A trail sloping above avalanche lilies
And ash-white glacier rivers.

Such men are fanciers of first editions
But never knew the ecstasy aroused
By an abundance of blank paper.

BKNB notes that the poem was sent to Pound on 20 January 1936 along with other poems that were first published with it the following month in *ND* ("Epicure," "Cold Heaven," "Mechanism," and "A Defense of the Poet's Method"). However, Barnard substantively edited "Provincial" during her first visit to Yaddo in the summer of 1936 after a conversation with the critic and philosopher Norbert Guterman. As she told her parents in a letter, "I'm amputating the last 7 lines of <u>Provincial</u> [. . .] Norbert Guterman [. . .] made me see the light. And I'm sure it's the thing to do. [. . .] he thinks Oregon must be a terrible place to live because it's so new, which us why I showed him <u>Provincial</u>," (*MB/Parents*, 22 June 1936, underlining Barnard's). Poem discussed in *SB/MBAI* 85–88, 134.

Published text: *CC* 13 (later *CP* 36) **Differences from *CP*:** *CC* version has initial capitals at the start of run-on lines.

Roots
1937; 1940

First published by Malcolm Cowley as "Northwest Anchorage" in *New Republic* 91.1183 (4 August 1937): 368, then alongside an earlier version of "Logging Trestle" in *Townsman* (London) 1.4 (October 1938): 6. Barnard noted in *BKNB* that the poem was sent to Pound on 10 February 1937, as well as to composer Edwin Gerschefski who Barnard met at Yaddo in her first stay in 1936, who set her poem "Lai" to music). Poem discussed in *SB/MBAI* 46, 78, 88, 109–10 (with reference to its Greek-derived prosody that formed Barnard's own measure—see, also, the note to the translation "The First Chorus from Oedipus King"), 136.

Published text: *CC* 14 (later *CP* 11) **Differences from *CP*:** *CC* version has initial capitals at the start of run-on lines.

Planks
1936; 1940

First published in *ND* 193 but also, in the same year, in *ND ONE* (no page). An early draft of this poem was called "Feet Striking Fine Gravel," dated "10 May 35" in Barnard's hand (there is also a copy entitled "Planks" in *LBN*), the title of which she incorporated into the first line of the version as it appears in *ND*. While there's no evidence to suggest Barnard sent this to her usual mentors Pound and Williams, her learning from them is evident in the two key changes she makes to the version that appeared in *Cool Country* in 1940 as presented here: (i) the distribution of whole phrases *over* lines, rather than *within* them, simulating the sustained walking rhythm depicted in the poem, in combination with (ii) a paring-down of language in order foreground this idea of gentle rhythm (the movement of "footsteps" in place of "feet striking" in "Feet striking fine gravel" and "Touching rhythmically [the hard earth]" in place of "In falling upon the dense earth" for instance), for "Planks," as it first appeared in *ND*, read like this:

Feet striking fine gravel drop sound into silence
Like pebbles dropping in water at close intervals.
Circles of air break on the dark mountains.

Strange how hard it is to balance in the pit of the evening,
Distances upward making the head light.
But walking feet have their own pleasure
In falling upon the dense earth.

Dry planks islanded in lush grass attract them.
The moment is completed neither by fragrance of wild lilac
Nor by the presence of the darkening river,
But by the feel of wood underfoot
And the sound of stepping upon thick planks.

(ND 193)

However, it's equally possible that Barnard's early East Coast encounters with other poets played their part, not least those she met at Yaddo, but also Marianne Moore, whose appreciation of the poem Barnard reported in a letter to her parents dated 15 May 1936.

Published text: *CC* 15 (later *CP* 20) **Differences from *CP*:** *CC* version has initial capitals at the start of run-on lines.

Prometheus Loved Us
1940
First published in *Furioso* 1.3 (Spring 1940): 23—see, also, note to "Road to Xanadu." As part of the submission, it seems that Barnard changed the poem's title to the one given—a draft exists of a version of the poem called "The Match," while in a letter of 15 June 1939 to her parents, Barnard refers to the poem as "the match one." Very possibly it's a poem inspired by her early experiences in Buffalo. *BKNB* notes that the poem was sent to Williams in September 1939 and, as Barnard said in a letter of 4 April 1940 to the editor of *Furioso*, James Angleton, the poem used to contain spaces—certainly the last lines of the second and third stanzas appear as their own, one-line stanzas in "The Match," so perhaps Barnard meant for there to be these spaces. Poem discussed in *SB/MBAI* 133–34.

Published text: *CC* 16 (later *CP* 75) **Differences from *CP*:** *CC* version has initial capitals at the start of run-on lines.

Blood Ritual
1937; 1940

Shared with Mildred Cline (see *MC*) where the title was punctuated "Blood-Ritual." First published in *ND TWO* (no page). As with "Roots," Barnard noted in *BKNB* that she sent this poem to Edwin Gerschefski (see note to "Roots,") but also to Babette Deutsch. The poem—and Barnard's friendship with Deutsch—is discussed in *SB/MBAI* 85; the Barnard-Deutsch "late modernist" connection is discussed at length in *SB/W.*

Published text: *CC* 17 (later *CP* 100) **Differences from *CP*:** *CC* version has initial capitals at the start of run-on lines.

The Axe
1940

Published text: *CC* 18 (later *CP* 12) **Differences from *CP*:** *CC* version has initial capitals at the start of run-on lines.

Playroom
1936; 1940

First published in *ND* 193 and *ND ONE* (no page). Subsequently published in *CC*, *CP*, and in *New Directions 50*, eds. James Laughlin, Peter Glassgold, and Griselda Ohanessian (New York: New Directions, 1986): 76–77. Poem discussed in *SB/MBAI* 106 where the first two lines of the second stanza are scanned for Barnard's appropriation of Greek metrics (see, also, the note to the translation "The First Chorus from Oedipus King").

Published text: *CC* 19 (later *CP* 3—as the opening poem) **Differences from *CP*:** *CC* version has initial capitals at the start of run-on lines.

Storm
1938; 1940

First published in *Poetry* 52.5 (August 1938): 256 and subsequently in *CC*, *CP*, and as part of a suite of poems in *NR*. One early draft of this poem was entitled "January 12" (which *PNC* dates as 1932), another draft appears in *LBN* with the date "June 1936" on the back of it in Barnard's hand. While both drafts show minor divergence from what was originally printed, it's notable that "January 12" includes a personalized element, which Barnard later omitted. "A pain burrows and consumes my day" begins the second line of stanza two of "January 12"; and "The music feeds my sickness" begins the second line of the last stanza, which in that draft is the penultimate line. Barnard came to expand the focus to include reference to the movement of the music across land and to add the line in Greek, perhaps reflective of her experiments with Greek rhythms and music in poems focused on the landscape that she did subsequently, in her initial years under Pound's tutelage (as in, say, "Lai" and other exercises in Sapphics like "Tranquil and shallow, spread across the flat stones . . . ," "A Defense of the Poet's Method," and so on).

"Bach from Philadelphia"—see discussion of Bach's influence on Barnard in the introduction, under "Mary Barnard: The Translations."

"ἀκτὰν πρὸς ἑσπέρου θεοῦ"—" 'towards the coast (or headland) of the god of evening' " (translated by Hamish Whyte in email correspondence). Whyte points to the metaphorical meaning of this line, suggesting that it points to Hesperus, the "god of darkness i.e., Hades, or death [. . .] so the phrase means 'towards the shores of death' ('the extreme coastland' as the poems says)." This line did not appear in the earlier version of "January 12." Whyte also points readers to Sophocles, *Oedipus Tryannos,* line 178. Readers may be interested in the Project Gutenberg section marked "vv.162–89 [Pg. 12]" (https://www. gutenberg.org/files/27673/27673-h/27673-h.htm, date last accessed 22 May 2024). See L43 of Barnard's "The First Chorus from Oedipus King," which reads "The coast land of the god of the evening." See, also, Barnard's fragment 16 in *S* (a tribute to Hesperus and his facility to "herd / homeward"), the note on the Hesperides in the notes for "Inheritance," as well as notes to "The Fool's Serenade." See, further, Henry Wadsworth Longfellow's "The Wreck of Hesperus" from *Ballads and Other Poems* (1842), which dramatizes the role of a captain's pride in the shipwrecking of the schooner *Hesperus,* with all its crew and his own daughter on board.

Published text: *CC* 20 (later *CP* 24) **Differences from *CP*:** *CC* version has initial capitals at the start of run-on lines; L11 of *CP* gives "towards" instead of "toward."

Cassandra
1935; 1940

First published in *NEW* then *WQ* 30 (carrying a typo in St 2, L7, giving "burried" instead of "buried.") *BKNB* notes that the poem was sent to

Pound on 28 July 1934 as well as to Genevieve Taggard, T. C. Wilson, and Yvors Winters on 31 August 1934. Poem appears in *MC*. Poem discussed in *SB/MBAI* 157, where the first four lines are scanned for Barnard's trademark balanced line as articulated in *ACOG*, reprinted in this volume.

Published text: *CC* 21 (later *CP* 96) **Differences from *CP*:** *CC* version has initial capitals at the start of run-on lines.

Winter Evening
1939; 1940
    First published in *Partisan Review* 6.4 (Summer 1939): 20 alongside "Fable from the Cayoosh Country" (21–22). *BKNB* notes that the poem was sent to Pound on 10 February 1937.

Published text: *CC* 22 (later *CP* 28) **Differences from *CP*:** *CC* version has initial capitals at the start of run-on lines.

Wine Ship
1935; 1940
    First published under the title "Faun un Exile" in *Poetry* 46.1 (April 1935): 25–26 (reprinted below), along with "Lai" and "Ondine" under the group title of *Spectral Tunes*, which won Barnard that year's Helen Haire Levinson Prize (see note to "Ondine"). Subsequently published as "Wine Ship" in *CC*, *CP*, and as part of a suite of poems in *NR*. The title, "Wine Ship," refers to the shipwreck of "the Alice" (see note for "An Evening by the Sea"). *BKNB* notes that the poem was previously sent to Pound—as "Faun in Exile"—on 28 July 1934. Numerous earlier versions exist, from a poem titled by EJB as "The Exile" and "Orlando," the latter of which appeared in *H*. Poem discussed, as "Faun in Exile," in *SB/MBAI* 33–35, 40, 42 as well as 104 where stanzas 4 and 5 are scanned for their impressive use of approximations of Sappho's signature Adonic colon form.

    Barnard significantly edited down "Faun in Exile" to arrive at the version known as "Wine Ship," losing the numerous color images that resonate with those in another Ocean Park poem "An Evening by the Sea." For the interested reader, "Faun in Exile" is reprinted below as it appeared as part of *Spectral Tunes* in the April 1935 edition of *Poetry*:

    In her eyes I saw her history written.
    Where brown disintegrated into green

And gold, with a red glint between,
I looked and understood.

There I read
The memory of a faun's pursuit
Through the myrtle wood;
How nymphs, aroused, had fled,
And he that followed after,
Bewildered by the talking water, led
By uncertain laughter,
Wandered far from his home.

His hunting thwarted,
Vineyards led him to the sea slope.
There were his eyes the warm pulsating gold
Of an inland sea.

Seeking wine on the wharves, a drunken faun
Rolled in a wine ship's hold
And was borne to this desolate coast.

Here were no myrtle groves,
No familiar shrines,
Only the splintered casks and the sweet wines
Spilt in the sea.
Here were no grapes,
But bitter berries grew in the marsh.

Here was no moss,
But sea-worn logs and the harsh
Grass on the dune-top.

Here was no mirth;
In this forlorn meeting of sea and land,
Eyes are the green of stormy water,
And the sand
Lies suddenly cold under the hand.

From this shore, always windy and roaring,
An exile learns
To keep where a fire burns.
And still by night the warm rhythm returns
From groves forgotten.

Then vain is the disguise
Of small hand or white throat.
The green and gold and red strangely appear
In a woman's eyes—
As if one were to hear
The tap of cloven hooves amid the rustlings
In convent corridors.

An earlier (unpublished) version of "Faun in Exile" can be found in *H*, where the poem was titled "Orlando" as well as in *LBN* where, on the reverse of this poem, appears the date of "Oct. 31, '31," in Barnard's hand.

Published text: *CC* 23–24 (later *CP* 94–95) **Differences from *CP*:** *CC* version has initial capitals at the start of run-on lines; L1 in the *CP* version ends on a comma instead of full stop; *CP* version hyphenates "sea wrack."

Lethe
1935; 1940
First published, with "Beyond Medusa" and "Cassandra," in *New English Weekly* (London) 6.17 (7 February 1935): 354, with "color" following British spelling, "colour." Subsequently reprinted in *AP V2* 660. This was one of the group of six poems that Barnard sent to Pound in her first letter to him dated 11 October 1933. "I know only one living poet whom I consider a master, and I am taking the liberty of writing to him," she wrote; "I don't write children's poems, or love poems, or surrealiste poems, although I can do the latter if absolutely necessary. Can you give me any advice, or any help, if you think the poems are worthy of it?" *(MB/EP;* see introduction for details of Pound's response). According to *BKNB*, the poem was also sent to a number of poet friends on 31 August 1934, including Genevieve Taggard, T. C. Wilson, and Yvors Winters. See also "Against Lethe," from 1932, for an earlier engagement with this theme, based on work from *H*. Poem discussed in *SB/MBAI* 95–96, speculating on why, in particular, the poem appealed to Pound's ideas for modern poetry.

Published text: *CC* 25 (later *CP* 101) **Differences from *CP***: *CC* version has initial capitals at the start of run-on lines.

Chanson Pathetique
1935; 1940

First published in *WQ* 31; there appears to be a corrective amendment from Barnard on her contributor's copy where in St 2, L1 an "s" has been inked over an indecipherable letter at the end of "stir" (thus giving "my hand stirs"). "Bannister" is Barnard's spelling. *BKNB* notes that the poem was on a list of poems titled "sent to Rapallo"—to Pound (no date). The title was connected to the last stanza (initially an alternative end), as she told T. C. Wilson ahead of its publication in *WQ*:

> I have been thinking of changing the title of the Chanson, but I can't very well do it until I know whether the alternate last stanza is still attached [gives last stanza as it was eventually given in *CC* and reprinted in this volume]. Is it still there? If it is, I don't see anything very wrong about the present title. If it is not, then I'd like to change the title. If there is time enough, will you please let me know the present condition of the poem, and I'll try to think up an appropriate name. (*MB/TW*, TS dated "January 25, 1934"—although this year seems incorrect; 1935 seems more chronologically accurate.)

See, also, note to "Ondine," "Beyond Medusa," and "Lament from the Shores of the Boorzh-wah Zee."

Published text: *CC* 26.

Lai
1935; 1940

First published in *Poetry* 46.1 (April 1935): 28–29, along with other poems that derive some of their imagery from Barnard's Ocean Park experiences (see note to "An Evening by the Sea," but also the note to "The Fool's Serenade"), "Faun in Exile" (later "Wine Ship"), and "Ondine" under the group title of *Spectral Tunes* (see note to "Ondine"). But also concurrently published in *WQ* 38 (where "her hands" of L4 appear in the singular "her hand," the "queens" of L6 carry an initial capital, "channelled meadows" of L8 is preceded by the definite article and there's a comma added between "the stripped" and "high-singing trees" in L9). Subsequently published as part of a suite of poems in *NR*. The version that appeared in the April 1935 edition of *Poetry* made more frequent and varied use of punctuation (additional commas after "by land," "refused to believe," "stripped," and "tideland," as well as a semicolon after "channelled meadows" in place of the full stop). *BIB* 198 specifies that the poem was set "as a baritone solo with piano accompaniment, by the late Edwin Gerschefski," (see note to "Roots"). Barnard seemed to have a copy of this setting in record form since she mentions it in a letter of 30 October 1944 ("I haven't got my radio fixed to take the turntable yet, but think I'll see about it today. Then I can play my 'Lai'—won't that be nice?" *MB/Parents*). Another poem on the list of poems titled "sent to Rapallo," "Lai" was sent to Pound with a letter of 2 January 1934 in response to Pound's suggestion that she "dig in DEEPER in greek" (letter of 2 December 1933, quoted in *AMH* 54–55). It was, Barnard wrote, "an exercise of the kind I can do 'now and any time,' and I want to know if you think that exercise profitable" *(MB/EP)*. Pound was curt—but instructive—in his reply: "LAI starts with something nearly a bad Sapphic line. Try writing Sapphics, and NOT persistently using a spondee like that blighter Horace, for the second foot" (letter of 22 January 1934, quoted in *AMH* 56). This instruction was to prove monumental in Barnard's career. Ahead of its publication in *WQ*, Barnard wrote to Pound: "Are you really going to use Lai? It ought to be the best metrically since no idea was present to disturb the meter. It was written by ear alone" (*MB/EP*, 14 January 1935). Poem discussed in *SB/MBAI* 34, 98–101 (of its demonstration of both the possibilities and difficulties of wholesale translation of Sapphics into English) and 124. See also note to "Raimon the Singer," arguably a precursor to this poem.

Published text: *CC* 27 (later *CP* 91) **Differences from *CP*:** *CC* version has initial capitals at the start of run-on lines.

Adversity and the Generations
1937; 1940
    First published in *ND TWO* (no page).
    "roots in the wrong places [. . .] Eden's east threshold"—Barnard described this as a New York poem, with her as a provincial within it (*KBOO*) where she stood out in her "home-made, too-colorful dresses" against the swathes of navy blue, standard for New York women in the 1930s (*AMH* 94). The poem was also sent to Pound on 20 January 1936, as well as to poet-critic Babette Deutsch (date unknown), who Barnard met at Yaddo during her first visit.

In a letter of 15 September 1937 Deutsch admired the poem's "dry humor," even if she berated its disregard for the wider chaos that was unfolding in the wider world; "lunch-counter chaos seems the merest fly-speck," Deutsch wrote (*BD/MB*; see also *SB/MBAI* 85).

Published text: *CC* 28 (later *CP* 69) **Differences from *CP*:** *CC* version has initial capitals at the start of run-on lines.

Drama
1940

First published in *WQ* 31, where in line four "third" is given an initial capital (thus "Third") and "about her head" in line ten is given as "around her head." *BKNB* notes that a poem called "Drama" was sent to Pound on 28 July 1934—it may be this poem, or the poem of the same name that appears in the *Uncollected* group in this section (no definitive answer has yet been found). See, also, note to the "Drama" that appears later in this volume (the different *Uncollected* poem that shares the same name).

Published text: *CC* 29 (later *CP* 40) **Differences from *CP*:** *CC* version has initial capitals at the start of run-on lines.

To a Lie-Adept
1935; 1940

First published in *WQ* 30. *BKNB* notes that the poem was sent to Pound on 28 July 1934. This curious poem is illuminated when considering what Barnard said about it to Pound in response to the revisions he suggested. Referencing various words eventually omitted from the *CC* version, Barnard wrote in a letter to Pound of 14 January 1935:

> I tried to leave "gusto" out of <u>To a Lie-Adept</u>, but if I did, it looked as though "skill" should come out, too. By that time there was no use in having the duke there except that I thought the poem held together better with him in it. As a result, "gusto" and the duke remain. If you think it would improve the poem very much to have those two lines left out altogether, I'm willing to take them out. (*MB/EP*; underlining Barnard's)

Published text: *CC* 30 (later *CP* 71) **Differences from *CP*:** *CC* version has initial capitals at the start of run-on lines.

Provincial II
1938; 1940
 First published in *Poetry* 52.5 (August 1938): 258, then in *CC* and *CP* and as part of a suite of poems in *NR*. *BKNB* notes that the poem was sent to Pound on 10 February 1937.
 Poem discussed in *SB/MBAI* 55–56 and 134.

Published text: *CC* 31 (later *CP* 37—directly after its companion poem "Provincial") **Differences from *CP*:** *CC* version has initial capitals at the start of run-on lines.

The Tears of Princesses
1938; 1940
 First published in *Poetry* 52.5 (August 1938): 257–58. *BKNB* notes that this poem was sent to Edwin Gerschefski (see note to "Roots").

Published text: *CC* 32 (later *CP* 5) **Differences from *CP*:** *CC* version has initial capitals at the start of run-on lines.

In Praise of Potted Plants
1940
 First published in *Furioso* 1.2 (New Year's Issue 1940): 20–21 with a minor difference in punctuation—there was originally a full stop after "intrude" in the second stanza—see, also, note to "Eavesdropper" and "Road to Xanadu." *BKNB* notes that the poem was sent to Pound on 10 February 1937 and also to Williams in January 1938. The poem is possibly a later version of "A cloud comes down," which shares numerous resonances, as well as of "Eavesdropper," which Barnard published in 1936 in *ND*. "May be several changes," Barnard appended in a note on a draft of "Eavesdropper," and clearly there were changes, with the reframing of what appears to be a poem about frustrated romance into something much more depersonalized, as well as the removal of excessive adjectives that Barnard was keen to eliminate as she cultivated her late Imagistic style.

Published text: *CC* 33 (later *CP* 77) **Differences from *CP*:** CC version has initial capitals at the start of run-on lines.

Hot Broth
1940
 BKNB notes that the poem was sent to Williams in September 1939.

Published text: *CC* 34.

The Orchard Spring
1940
First published in *CC*, then subsequently in *CP* and as part of a suite of poems in *NR*. *BKNB* notes that the poem was sent to Pound on 10 February 1937, but also to Deutsch (no date).

Published text: *CC* 35 (later *CP* 6) **Differences from *CP*:** *CC* version has initial capitals at the start of run-on lines.

Fable from the Cayoosh Country
1939; 1940
First published in *Partisan Review* 6.4 (Summer 1939), 21–22, alongside "Winter Evening" (20). *BKNB* notes that the poem was sent to Pound on 7 March 1938 and to Williams the next day, 8 March 1938, with the shorter title of "Fable from the Cayoosh." Pound complained that the poem was "mattressed and quilted down under the verbiage" (Pound cited in *AMH* 118). "[S]o far as I can remember, I did not revise; I pruned no verbiage from 'Fable from the Cayoosh Country,'" Barnard recalled, "but I did not forget the stricture, especially as Williams was writing in the same vein" (*AMH* 118). It was also a poem that spoke to her Buffalo experience—and especially the condition of contemporary poetry in a time of war. In an undated letter written on a Monday in October 1939 to her parents, Barnard wrote that "[a]ll the books that come into review are about the state of the world, till Anne [Anne McCarthy Ludlow, secretary to Charles D Abbott—see note to "Thinking of Yeats"] + I are going nuts. If civilization isn't saved, it won't be because enough isn't written on the subject. Vide <u>Cayoosh</u>" (*MB/ Parents*).

"Cayoosh Country"—area of British Columbia characterized by the Cayoosh mountain coastal range, as well as Cayoosh Creek, a tributary of the Seton River, which Barnard hiked with a couple of friends in the summer of 1937, a time when she was feeling a little despondent about poetry. It was, Barnard said, "a real wilderness trip [. . .] we went north in July, following the Frazer River to a hamlet called Lillooet, and hiked out from there into the steepest mountains . . . an experience that produced a number of poems eventually" (*AMH* 111–112). As she told William Stafford in her letter of 15 October 1978 (*MB/WS*), it was an experience not just reflected in this poem, but also in a poem from *AFP*, "Beds."

"a poet, whose love / If not his living was gravely endangered"—possible reference to the despondency Barnard felt upon returning home to the Northwest, in the summer of 1936, after her five months of travel to New York and then Yaddo "[W]ithin a very short time I had one immediate goal in mind, and that was to get back to New York to stay [. . .] I found my situation intolerable [. . .]," referring to the "depressing" resumption of social work duties at the Emergency Relief Administration where the "only two flashes of light" in the two "dreary winters" that followed were visits from James Laughlin and John and Xenia Kashavaroff Cage (see note to "Cream"), while "[t]he correspondence with Pound languished" (*AMH* 110–111). The hike into "Cayoosh Country" was, in part, a practical response to this "slough of despond" Barnard was experiencing (*AMH* 111).

Published text: *CC* 36–37 (later *CP* 98–99) **Differences from *CP*:** *CC* version has initial capitals at the start of run-on lines; L21 in *CP* is separated from L22 (beginning "Where my monologue runs") by a stanza break [Note: neither the version in *CC* nor *CP* has a closing set of speech marks at the end of L25, which ends "there is now only my voice," or at the end of L29, which ends "What legend could please her?"; in *CC* there is an opening set of speech marks at the beginning of L26, which opens with "Had the mountain goat," but these are not duplicated in *CP*].

Remarks on Poetry and the Physical World
1938, 1940

Barnard told fellow "Reedie" John Sheehy that this poem was a "memory of Reed Commons" (*MB/JS*, 19 October 1981). An earlier version of this poem (with minimal differences) was named after the first line, "After reading Ash Wednesday," dated, in the same typescript, in the bottom right corner of the TS "1 Feb.36," shortly before Barnard first left for New York (see, also, *MC*). First published in *Poetry* 52.5 (August 1938): 256–57, then subsequently in the *New York Herald Tribune* 25 September 1938, *Townsman* (London) 1.4 (October 1938): 6 (where there was no comma between "And' and "conversely"), in *Exile* (Reed College, 1982) (according to *MB/IC*) and as part of a feature by Susan Biskeborn, "Poetry of Place: If Other States Can Boast a Laureate, Why Can't Washington?," *Washington: The Evergreen State Magazine* 5.7 (May–June 1989): 58–61. Poem discussed in *SB/MBAI* 76–78 (with reference to Barnard's rejection of Eliot's poetics as represented by *Ash Wednesday*) and also page 82.

Published text: *CC* 38 (later *CP* 35) **Differences from *CP*:** *CC* version has initial capitals at the start of run-on lines. L13 in *CC* includes a comma between "life" and "than," an error that also appeared in the poem's earlier publications in *Poetry* and *Townsman* but was corrected in the *CP* version. The editor has carried this correction over to the version printed here. See also the corresponding notes to "Shoreline" and "Note to a Neapolitan," which also flag possible typesetting issues.

Suggested Miracle
1937, 1940

First published in *ND TWO* (no page).

Published text: *CC* 39 (later *CP* 39) **Differences from *CP*:** *CC* version has initial capitals at the start of run-on lines.

Note to a Neapolitan
1940

Barnard's own records note that the poem was sent to Pound on 10 February 1937, to Williams in January 1938, and to Deutsch on 30 March (year unknown) but, judging by Barnard's annotations, most probably in 1938, following a suite of other poems she had sent to Deutsch on 1 February 1938 [See *BKNB*]. Poem discussed in *SB/MBAI* 40, 52.

"Miranda"—character in Shakespeare's *The Tempest*, daughter of the exiled Prospero.

Published text: *CC* 40 (later *CP* 38) **Differences from *CP*:** *CC* version has initial capitals at the start of run-on lines; L3 in *CC* omits a full stop at the end, after "private beaches," whereas *CP* adds it. The editor has carried this correction over to the version printed here. See also the corresponding notes for "Shoreline" and "Remarks on Poetry and the Physical World," which also flag possible typesetting issues.

A FEW POEMS (1952)

Beds
1941, 1952

First published as "Beds of My Fathers" in *PJ*. See note for "Fable from the Cayoosh Country" for a discussion of this poem's origins from a hiking trip in British Columbia. The poem resonates, imagistically and emotionally, with fellow *AFP* poem, "Inheritance," in the reference to the "ancestral beds," "my grandmother's beds," and the image of the grave implied in "bone to earth, I lay down."

Published text: *AFP* (no page) (later *CP* 13) **Differences from *CP*:** *AFP* version has initial capitals at the start of run-on lines; L11 in *CP* replaces the colon after "olive" with a comma, thus "the rooted olive, sham walnut."

The Fitting
1942, 1952

First published in *Harper's Bazaar* (July 1944); subsequently reprinted in *AFP*, *CP*, as part of group of poems in *ENC* 7, as part of a suite of poems in *NR* and, according to *MB/IC*, in *The Columbian*, Sunday, May 28, 1978, with "Probably Nobody."

Published text: *AFP* (no page) (later *CP* 4) **Differences from *CP*:** *AFP* version has initial capitals at the start of run-on lines; L15 in *AFP* gives a colon after "mirrors," but this seems an error that was corrected in the *CP* version. The editor has carried this correction over to the version printed here.

Dick
1952

Barnard said that this poem was inspired by the central courtyard of the University of Buffalo (*KBOO*), which had "a clock tower with nice chimes (every ¼ hour)" that she could hear even from her apartment (*MB/Parents*, 16 August 1939). "Doesn't play tunes + isn't loud," she added. However, she may also have been partly thinking of her time in the previous year in Norfolk, Connecticut, when she was working at New Directions with James Laughlin sending out catalogues where, similar to the Buffalo clock and the belltower of "Dick," "the bells in the Norfolk church sound the hour + ¼ hour'" (*MB/Parents*, 10 November 1938).

Poem discussed in *SB/MBAI* 114–115. See, also, the note to "Bay Beach."

Published text: *AFP* (no page) (later, as "Carillon," *CP* 41) **Differences from *CP*:** *AFP* version has initial capitals at the start of run-on lines.

Height Is the Distance Down
1944, 1952

First published in *Poetry* 63.5 (February 1944): 262–63.

The imagery of this poem was worked out in what appears to be an earlier—unpublished poem—called "Low Tide," not least the likening of north-western sky to whirlpool, its sharp sunset colors to a knife, and the presence given to a portentous wind not too dissimilar from that in "Fire." One version of "Low Tide" (named elsewhere as "Bright Side") reads:

> In the hour of undivided light and darkness,
> The sea ebbed and climbed into the misted sky;
> The sky, whirling, curled under the edge of the land
> And swirled all, formless, in a narrowing funnel
> Measureless out from us, sided with dark silver,
> Lined with winds unending out of the northwest.
> Out of a red scar thin as a knife blade,
> Crimson incision into the walls of hell,
> Came winds to rake the world of the living,
> To sift sand with the spirit and mist
> With the sifted body dissolved in the wind.
> Fragments of faces were cold in the wet wind,
> In the dull sound. In another world
> Feet struck the hard wet sand as though they walked.
>   (Ms/Ts: *U*)

See, also, notes for "Cold Heaven" and "Altitude."

Published text: *AFP* (no page) (later *CP* 52) **Differences from *CP*:** *AFP* version has initial capitals at the start of run-on lines; L4 of *CP* omits the hyphen in "knife-rim."

The Whisperer
1947, 1952

First published as "This Poor Soul" in *Tiger's Eye* 2 (December 1947): 19; subsequently reprinted in *AFP*, *CP*, and as part of a suite of poems in *NR*.

Published text: *AFP* (no page) (later *CP* 30) **Differences from *CP*:** *AFP* version has initial capitals at the start of run-on lines.

Persephone
1948, 1952

First published in *Harper's Bazaar* 2842 (October 1948): 262, where a stanza break is given between the line ending "Brought no news" and the one beginning "Homesickness here." Given subsequent variations in *AFP* and *CP* (see "Differences from *CP*" below), it seems Barnard changed her mind about the poem's layout each time it was printed.

Published text: *AFP* (no page) (later *CP* 53) **Differences from *CP*:** *AFP* version has initial capitals at the start of run-on lines; L14 of *AFP* begins the ellipses immediately after "wood," with no space, whereas in *CP* there is a space given between the two (e.g., "wood . . ."); *CP* version has a stanza break between the line ending "surrender is death" and "How many times it is said to the living."

Fable of the Ant and the Word
1944, 1952
First published in *Poetry* 63.5 (February 1944): 262. Reprinted in *ODY* (no page), along with "E.P.: Sant' Ambrogio, 1964" (see notes to "Two Visits"), a version of "Later: Four Fragments" entitled simply "Fragments" and "The Spring," as well as in *The Poetry Anthology, 1912–2002: Ninety Years of America's Most Distinguished Verse Magazine*, eds. Joseph Parisi and Stephen Young (Chicago: Ivan R. Dee, 2002), 124.

Published text: *AFP* (no page) (later *CP* 49) **Differences from *CP*:** *AFP* version has initial capitals at the start of run-on lines.

Anadyomene
1952
First published in *AFP*, then subsequently in *CP*, and as part of a suite of poems in *NR*. "Anadyomene" is an epithet of Aphrodite shown emerging from the sea in a painting by Apelles, according to Book XXXV of Pliny's *Natural History (PLINY* 329); indeed, the Greek word *Anadyomene* means "rising from the sea." See, also, L360 of *TI* (and the note to it), which dramatizes the sea goddess Thetis's rise out of the sea like sea mist, as well as "The Pathetic Fallacy," "The Fool's Serenade," and "Blanchefleur" (and the notes to them), which also resonate. Barnard sent a copy of the poem to her parents in a letter of 8 December 1943 with very little changed by the time the poem was finally printed in *AFP* other than to edit down the presentation of the "Cloudself" so that there is less personification and more focus on a distilled image, as can be seen in the original middle stanza:

> See where the sunlit headland
> Changes! Light-dazzle on rock fades
> And shadow softens. Cliffs, rising,
> Widen in encircling vapor—
> Cloudself. Half-obscured
> The bulk looms larger, gleams
> Radiant with an unknown
> Attribute of mist's being.

(MB/Parents)

Published text: *AFP* (no page) (later *CP* 50) **Differences from *CP*:** *AFP* version has initial capitals at the start of run-on lines.

Encounter in Buffalo
1942, 1952

First published in *Harper's Bazaar* (December 1942): 106 (where "theater" in L3 is spelled "theatre"). Poem discussed in *SB/MBA!* 53–54, 78, 134. Poem explores some of Barnard's dissatisfaction with the city of Buffalo. "While my work at the library was as interesting and stimulating as I had been assured that it would be, life outside working hours continued to offer no stimulus at all," she wrote in *AMH* 188.

"all crossings at sunset"—see note regarding "the late sail" in "Shoreline."

"The city / [. . .] where no doors open"—possible reference to the impact of hazardous weather through harsh Buffalo winters. "During the frequent blizzards," Barnard recalled, "pedestrians clung to ropes on downtown streets. The combination of ice and wind made it impossible to stand up, let alone proceed, without the assistance of the ropes. Doors on the windward side of public buildings were kept locked when the wind rose, because once opened they could not be closed again" (*AMH* 172).

Published text: *AFP* (no page) (later *CP* 29) **Differences from *CP*:** *AFP* version has initial capitals at the start of run-on lines.

Inheritance
1947, 1952

First published in *Furioso* 2.3 (Spring 1947): 24, with no comma after the second line of the second stanza (see note to "Road to Xanadu" for background on *Furioso*). Subsequently reprinted in *AFP*; *CP*; *Agenda* (London) 13.4–14.1 (Winter-Spring 1976): 11 (along with "The Pleiades" over the page); as a feature of a profile by Lana Roberts in *Prism: The OSU Magazine* (Winter 1976): 2–4, 4 (a student publication) where the second and third stanzas were run together; as well as reprinted as part of a suite of poems in *NR*. This poem is a tribute to Barnard's sense of inheritance through the ancestry of her parents (see, also, note to "Beds"), mostly through her mother's line. As she wrote in the introduction to *NG*, Barnard had grown up with an understanding about her ancestry that tapped into national narratives about Daniel Boone's expansion as articulated in this poem ("I persisted in thinking of my ancestry as wholly southern—from Virginia and Kentucky on my mother's side, and North Carolina on my father's" *NG* 144). But the poem also references, in

Mary Marshall, a line (from her father's side) that stretches back to Nantucket. An excellent source document for this poem is an unpublished memoir piece Barnard left among her papers, called "The Distaff Side" (*DS*). Running to twenty-five pages, the work opens with a section title ("I. A Letter to a Friend Concerning a Ring, a Shoe and a Book"), although it doesn't appear to otherwise follow the letter format, nor do there appear to be any other sections. *DS* traces Barnard's mother's line back several generations; the ring, shoe, and book of the section title belong to her maternal grandmother, Lillie May Hoard, whose dramatic story—detailed below—lies at the heart of the piece. The specific naming of "those women" is important to Barnard, as an act of recuperation, since she only refers to them by their maiden names. This seems a response to William Maxwell's *Ancestors* (New York: Knopf, 1971), of which Barnard writes:

> Maxwell says that the women of past generations are shadowy creatures compared to the men, and it is true that as we work our way back in time, especially in the early days of the American Colonies and the frontier, the maiden names of the wives are often lost. [. . .] I was surprised by his remark because I knew so much more about my mother's family than my father's and I had heard other women say the same thing. But then, I thought William Maxwell was a boy and didn't hang around in the kitchen, where the oral history of families has most often been transmitted. Later, on television, I heard Daisy Zamorra say the same thing about shadowy women, but her male ancestors were educated and active in public life. Most of mine were unlettered farmers, and when I think of them, I imagine them off somewhere plowing the north forty with no one to talk to but their horses. (*DS* 19)

"One teaspoon / out of a Virginian dozen"—the teaspoon is a possible reference to "a small coin silver teaspoon" passed down to Barnard from her great-great-great grandmother, Jane Carroll, "broken up among the daughters and then the granddaughters until this one finally came to me," (*DS* 5).

"Boone's / Bold star into Kentucky"—Daniel Boone, frontiersman, led Virginians into Kentucky in 1775 through the Wilderness Road, "which soon became white settlers' primary route to the West. Just months after its completion, Boone's wife and daughters traveled the new thoroughfare to the new settlement of Boonesborough, becoming the first Anglo-American women to settle in Kentucky" (https://www.loc.gov/item/today-in-history/june-07/, date last accessed 22 May 2024). Barnard's mother, Bertha Lee Hoard, came from Boone County, Kentucky (*NG* 56), "the little knob on top of Kentucky where the Ohio River makes a thrust northward into the underside of Ohio," (*DS* 4).

"Hesperides"—in Greek mythology, goddess-nymphs of the evening associated with the west. Graves writes: "[t]he three Hesperides, by name Hespere, Aegle, and Erytheis, live in the Far-Western orchard which Mother Earth gave to Hera. Some call them daughters of Night, others of Atlas and of Hesperis, daughter of Hesperus; sweetly they sing" (*TGM* 126). See, also, notes to "Storm."

"Mary Marshall"—maiden name of Mary Melissa Marshall, Mary Barnard's paternal grandmother born in Indiana in 1840 and married to Samuel Lee Barnard, born in North Carolina in 1835. The couple had five children, including Samuel Melvin, Barnard's father. See, also, L104–108 in "After Nantucket" (*NG*). *NG* specifies that Mary Melissa Marshall "died in Vancouver, Washington, in 1927" (*NG* 56), the year before Barnard entered Reed College; she had lived with the family for many years.

"Mary Noel"—from Boone County, one of Barnard's great-great-grandmothers. "The Noel line is one of the few lines in my mother's family that has been convincingly traced back to Europe," wrote Barnard in *DS* (6).

"Polly Connor"—Mary Pullilove, another of Barnard's great-great-grandmothers, known as "'Aunt Polly Conner'" (*DS* 20).

"Susan Carroll"—Susannah Hall Carroll, also one of Barnard's great-great-grandmothers. "Of these women," Barnard writes in *DS*, "Susannah Carroll is the most alive to me: I have pictures of her, silver that belonged to her, and my mother's reminiscences of a warm, loving woman [. . .] if my mother had a rôle-mother for her own mothering, it was surely Susannah," (*DS* 20).

"that willful girl, / Proudest of all, who turned / Twenty on her deathbed"—almost certainly a reference to Barnard's grandmother, Lillie May Hoard. *DS* recounts Lillie's supposed "treachery" in terms that foreground the love and "night ride" of the final stanza:

> I know that Lillie gave informal schooling to some of the neighbouring children from the time she was sixteen, and their mothers paid her with a quilt [. . .] Then one night this young woman climbed out of an upstairs window, descended a ladder and rode away on horseback with Orren Hoard. They spent the night with the Hoards and were married the next day. However did she come to do such a harebrained thing? Decent young women in Boone County in the 1880's [*sic*] were married in their father's homes in the presence of friends and family. (*DS* 13)

After around three years in their Florida "Eden" (*DS* 15), where Barnard's mother, Bertha, was born in Tangerine, Orange County, tragedy struck:

> [O]ne evening a Walton [city in Boone County, Kentucky] family living near the train station heard the train stop, and a little later heard a knock on the door. When they opened it, Lillie fell full length into the room with her child in her arms. She had come home to die, though perhaps she still hoped to live. Both Lillie and Orren had tuberculosis [. . .] Lillie died in 1886 and Orren died a few months later in the same year. They are buried side by side in the cemetery at Walton. (*DS* 15–16)

Barnard perhaps identified, too, with Lillie's willfulness, evoked in her unpublished poem which began "The slenderly poised clean shaft of your fir . . ." in the image of the "the wilful water / Of my life, flowing so contrarily eastward" (like Lillie's from Kentucky to Florida) in the name of love. Referring to Lillie's love of words, Barnard certainly thought her "a girl after my own heart," speculating that it was "the poetry" in the Hoard family's "speech and in their outlook on life [. . .] that [. . .] called to Lillie so powerfully that she rode off into the night with one of them [Orren]" (*DS* 25).

"the pride of / her love"—a reference to the Lillie May Hoard's love for Orren Hoard, but perhaps also a sense of family pride Barnard snapshots in *DS:* "There is one more glimpse of Lillie, now on her death-bed. Her child [Barnard's mother] is running about the room, and the grandmother says disapprovingly: 'She's going to be proud. She holds her chin too high.' And Lillie answers: I <u>want</u> her to be proud" (*DS* 15; underlining Barnard's).

"stronger than silver"—as well as the "coin silver teaspoon" (see above), according to *DS* Barnard inherited other "pieces of coin silver" engraved with names in the family line (*DS* 6) as well as Susannah Carroll's silver (*DS* 20). Clearly none of this is as important to Barnard, if we go by the poem, than the very power of the "pride of [. . .] love" modeled by Lillie May Hoard.

Published text: *AFP* (no page) (later *CP* 51) **Differences from *CP*:** *AFP* version has initial capitals at the start of run-on lines.

Midnight
1949, 1952

First published in *Saturday Review of Literature* 32.12 (19 March 1949): 7; subsequently reprinted in *AFP, CP,* and as part of a suite of poems in *NR.*

According to *MB/IC*, the poem was translated "into Italian by Carlo Izzo, and published in Italian anthology of English and American poetry."

Barnard explained the origins of the poem in a letter of 30 October 1944 to her parents: "Probably I should say, since Helene was very upset when she read the first draft of 'Midnight' that I was dwelling on such lugubrious subjects, that I got the idea out of what was probably a mis-reading of Chaucer. When I explained, it was all all right, and she liked the poem. Anyway, I think it's a cheerful poem, in a very serious way" (*MB/Parents*).

Published text: *AFP* (no page) (later *CP* 54) **Differences from *CP*:** *AFP* version has initial capitals at the start of run-on lines.

The Field
1952
> Reprinted in *AP V2* 657.

Published text: *AFP* (no page) (later *CP* 55) **Differences from *CP*:** *AFP* version has initial capitals at the start of run-on lines.

FROM *COLLECTED POEMS* (1979)

Ondine
1935
> Titled after a water spirit, "Ondine" was first published in *Poetry* 46.1 (April 1935): 27–28, along with "Faun in Exile" (later "Wine Ship") and "Lai" under the group title of *Spectral Tunes*, a title assigned by Harriet Monroe. "I cringed when I thought of it, but did not dare to protest," Barnard recalled in *AMH* 71, although this was putting it mildly when considering the wry humor of a letter of 19 March 1935 to T. C. Wilson: "Miss Monroe inflicted the general title of 'Spectral Tunes' on the three which are to be in POETRY. It was too late to tactfully suggest something else. I can't see anything spooky or tuneful about any of them. She might have an idea for the Chanson ['Chanson Pathetique']: Ghostful Chaunt or something" (*MB/TW*). As she wrote of Monroe's acceptance letter she received on 8 March 1935—"Letter from H.M saying she would use Faun in Exile, Ondine, + Lai—under the general title Spectral Tunes. Ow! Wot an idea" (*JSN*; punctuation Barnard's). The poem was subsequently republished a few months later in *Poetry* 47.2 (November 1935): 111–112, in conjunction with the journal's award of the Helen Haire Levinson Prize to her for the *Spectral Tunes* (see, also, Barnard's poem "On Arriving," as well as *AMH* 81, 110). The following summer, when Barnard

attended the Yaddo artist's colony for the first time, the poem's appearance in *Poetry* caught the attention of the writer David Greenhood, who remarked to her one evening at dinner that of her group in the magazine "he liked Ondine best." Barnard said in a letter of 25 June 1936 to her parents that: "I was particularly interested because [he] had a very good reason for liking it best. He said that that was the one in which it would have been easiest for me to fall into someone else's style, especially H.D.'s or Yeats', and I didn't, but kept it entirely my own" (*MB/Parents*). Poem discussed in *SB/MBAI* 33–34 and 40. See, also, notes to "An Evening by the Sea," "The Fool's Serenade," and to L52 ("thick on the beach the pyres of the dead burned always") of Barnard's *TI*.

Published text: *CP* 92 **Differences from *CP***: *Poetry* version has initial capitals at the start of run-on lines. L34 in the *CP* version replaces "Come toward" with "Come towards."

The Pleiades
1966; 1979; 1986

In a letter of 15 October 1978 to William Stafford concerning the introduction to *CP*, Barnard told him that the poem reflected the reading she had done for *TM* (as did "Picture of the Moon" and the first part of "Two Visits," entitled "E. P.: Martinsbrunn, 1961") (*MB/WS*). A much reprinted poem of Barnard's, "The Pleiades" was first published in *The New Yorker*, 42.27 (27 August 1966): 38, with some very minor punctuation differences. It was subsequently published in: *The New Yorker Book of Poems,* ed. the Editors of The New Yorker (New York: Viking Press, 1969): 566; reprinted also in *The Sallyport* (January 1971): 21 (according to *MB/IC*) as well as *Agenda* (London) 13.4–14.1 (Winter–Spring 1976): 11–12 (along with "Inheritance"); "Dialogues with Northwest Writers," (Vol. 20, Nos. 2 and 3), *Northwest Review* (1982): 187; *Testo a fronte* 6 (Milano, Marzo, 1992): 130–31 with a translation into Italian by Mary de Rachewiltz; and then as part of *TIME* (Section III of the third fytte, reproduced in this volume); as well as reprinted in *HAT* 34–35 and *AP V2* 659–60. *BIB* 198 specifies that the poem was set "for orchestra, mixed chorus, solo soprano, tenor and baritone by Tibor Serly" performed in Portland, OR, in 1978—according to *MB/IC* this was reprinted in the Portland Symphonic Choir program, for 6 May 1978 in connection to Serly's setting for the poem; Serly knew Pound in Paris and Rapallo and set this poem when he became a Washington State resident—see *SB/MBAI* 124–25.

"The Pleiades"—star cluster, one of the closest to Earth.

"the Seven Little Sisters"—alternative name for the Pleiades star cluster, named after the seven Greek mythological sisters Alcyone, Celaeno, Electra, Maia, Merope, Sterope, and Taygete, whom Zeus turned into stars. "The name Pleiades, from the root *plei*, 'to sail,' refers to their rising at the season when good weather for sailing approaches" (*TGM* 150).

"Spartan / dancing grounds"—reference to Sparta, ancient Greek city-state.

"Electra's weeping over Troy is stilled"—Electra was said to be the faintest star, for her grieving for Troy, home of her son (Dardanus) with Zeus (https://www.britannica.com/topic/Pleiades-Greek-mythology, date last accessed 22 May 2024); *TGM* 150 says she "disappeared in grief." See note, also, to "Chronos."

"Yellow River"—second largest river in China.

Published text: *CP* 89; *TIME* 18.

They Are Excited
1966; 1979

First published in *Origin* 3rd series, 2 (July 1966): 53 (with no full stop after " 'and comprehend' " and no comma after "brushwork") and, according to *MB/IC*, translated "into Japanese, and published in Japanese magazine, [summer] 1970" and reprinted in *TA* (no page).

See, also, note for "The Pump."

Published text: *CP* 42.

The Spring
1972; 1979

First printed in *ODY* (no page), along with "E. P.: Sant' Ambrogio, 1964" (see notes to "Two Visits"), "Fable of the Ant and the Word" and a version of "Later: Four Fragments" entitled simply "Fragments."

"nameless [. . .] poet" with "two small collections of verse"—at the point of first publication, Barnard had two collections of poetry out. This line makes interesting comparison with the first line of the second section of "Two Visits," which followed this poem in *CP* as it does here where, writing about Eliot's death, Barnard writes "Names make news."

See, also, the notes to the uncollected poem "Bay Beach," *CC*'s "Highway Bridge" and *CP*'s "The Pump."

Published text: *CP* 43.

Noon Hour
1976; 1979
First published in *New Letters* 42.4 (Summer 1976): 7–8 and reprinted in *TA* (no page). One typescript for the poem evidences Barnard's well-honed Imagist trimming and condensation—for instance, manually creating a line break between "eating" and "pears," replacing "trailing" with "trail" (*U*; but also see note to "Blanchefleur").
See, also, note for "The Pump."

Published text: *CP* 79.

The Solitary
1976; 1979
First published in *New Letters* 42.4 (Summer 1976): 7–8 subsequently in *CP* 82 and *From A to Z: 200 Contemporary American Poets.*, ed. David Ray (Athens, OH: Swallow Press/Ohio University Press, 1981), 6–7 and *AP V2* 658. According to *PNC*, this poem also featured in an audiovisual piece called "Bird Verse Portfolio" Series 1 No. 4, attributed to the Poetry Foundation.
"spillway"—"hydraulic structure built at a dam site for diverting the surplus water from a reservoir after it has been filled to its maximum capacity," (https://theconstructor.org/water-resources/hydraulic-structures/different-types-spillways/32484/, date last accessed 22 May 2024).
See, also, note for "The Pump."

Published text: *CP* 82.

Probably Nobody
1978; 1979
First published as part of group of poems in *ENC* 9 (with no full stop at the end of the second stanza) and, according to *MB/IC*, in *The Columbian*, Sunday, May 28, 1978, with "The Fitting," although in this instance Barnard adds it was published "but without title." Reprinted in *AP V2* 659.
"haws"—red fruit of the hawthorn
See, also, note for "The Pump."

Published text: *CP* 83.

Seedlings
1978, 1979
First published as part of group of poems in *ENC* 6.

Published text: *CP* 7.

Eternal She
1979

First appearance in print in *CP.*

This poem draws on one of Barnard's many visits to Italy. Her first, a three-month trip in 1949, took in Ravenna, the setting of this poem, as well as numerous places that Pound suggested she visit on an itinerary that ran to "three typed pages"—or, as Mary de Rachewiltz put it in *Discretions,* "a '*Cantos* tour of Europe'" (cited in *AMH* 251). Both the extensive consultation with Pound, including in person at St Elizabeths just before departure (Pound "approved of my hatbox, saying that it was exactly the right amount of luggage to take to Europe," *AMH* 257), and the trip itself, including Barnard's meetings with Rudge and her daughter Mary de Rachewiltz, are engagingly detailed in chapter 7 of *AMH.* "No other three months of my life left a deeper impression," wrote Barnard (*AMH* 257). See, also, the note for "Preacher," which very possibly presents a memory of Barnard's return visit to Pound following this specific trip.

"the brick tomb that protects / Placidia's dust"—reference to the Mausoleum of Galla Placidia, (386–450 AD), "commissioned [. . .] by empress Galla Placidia, daughter of Theodosius and sister of emperor Honorius [. . .] This little building was meant to be her last home; she wanted to be buried here with her brother and second husband, Constance III. However, the mausoleum never fulfilled that purpose—in 450 AD, the empress died in Rome and was buried there," (https://www.turismo.ra.it/en/culture-and-history/unesco-world-heritage/mausoleum-of-galla-placidia/, date last accessed 22 May 2024).

"certain mosaics"—art historian and friend of Barnard's, Sue Hennum, notes that there are numerous mosaics in Ravenna (conversation with the editor 13 April 2022; see also note for "Ravenna" below).

"clarion"—narrow war trumpet that emits a shrill sound.

"Roman / lawgiver and barbaric invader"—refers to the tensions of the period when the Roman Empire was collapsing, between the "external barbarians" and those "landed aristocrats and Byzantine emperors" who strove to uphold Roman values, codes and laws (see *OX* 811), such as Justinian (see note below); a "barbarian" was "one who spoke another language" (*OX* 40) or "national enemy" (*OX* 48).

"Alaric"—Alaric of Visigoth, who sacked Rome in 410, the same year that Rome formally renounced Britain (*OX* 860).

"Justinian"—Emperor who sought to reconquer Italy and Africa over 527–65 (*OX* 860) and, for a short time, reunited Italy to the Eastern Empire. Both acclaimed and derided for his achievements within the areas of the law and architecture, "one cannot help feeling about him as the Anglican John

Bramhall in 1658 felt about Henry VIII—that great good could come of the deeds of dreadful men" (*OX* 812). See also note on "Ravenna" below.

"Theodoric"—possibly pertaining to Theodosius, "the Great Emperor," who ruled the Late Roman Empire 378–95 (*OX* 860) but may also be a different spelling (or misspelling) of Theoderic, who, according to *OX*, was "the Ostrogothic king [. . .], educated at Byzantium" who was sent to remove the "barbarian army commander Odovacer" in 493 (*OX* 810).

"Ravenna"—city in northern Italy that became the capital of the Western Roman Empire after Milan and Rome and site of "the exquisite church of San Vitale." Barnard's "new egg in Ravenna" (*OX* 811) might possibly be a reference to the Mosaic of Justinian and retinue, reproduced in *OX* 812 and located in the church of San Vitale. In this mosaic, Justinian wears a halo and carries a golden egg-shaped vessel at the consecration of the church. The "new egg" may also be a reference to Barnard's own traveler self, greatly energized, as noted earlier, by the three-month tour of Italy that generated the poem—as she writes in chapter 10, "Second Thoughts on Egg Symbolism," in *TM*, eggs have long been mythically been associated with creation across cultures.

Published text: *CP* 70.

Fawn
1979
First appearance in print in *CP.*

Published text: *CP* 76.

Journey
1979
As with "The River Under Different Lights," this poem was published as part of a group of poems in *WP,* scheduled to be published ahead of *CP. BIB* 198 specifies that the poem was set "as a cantata for mezzo soprano, baritone, choir and orchestra (Opus 127), by Tomas Svoboda" as part of a residency at Portland State University, with the poem performed in Portland in 1987. Poem also referenced as part of a wider discussion of the adaptability of Barnard's work by composers in *SB/MBAI* 124–25.

Published text: *CP* 25–27, where each section appears on its own page.

Letter from Byzantium
1979
First appearance in print in *CP.*

"Byzantium"—former Greek colony, known as Constantinople, then later as Istanbul.

"Priam"—last king of Troy in Greek mythology; first referenced in L19 of *TI*—see, also, annotation to this line.

Published text: *CP* 68.

A Picture of the Moon
1979

First appearance in print in *CP.* See note to "The Pleiades."

"Heng O"—as Barnard writes of Chinese mythology in *TM*, the name refers to "the goddess Heng O, who stole the elixir of immortality, floated up to the moon and was changed into a toad" (*TM* 116).

"The Snowy Tiger of the West"—in Chinese mythology, the White Tiger (also known as Bai Hu) is the name of one of the four symbols for the constellations, which represents the west and the season of autumn. See, also, lines 40–43 of the first fytte of *TIME*, which introduces the "White Tigress who prowled / Time's hinterlands once / in the Age of Dragons" that gives rise to the title of *TIME*.

"the Cassia Tree"—another reference to Chinese moon mythology, this time to a tree that grows on the moon and cannot be cut down; also known as the Tree of Life. Curiously, Williams took part in a translation project with David Rafael Wang over 1957 to 1961, resulting in a collection of poems called "The Cassia Tree" published posthumously in the same year as Barnard's *TM*, in 1966 in *New Directions* 19—see Stephen Field, " 'The Cassia Tree': A Chinese Macropoem," *William Carlos Williams Review* vol. 18, no. 1 (Spring 1992): 34–49.

"the Toad of Time"—as well as the myth of Heng O being changed into a toad, Barnard writes of another Eastern moon myth that features a toad in chapter 11 of *TM*, which considers mythologies surrounding the phenomenon of the eclipse:

> There is a story from Annam to the effect that eclipses of the moon are caused by an enormous moon-eating toad which the Lord of the Han Lake keeps chained on the lake bottom. Occasionally, when the god is sleeping, the toad breaks his chain and escapes. He straightaway makes for the moon and swallows it. The Moon Girls, who guide the moon across the sky, then run to awaken the toad's keeper; and it is to help them that young women everywhere make a racket by striking pestles on rice mortars. The Lord of the Han

> Lake, being roused by the clatter, rescues the moon and rechains
> the toad to the lake bottom. (*TM* 111)

No initial capital is given for the phrase "the Toad of Time" in the *CP* version; the editor has decided to retain this idiosyncrasy given the similar lack of initial capital on the "oh" following an em dash in the final stanza.

Published text: *CP* 90.

Picture Window
1979
> First appearance in print in *CP*.

Published text: *CP* 81.

The Pump
1979
> Poem also published as part of a group of poems in *WP* scheduled to be published ahead of *CP*. As with other poems that followed "The Pump" in *CP* ("Noon Hour," "Real Estate," "The Solitary," "Probably Nobody," "Soft Chains," and "Now"), the influence of Barnard's translation of Sappho can clearly be seen in the visual (spare, ribbonlike) layout of the poem—a layout also shared by other poems in *CP* that preceded it ("They Are Excited" and "The Spring").

Published text: *CP* 78.

Real Estate
1979
> Another poem that was published as part of a group of poems in *WP*, which were scheduled to be published ahead of *CP*.
> "vetch"—scrambling plant with pink flowers.
> See, also, note for "The Pump."

Published text: *CP* 80.

The River Under Different Lights
1979
> The first fragment, "The Gorge," was published as part of a group of poems in *WP*, which were scheduled to be published ahead of *CP*. However, the individual fragments had been worked on in the 1930s but, strangely, not collected into *Cool Country*—see, also, notes to "Estuary," "Road to Xanadu,"

"Shoreline," and "The Fool's Serenade." An early version of "The Gorge" was an expanded piece entitled "September" with different spellings of "luster" and "gray," dictional change from "resting" to "beating" in L3, and the final image concentrated in one line rather than two:

September

Light has the dull lustre of pewter
And the clouds move sidewise clawing the tops of the crags,
Beating their soft grey bellies
Briefly in high valleys.
By the climbing road vine maple is frosted to fire
And elderberries are ripe with woodsmoke's blue.
A glittering wire
Laces the river water from mountain to mountain.
Foam plowing against the rapids gathers all brightness.
(Ms/Ts: LBN)

"The Gorge"—Columbia River Gorge (see note to "Altitude").

Poem discussed (with reference "September," the poem's relation to Sappho's oppositional poetics, and as an extension of "Fire, snow, and the night . . .") in *SB/MBAI* 72–73, 78–79, and 82.

Published text: *CP* 21–23, where each section appears on its own page.

Two Visits
1979

Section 1 first published as "E.P. Martinsbrunn, 1961" in *Odysseus* 1.2 (October–November 1971) (no page); see, also, note to "The Pleiades." Section 2 first published as "E.P.: Sant' Ambrogio, 1964" (with a space given between "Sant'" and "Ambrogio") as part of a suite of poems in *ODY* (no pag.), along with "Fable of the Ant and the Word," a version of "Later: Four Fragments" entitled simply "Fragments," and "The Spring." Barnard gives a compelling account of the visits that inspired these poems in *AMH* 305–308, including a lunch with Pound and Olga Rudge where they receive news that T. S. Eliot had been awarded the Presidential Medal of Freedom.

"Martinsbrunn"—private clinic on the outskirts of Merano (and near to Brunnenburg) where, in the time period of this poem, Pound was recuperating for a second time following his release from St Elizabeths.

"death-mask [. . .] his jaws unhinged by death will sing"—see note to L536 of *TI*.

"Sant'Ambrogio"—village on an escarpment above Rapallo, where Rudge had a house.

"the name / is the Possum's"—Pound's nickname for T. S. Eliot, the racial politics of which have been discussed by Michael North in *The Dialect of Modernism: Race, Language, and Twentieth-Century Literature* (New York and Oxford: Oxford University Press, 1994). Of the nickname's origins, North writes: "[Pound] no doubt meant to his mock his friend's caution and reserve, but he also used the name, which he had found in Joel Chandler Harris's *Uncle Remus*, to turn Eliot's timidity into a subversive mask" (North p. 77). See, also, notes to Barnard's essay "Ezra Pound, Sappho and My Assault on Mount Helicon."

"*salita*"—Italian for uphill slope, this refers to the escarpment that leads to Sant'Ambrogio.

"Parnassus"—see notes to "Fable" and "Ursus Parnassus."

Published text: *CP* 44–45, where each section appears on its own page.

TIME AND THE WHITE TIGRESS (1986)

Barnard began the research for what became *Time and the White Tigress*—and, in concert, *The Mythmakers*—sometime around September 1954, although, given the overlap of some of the subject matter with her *Sappho* (religion, mythology), the seeds were probably sown a little earlier. Barnard told Pound in a letter of 3 January 1955:

> I have decided perhaps I had better let you know what is going on. I seem to be writing the new <u>Golden Bough</u>, not because I am particularly interested in the origins of religion, but because—well, possibly because this stuff is lying around all over the top of the ground and nobody notices and I have a tidy mind and feel impelled to pick it up and put it together. I didn't know I was going to do it until I got back to New York in September and put my notes together and saw what I had. Since then, I've been invisible except to the librarians in the Art Room, the Oriental Room, the Photostat room, and so on. It could run to 20 volumes, I suppose, but I hope to keep my share down to one—anyway, for present publication. (*MB/EP*; "September" is manually corrected by Barnard from the typed "October")

She goes on to write about her overall approach, and, curiously, the dual support of science and poetry:

> It contains large doses of—or rather, [*sic*] attacks on the accepted views as regards mythology, anthropology, archaeology, and religion (origins of). Lots of symbols and lots of circles. I confess I can't read Jung let alone his disciples, but he seems to be interested in symbols and circles. He might not like what I've done with them, because I turn them into diagrams and make them function. I work with astronomy books at my right hand and Dante at my left. (*MB/EP*)

A version of Barnard's notes and diagrams to the second fytte: *The Year into Quarters* can be found in her letter to Pound of 27 May 1955 (*MB/EP*); this letter provides additional diagrams, which may be of use to the interested reader.

Barnard discusses the process by which some of material was transformed into poetry, into *TIME,* in *FN* in the paragraph that begins "After a hiatus of about ten years," including the metric used, explaining that her earlier development of the five-beat line in her translation of *TI* formed "the backbone of the book" (*FN* 156–57).

Section III of the third fytte: *Time Slips a Cog* was published numerous times under the title "The Pleiades" (see earlier note to "The Pleiades"); the sixth fytte: *Song for the Northern Quarter* was first published in *The Paris Review* 99 (Spring 1986): 166–68 (the only differences being that arabic numerals are used to divide the sections and some indentations are of slightly different breadths); the ninth fytte: *La Donna* was reprinted in *Annual Survey of American Poetry*: 1986, edited by the Editorial Board, Roth Publishing (NY: Roth, 1987) 30–32; the coda: *Song for the New Year* was first published in 1985 as a Christmas broadside by the University Libraries, State University of New York at Buffalo, where "time" in the third stanza has an initial capital and in the fourth stanza there's no comma after "shells."

FROM *NANTUCKET GENESIS: THE TALE OF MY TRIBE* (1988)

This work has its origins some forty years earlier than publication in the research Barnard did between 1945 and 1950, assisting Carl Van Doren with *his* research around Benjamin Franklin's Nantucket connections. Barnard made a tongue-in-cheek reference to her Nantucket origins in a 1991 poem called "Limerick":

> A famed poet of ancestry Nantucket
> Asked: "Judge our limericks?"
> She sure didn't duck it.
> "Favorite limericks," she said
>   "I keep in my head"
> Like Kool-Aid in a champagne
>   Ice bucket

Ms/Ts: *U*

The typescript adjusts the capitalized "I" in "Ice bucket" to lowercase in pencil and carries a typed note: "Appeared in the Vancouver, Washington newspaper <u>The Columbian,</u> February 1991 in an article on a Valentine's Day limerick contest."

Introduction

"William Byrd II"—Virginian colonel who wrote disparagingly of North Carolinians in his colonial work *The History of the Dividing Line Run in Our Year of the Lord 1728.* See James R. Masterson, "William Byrd in Lubberland," *American Literature* vol. 9, no. 2 (May 1937): 153–70.

"In the 1940s, when I was assisting Carl Van Doren in the editing of Benjamin Franklin's papers"—Barnard's employment as a researcher is detailed in *AMH* (205–10). Van Doren was friends with Barnard's history professor at Reed, Victor Chittick.

"Weymouth"—town on the south coast of England, in the county of Dorset (not "Dorsetshire" as Barnard goes on to say), used by some of the first emigrants to the US as an embarkation point, in addition to more popular ports in Bristol and Plymouth.

"Cape Ann"—cape thirty miles north of Boston, at the north tip of Massachusetts Bay.

"From time to time someone would ask me whether I was descended from the Nantucket Barnards. One man assured me that Nantucket was covered with Mary Barnard gravestones"—a family myth, shared by Barnard's parents, as she recounted in a letter to them of 16 January 1949: "I've probably told you that I've been asked if my family came from Nantucket, because the island is said to be covered with Barnard gravestones, and I said, no, they came from North Carolina; and I asked you people and you said yes, both sides of the family, Barnard and Marshall, came from North Carolina" (*MB/Parents*).

"W. O. Stevens, in *Nantucket: The Far-Away Island*"—see W. O. Stevens, Nantucket: The Far-Away Island (1936. Repr. 1947), 286.

" 'Crèvecoeur speaks . . .' "—reference to J. Hector St. John de Crèvecoeur's *Letters from an American Farmer* (1782), which contains a sequence of five letters to Nantucket.

"Obed Macy, the first Nantucket historian (1835)"—see Obed Macy, *The History of Nantucket* (1835, 2nd ed. 1880), 53.

"the deed of Wanack-Mamack (1671)"—also mentioned by Mary de Rachewiltz in the foreword to this volume, Wanack-Mamack was the Chief Sachem of Nantucket who signed the deed of sale to Barnard's settler ancestors mentioned in "II. Nantucket" (who bought from Nantucket's Algonquian-speaking Native American population "the right / to own and to settle one fourth of Nantucket Island" (*NG* 31). The deed is excerpted in "Nantucket II."

"One of the earliest Quaker preachers to visit Nantucket said of her that 'the islanders esteemed her as a Judge among them, for little of moment was done there without her' "—while no specific reference is given in the text, a useful study that gives some consideration to Mary Coffin Starbuck's influence, and such appraisals by Quaker ministers, is Alison M. Gavin's essay "Quaker Revivals as an Organizing Process in Nantucket, Massachusetts 1698–1708," in *Quaker History* vol. 79, no. 2 (Fall 1990), 57–76 (see 60–61 especially).

"Kezia Coffin, whose life has inspired more than one novel"—Kezia (Folger) Coffin (1723–1798) was, according to Nathaniel Philbrick, one of the "influential merchants" on the island who "[clung] to their royal connections (financial and otherwise)"—see Nathaniel Philbrick, *The New England Quarterly* vol. 64, no. 3 (September 1991): 414–32: 428. Philbrick spells Keziah Coffin's first name "Keziah." Barnard also seems to make reference to her in *AMH* when discussing her work with Van Doren on Franklin's papers, with another spelling of Coffin's first name: "after I found that the mother of Franklin's cousin Kezian [*sic*] Coffin was named Mary Barnard, [Carl Van Doren] invariably referred to that controversial female as 'your kinswoman Kezian' " (*AMH* 273). Deemed an "infamous" " 'she-pirate' " (https://www.mariamitchell.org/what-lies-beneath-15696, date last accessed 3 December 2024), one such novel Coffin inspired was Diana Gaines's *Nantucket Woman* (Random House, 1977).

"Crèvecoeur, in his *Letters from an American Farmer* (1782)"—there is no comma after "1782" in the published *NG*; the editor has treated this as an error and added one in the version that appears here.

"the Merrimack Valley"—region around the Merrimack River, spanning both Massachusetts and New Hampshire, mentioned, also, in "I. Before Nantucket."

"Tristram Coffin came from Devonshire [. . .] Thomas Gardner from Dorsetshire"—the correct British spellings of these southern English counties are "Devon" and "Dorset" respectively, but are presented here as Barnard knew of them. See, also, the earlier reference to "Weymouth."

"[Robert] Pyke was one of the First Purchasers of Nantucket, but never lived on the island. He has a modest monument in Salisbury"—"Pyke" may also appear as "Pike" in other publications; "Salisbury" is a town in Massachusetts where Pyke lived, mentioned, also, in "I. Before Nantucket."

I. Before Nantucket

L27–28 "New England's estuaries: / the Merrimack and the Piscataqua"—see note to "the Merrimack Valley" in notes to *Introduction*; running to just over twelve miles, the Piscataqua River flows out into the Gulf of Maine through numerous towns in New Hampshire and Maine, including Dover, mentioned in L21.

L32–33 "Six of our seven / emigrant ancestors seem to have been 'the others' "—since by "the others" Barnard means those whose "freedoms" had been "curb[ed]" by those who assumed "God-given power" mentioned in L31, then we can infer that the "[s]ix" she is referring to are Thomas Macy, Thomas Barnard, Robert Barnard, John Severance, Edward Starbuck, and Tristram Coffin. The seventh of this group, Thomas Gardner, was chiefly attracted to Nantucket "not for religious reasons, but in the hope of establishing a lucrative fishing station on Cape Ann," the introduction tells us.

L58 "Oliver Cromwell"—for five years between 1653 and 1658, Cromwell governed the British Isles as Lord Protector of England, Scotland, and Ireland, overthrowing King Charles I during the English Civil War (1642–1651) in order to form a Republican commonwealth where he dually served as head of state and head of government. Cromwell's leadership inspired waves of puritanism in both Britain and North America, as evidenced in L59 by the "the colonists [who] passed repressive religious laws."

L63 "the Roundheads"—Parliamentarians whose armies assisted Cromwell in the English Civil War, so-named after the shape of their closely cropped hair.

L69 "EDWARD STARBUCK, a prosperous Dover citizen"—see note to L27–28.

L85 "Not that they fled in the night, as Whittier has it"—see John Greenleaf Whittier's poem "The Exiles" (1841); Whittier was a descendent of Nantucket Coffins.

L95 "Andover"—Massachusetts town in the Merrimack Valley (see note to L27–28).

L140 "they might marry Folgers, Colemans, Husseys or Swains"—Peter Folger, II. Nantucket tells us, was already living on Nantucket as a preacher when the settlers arrived, and served as a witness to the deed of Wanack-Mamack; Thomas Coleman was among one of the twenty First Purchasers who had been taken on as a partner of "the original ten" mentioned in L76, and is named in the deed of Wanack-Mamack in II. Nantucket, as are Christopher Hussey and John Swain, who were both part of "the original ten."

II. Nantucket

L3 "Eddystone lighthouse"—lighthouse situated on the treacherous Eddystone rocks in the English Channel, nine miles out from the southwestern English mainland.

L5 "So says Melville, or Ishmael says it for him"—see chapter 14, "Nantucket," in Herman Melville, *Moby-Dick* (New York: Norton, 1967), 61–62.

L19 "The deed was signed by Wanack-Mamack, head Sachem"—see *Introduction*, reprinted here, and relevant note to "the deed of Wanack-Mamack (1671)" in the notes to *Introduction*, above.

L27 "Philip's rebellion"—reference to war of resistance led by Metacom (1638–1676), also known as Metacomet, King Philip, or Philip of Pokanoket. Metacom was sachem of a coalition of indigenous peoples who, during "King Philip's War" (1675–1676), suffered huge loss of life, including Metacom himself.

L47 "selectmen"—members of New England local governing bodies.

L184–85 "a bride on Nantucket, a housewife, mother and widow / in North Carolina, she died at last in Ohio"—this kind of female biography is explored in Barnard's poem "Inheritance," in *AFP,* reprinted in this volume.

III. After Nantucket

L10 "the Piedmont"—area in North Carolina between the Atlantic ocean and the Appalachian mountains, known in the seventeenth and eighteenth centuries for its communities of Quakers and other religious groups seeking religious freedom.

L11 "New Garden Quakers"—as the New Garden Friends website explains of their activities in Greensboro, North Carolina, "Friends first gathered here in the mid-1700s to worship outdoors on First Day (Sunday) while seated on fallen trees. In 1754, New Garden Friends Meeting was established as a Monthly Meeting (the Quaker term for a regular congregation)," (https://ngfm. org/about/, date last accessed 3 December 2024).

L35 "John Woolman's *Journal* [. . .] and Barclay's *Apology*"—influential Quaker works by John Woolman (1720–1772), whose autobiographical *Journal* was published posthumously in 1774, and Scotsman Robert Barclay (1648–1690), one of the first colonial settlers of East Jersey whose *Apology for the True Christian Divinity* was published in 1678, one of the first—and among the most enduring—expositions of Quaker belief.

L83 "His land, worth twelve hundred dollars in 1850"—there is no comma after "1850" in the published *NG*; the editor has treated this as an error and added one in the version that appears here.

L99–103 "There is no indication [. . .] for instance"—reference to the abolitionist stance of the Quaker movement in Europe and the US.

L104 "MARY MELISSA MARSHALL"—Barnard's paternal grandmother; see notes to "Inheritance" for further biography.

L107 "before Fort Sumter"—the Battle of Fort Sumter, which took place at the sea fort protecting Charleston in South Carolina between 12 and 14 April 1861, beginning the American Civil War.

L124 "Elizabeth Bennet's father"—father of the main protagonist in Jane Austen's *Pride and Prejudice* (1813).

L130 "ours was a tribe of no especial distinction"—similar humility can be found in Barnard's own foreword to her memoir: "I can still think of a number of reasons against writing such a book as this: First, a life singularly lacking in dramatic incident" (*AMH* xvii).

Published text: *NG*.

UNCOLLECTED

"I found my grief . . ."
No date
Along with the poem that begins "My mind is a hall where walk . . . ," this untitled poem appeared on a manuscript draft with the heading "For my Valentines" followed by the subheading "Not the title of the pieces" in brackets beneath it. It's possible, therefore, that the poem is from around 1932 since this date was given for copyright purposes for the companion piece, "My mind is a hall were walk . . ." It's not clear who the "Valentines" were.

Ms/Ts: *U*

Thirst
No date

   PNC once speculated that the TS is from 1932, but Bell has subsequently informed the editor that this has been crossed out.

   "cloudy curtains" and "the cloudy dust"—Bell's annotation on a copy of the TS points the reader to *AMH* 44 for Barnard's account of a Portland dust storm one spring afternoon in 1931 on which this poem might be based. Barnard recalled a "yellow cloud extending itself half across the sky, approaching from the east" accompanied by a "furious wind," which struck as she was studying in her dorm at Reed College.

   "drys"—this is Barnard's spelling.

   "drouth"—means both drought and thirst (n.), from Scottish dialect.

Ms/Ts: *U*

Thinking of Yeats
No date

   This is another poem whose date is not entirely clear (1933 has been given for copyright registration), not least because the TS typeface resembles the kind of typefaces Barnard was using in at least the mid-late 1930s (similar to that used in for "The Colored Stone" and "Ursus Parnassius"—see relevant notes), but also because the poem practices Barnard's later use of dropping the initial capital from the beginning of each line, which she adopted after *A Few Poems* (1952). While it does not appear that Barnard knew Yeats, there are several brief references to him in *AMH* (35, 51, 54, and 175) as well as a description of Barnard's appreciation for Yeats (and, surprising to her, a new appreciation of Cummings) in a letter Pound of 1937, two years before Yeats died. Discussing her response to the *Faber Book of Modern Verse*, edited by Michael Roberts, on 14 June that year Barnard wrote:

> I found there were only three poets represented whom I could read. It was not only that they were the only ones I had any real pleasure in reading. I couldn't keep my mind on even the briefest poem by anyone else. The three poets were Yeats, Cummings, and yourself. I had realised that an enthusiasm for Yeats was slowly developing during the last year, but I had certainly never expected that I would place Cummings on a level above all the other contributors. There are others that I like at certain times, admire for special qualities, etc. They don't, however, exhibit the one quality I find of first importance. *(MB/EP)*

"We'll see him, not lonely, riding as one / central in Chaucerian company"—these lines reflect how important Barnard considered Yeats's work to be. Her 14 June 1937 letter to Pound further illuminates on the other members of this "Chaucerian company," and why their work is deserving of such status and attention. "You wrote me more than year ago that you would like me to make an anthology ('as an exercise, if nothing more') of 64 pages of contemporary work," Barnard explained to Pound, before describing how she would add Williams—who was not in the Faber anthology—to the group of Cummings, Pound, and Yeats to make an "Anthology to End Anthologies." Critically, the letter continues:

> What troubles me is my difficulty in identifying the quality that distinguishes these poets from the others. Since it also distinguishes the poets you recommend highly, you ought to know what it is: Catullus, Villon, Heine, Propertius, Li Po, Cavalcanti, Chaucer, and the best Provencal. Sometimes it appears without technical discipline. I think it did in D. H. Lawrence [. . .] From what I have heard, Dante had this quality I am looking for, but it is lost in the translations I have seen. Emily Dickinson had it, and Shakespeare of course. It manifests itself in both imagination and speech. In imagination it "surprises with a fine excess" and in speech with a sudden simplicity (simultaneously). I don't think it is a combination of qualities. Sometimes I think it is nothing more complicated than sincerity. It never appears wholly separated from either humor or bitterness. Do you have any idea what I am talking about, and if you do, am I not right in thinking it is not one characteristic but a combination?

Such sentiments with regards to Yeats's work were certainly shared by Charles D. Abbott, Director of Libraries and Professor of English who initiated the Poetry Collection at Buffalo and appointed Barnard as the first Poetry Curator, the result of "Pound [having] made the connection between me and the one job in the country that I was best fitted to do" (*AMH* 167). As Barnard writes in *AMH*, the Buffalo collection began chronologically with Yeats's first volume (*AMH* 175). She subsequently read a biography of Yeats in the year she left Buffalo—which, combined with reading "a good deal of Shakespeare" triggered an "attack of poetry [writing]" (*MB/Parents*, 8 December 1943)—as well as cited Yeats's work in the tenth fytte of *TIME*. For a full and engaging account of Barnard's time as Curator of the Poetry Collection at the Lockwood Memorial Library of the University of Buffalo, see *AMH* 168–201.

Ms/Ts: *U*

The Carver
c. 1927

Poem first published in *G* titled "The Carver" then subsequently in *TG* with no title, minor punctuation changes and illustrated with a wood linocut on an adjoining foldout page; poem appears here as in the latter *TG* version, with title restored. *MB/IC* notes that this poem was sent out to numerous journals prior to its eventual publication, including, in 1927, *Saturday Evening Post*, then in 1928, to *Harper's Bazaar*, *Poetry*, and *Scribner's*. Barnard recollected in her memoir:

> When I was sixteen, at the instigation of a woman visitor from the East, who praised my work highly, I submitted some of my poems to magazines for the first time. They were returned from *Poetry* (Chicago) with a penciled "promising" in the corner of the printed rejection slip. I was sad, but at the same time I felt encouraged by the "promising" and the little note. It was my first editorial encouragement, and I felt hopeful. As it turned out, that was the last editorial encouragement I was to receive for a long time. This was in 1926. I continued to send poems out until, in 1935, I saw my first poem in *Poetry* after Marianne Moore had opened the door for me." (*AMH* 30)

On this experience with *Poetry*, see, also, Barnard's poem "On Arriving," published in the 1987 edition to mark *Poetry's* seventy-fifth anniversary. Other magazines and journals Barnard tried—also unsuccessfully—during this period include *Forum* and *Good Housekeeping* (for an unpublished poem called "Sunset Clouds," 1927) and *Delineator* and *St Nicholas* (for an unpublished poem called "Clouds," 1926). No copies seem to have survived, but *PNC* refers to these poems with reference to "A cloud comes down . . . ," entertaining the idea that they were earlier versions of this poem. "The Carver" is discussed in *SB/MBAI* 23–24.

"a silver spoon"—unlike "Impassioned Sonnet" (see next note), her professor Lloyd Reynolds's view of the poem was that it was "[n]ot so good.

The 'spoon' made it ridiculous—a hunch I'd always had" (*MB/Parents*, 27 October 1930). The spoon, however, stayed in publication and is thus retained here.

Published text: *G*; *TG*.

Impassioned Sonnet
c. 1927

Bell dates a copy of the *LBN* TS as October 1927. A slightly different version of the poem—in terms of layout and punctuation only—was published in the Barnard special issue of *Paideuma*, as part of an essay by Molly O'Hara Ewing. O'Hara Ewing writes that Barnard sent her a copy of the poem in a letter dated 9 January 1992, with a note explaining that she believed the poem was published in the school paper when she was sixteen or seventeen years old (thus, 1925/1926) and then a little later in the Reed College *QUEST* when Barnard was freshman at Reed (*MOHE* 65). It was a poem that had attracted some attention for its musicality. As she told her mother during her very first semester in a letter of 7 November 1928:

> Miss Thompson said that she wanted the sonnet if I would change the name of it. It seems she doesn't like "impassioned" [. . .] she said that [. . .] I had mastered my technique of rhyme and rhythm [*sic*] so well that it seemed effortless [. . .] And then she wanted to know, did I ever write songs? I told her, no, I never had, but just the same she thought I was just the person to win twenty-five dollars writing the words to a new Reed Song. (*MB/Parents*)

The poem was among a set that Barnard later shared with Professor Lloyd Reynolds in her junior year at Reed while taking his creative writing course (for background on Reynolds, see notes to the poem she wrote for him, "Odysseus Speaking"). Reynolds's comments were relayed in a letter to her mother of 27 October 1930, showing he was clearly in agreement with the poem's sentiment: "Impassioned Sonnet—Quite agreed. Was expressed gracefully" (*MB/Parents*). Reynolds was, however, less in favor of other poems in the set—see, for example, the note for "The Carver." *PNC* notes that the poem was read by Elizabeth J. Bell at Mary Barnard's memorial service, 4 September 2001.

Ms/Ts: *LBN*

The Pathetic Fallacy
c. 1928–1930

Elizabeth J. Bell dates this poem as from 1928 on one copy of the TS and from 1930 on another; *PNC* crosses through "ND" (for "no date") replacing it with "1928." In *BKNB*, Barnard notes that the poem was sent to Pound on 28 July 1934 and T. C. Wilson on 31 August 1934, where it is listed as simply "Pathetic Fallacy."

"Thetis"—in Greek mythology, variously a sea nymph, goddess of water and, as one of the nereids, daughter of the sea god Nereus, who married the mortal Peleus of Thessaly, with whom they had a son, Achilles, hero of *The Iliad*. See note to "In the bridal . . ." (four fragments) and L358 of Book 1 of *TI*, where Thetis first appears in the text, as well as the notes to L34 and L359–60 of the text. See, also, notes to "Anadyomene" and "The Fool's Serenade."

Ms/Ts: *U*

An Evening by the Sea
1930

Poem included in the set Reynolds read in the autumn of 1930 (see note for "Impassioned Sonnet"). Barnard reported that he had "[n]o comment that I can remember. In other words not worth talking about" (*MB/Parents*, 27 October 1930)—a view not shared by this editor.

"the Alice"—wreck of a French square-rigged ship that, in 1909, washed up on the Long Beach peninsula, a twenty-eight-mile slim stretch of land in Washington State. According to a website for tourists, the *Alice* was a "square-rigged ship [which] ran aground near Ocean Park with 3,000 tons of cement. The entire crew made it to shore, but the cement hardened, causing it to sink deep into the sand. The mast and rigging became a landmark and tourist attraction until about 1930. Today, the *Alice* makes rare appearances during extreme low tides" (https://www.visitlongbeachpeninsula.com/graveyard-pacific/, date last accessed 22 May 2024).

From the perspective of Sappho's influence on Barnard, and how that might be apparent in this poem, see note to "The Fool's Serenade."

Ms/Ts: *LBN*

Against Lethe
1932

LBN on reverse of this poem gives the date of "May 8, 1932," in Barnard's hand. *PNC* notes that this poem was found in *LBN* and dated 5/8/32, but also appeared in *H* with no title. Bell also speculates that the poem was "perhaps inspired by MB's paternal grandmother who lived w/them" (*PNC*). The image presented in the poem certainly resonates with the image Barnard presents in the opening paragraph of *AMH* of her paternal grandmother, Mary Melissa Barnard (née Marshall):

> During the last years of my grandmother's life we could always quiet her restlessness by placing a book in her hands, although she had long ago lost the ability to read or even to recognize her family. She would sit in the rocker by her bedroom window, rocking contentedly and occasionally following a line of print with her forefinger. It broke my heart. Sometimes I thought that the unslaked thirst for books of my female forebears had culminated in my own passionate reading and singleminded desire to write books as well as read them. (*AMH* 1)

Barnard sent the poem to *Poetry*, *Harper's Bazaar*, and *Ladies Home Journal* (twice) between July and December 1932; "[a]ll returned it," notes Bell, as per Barnard's experience of the big magazines at this time (*PNC*). See also notes to "Cupbearer," "Moonstone," and to "Lethe," the latter a poem Barnard sent to Pound when she first reached out to him in the autumn of 1933, which may be an entire reworking of this poem.

Ms/Ts: *LBN*

Aquarelle
1932

Another medieval knight poem, also sent to Pound on 28 July 1934, along with all the other poems that appeared in *CV* (*College Verse*) over 1932–1933 and many others, in the hope that the group may open some doors. It did—shortly after, Barnard heard from T. C. Wilson about submission to *The Westminster Quarterly* in a showcase of contemporary American poems coedited with Pound (Wilson took fourteen from her); Pound wrote to say he had sent some of her poems to T. S. Eliot at *The Criterion* (Eliot took none); and Marianne Moore wrote to suggest Barnard mention her name when submitting poems to *Poetry* (which led to her first national publication the following February—see notes to "Shoreline"). As with many others from Barnard's *CV* group, the poem evidences Barnard's pre-free verse style initially honed at Reed during her days as a member of the Gawd-Awful Society, "a very informal organization" of writers where she stood out for being "the only rhyming poet on campus. Everyone else wrote free verse" (*AMH* 35–36)—until, that is, she read in the moderns in her junior year (see Introduction).

"Aquarelle"—a painting composed using transparent watercolors.

Published text: *CV 2.1* 12–13.

Bay Beach
1932

Line breaks, indentations, and justification are preserved as they appear on Barnard's original MS, dated in the same TS as "9/32." This is one of a few prose poems that Barnard appears to have been writing at the time (the others being "Ash-Thursday" and "The King's Mistress," both of which she appeared to give, as with "Bay Beach," to her friend Mildred Cline—see *MC*). While Barnard wrote prose fiction, she did not publish any prose poetry. However, while interesting for its formal departure from her usual style, "Bay Beach" contains images and ideas that were to become key to Barnard's later published poems. The "abandoned wharf, and the piling [which] marches out into the bay, bearing tumbled / shack at the head of its column" anticipates images of "the piling lengthening its stroke / Where ground slopes riverward" and "The broken column stands against cloud / As though an abandoned wharf extended into wind" of "The Trestle," first published in 1938, then in 1940 as "Logging Trestle" in *CC*. The image of the "thin tide" moving "without a whisper" anticipates the "stillness" of stream water "welling / Between grass blades" in the "quiet" under "Highway Bridge," also from *CC*, but also anticipates "The Spring" from *CP* in 1979 where "the water whispers [. . .] to moisten the thick-standing mint [. . .] a mere trickle still." The call to "Remember?" is central to "Dick" (later "Carillon"), first published in *AFP* in 1952: "Remember? / Remember wondering: oh what will the day bring?" See, also, note to L52 ("thick on the beach the pyres of the dead burned always") of Barnard's Book 1 of *TI*.

Ms/Ts: *U*

Cream
1932

Poem first appeared in *H* and, according to *BKNB*, was sent to Pound on 28 July 1934, along with all the other poems that appeared in *CV* (*College Verse*) (see "Aquarelle"). Of some interest is an unpublished love poem Barnard wrote around the same time, entitled, curiously, "To X______." The poem also takes the metaphor of cream as its starting point, but in this instance the object of attention is an unnamed princess (which Barnard marks with an accent, as below). Here is the opening:

> Your skin is cream
> In a gold glass,
> Princéss.
> But your hair is brass
> Like cymbals and bowls
> Polished to a red gleam.
> On either high cheek-bone
> Flutters an orange moth.
> With smoke blown
> Like incense from your lips [. . .] (*U*)

The poem ends with an image of a ship "rolled ashore in the sea-foam" to greet the princess—reminiscent of Barnard's recurrent fixation on Aphrodite's rising from foamy waves (see note to "The Fool's Serenade"—with mention of the "the emerald wave" and the likening of the foam to "plump white snow" reminiscent of the monarchical love scene in "North Window.") On one copy of the poem, which Bell has transcribed, Bell has written "Xenia K" at the foot of the first page—suggesting Xenia Kashavaroff, later Xenia Kashavaroff Cage (Mrs. John Cage), one of Barnard's friends from Reed. Archive copies exist of a touching exchange of sketches between Barnard and Cage, where it appears Barnard has sketched Kashavaroff Cage in imitation of the opening stanza, to which Kashavaroff Cage replied with her own take on the imitation.

Published text: *CV 2.1* 11.

Cupbearer
1932

   LBN on reverse of this poem gives the date of "May 3, 1932," in Barnard's hand. *PNC* gives the date of this poem as 5/3/32 (also annotated as such by Bell on the TS) and notes that the poem was sent to *Harper's Bazaar* in July 1932 (perhaps with "Against Lethe" and "Moonstone") and returned the following month. As the poem appeared in *H,* as did "Against Lethe," it's possible that Barnard sent out a clutch of her senior thesis poems upon graduation. See, also, Sappho's Fragment Four (Barnard's 37. "You know the place: then . . . ," reprinted in this volume, where Aphrodite—the "Cyprian"—is invited to fill gold cups with nectar), as well as the opening of the sixth fytte and Section II of the eighth fytte of *TIME*. Poem discussed in *SB/MBAI* 67–68 and 70–72.

Ms/Ts: *LBN*

"Fire, snow, and the night . . ."
1932

 PNC dates the poem as "Jan. 17, 1932," followed by the attribution "MB" and speculates "perhaps second stanza of Mood Shatula," a poem in *H*; nevertheless, both poems stand solidly as individual pieces. Poem discussed in *SB/MBAI* 67–74, 78–79, 82, and 89–90. There's also a typescript made available by Elizabeth J. Bell, which is slightly longer, with a different ending, and gives "gray day" (repeating on the earlier "one gray") in place of "common day." Here it is in full:

> Fire, snow, and the night
> Create a world
> Where two may come together.
> But violet, gold, and white
> Are one gray
> With the rain, the light,
> And the thawing snow.
> In the gray day
> We walk again remote,
> Hardly aware of that thin plaintive note
> Of memory, a colored cord to bind us.
>
>   (Ms/Ts: *U*)

 "violet, gold, and white"—colors associated with Aphrodite in Sappho's fragments, an allusion also made in "Departure," one of Barnard's poems in Sapphics that appears in Section II, and, partially perhaps, in "A cloud comes down . . ."

Ms/Ts: *LBN*

Knight-Errant
1932

 Named after the kind of Middle Ages knight associated with adventure, this poem appeared first in Barnard's *H*. See, also, note to "Cream."

Published text: *CV 2.1* 12.

Moonstone
1932

On the reverse of this poem in *LBN* the date of "June 16, 1932" is given in Barnard's hand. *PNC* dates the poem as "6/16/32" (although Bell's annotation on a copy of the *LBN* TS dates it two days later—"6/18/32"). As with some other poems of the period, Barnard sent the poem to *Harper's Bazaar* and *Ladies Home Journal* in July and December 1932 respectively from which it was swiftly returned (*PNC*). Poem listed in *MC*.

Ms/Ts: *LBN*

Shriek of Defiance
1932

PNC and Bell annotation on a copy of the *LBN* TS date the poem as "4/12/32," following Barnard's note on the back of the poem in *LBN* giving "April 12, 1932." The poem also appears in *H*, completed around the same time in Barnard's senior year at Reed. Poem discussed in *SB/MBAI* 56.

"Come, my songs" and "Let us" riff on lines from Pound's 1914 poems from *Blast* (such as "Salutation the Third" and "Come My Cantilations"); I am grateful to Ian F. Bell for this observation. Around the time of composition Barnard had been profoundly impressed by Pound's *Personae*, which included the *Blast* poems that she studied intently after reading "Homage to Sextus Propertius" in her third-year literature class at Reed (*AMH* 39). See, also, note to "Adonis Dying."

Ms/Ts: *LBN*

". . . Without whose untender criticism this book . . ."
1932

The double quotation marks and ellipses before and after the title are Barnard's. *PNC* dates the poem as 4/23/32 followed by the attribution "MB," adding "dated by author." First appeared in *H*.

"slight wind of your breath"—possible reference to some accounts of the destruction of the Tower of Babel, which attributed it to a wind sent by God.

Ms/Ts: *U*

Gourmand Before an Oyster Can
c. 1932

PNC notes that the poem was found on "3-holed notepaper" and suggests it could be a poem from 1932—as with other poems typed on the same notepaper with the same typeface, such as "Moonstone."

"Willapa"—Willapa Bay, situated on the east side of the Long Beach peninsula (on the opposite side to Ocean Park) once populated by oyster boats, which sold their produce at the bay's Oysterville. See, also, note to "An Evening by the Sea."

Ms/Ts: *U*

"My mind is a hall where walk . . ."
c. 1932
1932 was given for copyright registration. See note for "I found my grief."

Ms/Ts: *U*

Sonnet for Dorothy
c. 1932
Like "Fable" and "Fatigue," this is an early 1930s poem that Barnard may have given to her friend Mildred Cline (see *MC*); Bell dates a copy of the TS as 1932. It is more explicit than "Fatigue" in its romantic over-tones, and there is deployment of a foam image that recurs in several of Barnard's poems after Sappho (see note for "The Fool's Serenade"). A draft of the poem was included in the set Reynolds read in the autumn of 1930 (see note for "Impassioned Sonnet") where he "[l]iked the sestet better than the octet. That was all the comment on that one" (*MB/Parents*, 27 October 1930).

"Dorothy"—while it is uncertain who this is, Barnard knew at least three Dorothys at this time, Dorothy Blair, Dorothy Johansen (who grad-uated from Reed in 1933 and was Reed Professor of History 1934–1984), and Dorothy Wikelund (Barnard's roommate and friend who graduated from Reed in 1929). Both Johansen and Wikelund (known as Dorothy Gill) were members of the Gawd-Awful poetry group at Reed, along with Barnard, whose early poems such as "The Carver" first appeared in their anthology *G* (see *JS/MB*, *Reed Magazine*, February 2003, inside of cover page and *SB/MBAI* 23).

A further, but perhaps less accomplished, poem addressed to Dorothy exists from around the same time, entitled "To Dorothy, in Autumn," which speaks of the connection between the speaker and Dorothy in more emboldened terms, ("Doro, I want the rare, sweet wine your hand / Alone can give to me. I want you near.") See, also, note to "Letter from the Country."

Ms/Ts: *U*

Estuary
c. 1932–1934

Bell's annotations on the TS speculate that this poem is from 1932 or 1934 (with 1934 given for copyright registration); the style suggests it is perhaps a little later—it is certainly in keeping with the cool, restrained, imagistic temper of the poems of *CC* yet appears with a typescript and on paper associated with Barnard's early 1930s work. In its examination of the estuary as a subject for poetry (as signaled by the "silent pencil" of the boat mast that "inscribes the cloud"), the poem foreshadows, but is distinct from, the third section of "The River Under Different Lights" (undated), entitled "The Estuary," which appeared in *CP* 23.

Ms/Ts: *U*

Alms
1933

An early foray into free verse by Barnard, this love poem first appeared in *H* and was among those sent to Pound on 28 July 1934 (see note to "Cream" above).

Published text: *CV 2.6* 17.

Bay Road
1933

Another early example of Barnard's free verse, its focus on the Northwest landscape anticipatory of the style she would cultivate for *CC*. It was also sent to Pound on 28 July 1934 (see note to "Cream" above). Published alongside "Blanchefleur" and "Inspiration."

Published text: *CV 2.7* 18.

Inspiration
1933

Also a free verse love poem, a version of "Inspiration" appeared in *H* and was in the group sent to Pound on 28 July 1934 (see note to "Cream" above). Published alongside "Blanchefleur" and "Bay Road."

Published text: *CV 2.7* 17.

Raimon the Singer
1933

Poem first appeared in *H* and also sent to Pound on 28 July 1934 (see note to "Cream" above). The images of "the Queen," riding at night by horseback, and shore scenes anticipate the more abstracting character of "Lai" with its "queens who ride fast along dark roads" amid the "furtive song in the spread foam."

"Raimon the singer"—one of the French troubadour poets, possibly Raimon de Miraval or Peire Raimon de Tolosa.

"chrysolite"—mineral, yellow-green in color.

Published text: *CV 2.3* 16–17.

Reverdie
1933

On the reverse of this poem in the *LBN* the date is given as "June 23, 1933," in Barnard's hand. *PNC* dates the poem as "6/23/33." Barnard noted in *BKNB* that the poem was "Sent to Gerschefski" (see note to "Roots").

Ms/Ts: *LBN*

Uninspired to the Uninspiring
1933

PNC records the following "dated by MB 4/16/33."

This is a small poem and yet it draws on many of Barnard's Ocean Park experiences, its images and thread of narrative reflecting Barnard's descriptions of domestic fire-making when staying with her friends in "Utopia" (see note to "An Evening by the Sea"). One letter recounts: "This evening I tried my hand at making a fire in the kitchen stove—the first time. The other girls have been struggling to learn ever since they have been down here + with almost unfailing unsuccess [*sic*]. My first fire burned—went whooping up the chimney, in fact, + when complimented, I said 'Oh, well, I guess I wouldn't be my father's daughter if I couldn't make a fire burn!'" (*MB/Parents*, date unknown). Another letter records a day that began with clamming from 4.30 a.m., cleaning "the little diggers" up for a noontime clam stew, dozing and lazing around in the dunes in the afternoon, having dinner then going "back out on the dune to watch the sunset," before Barnard enacted the kind of listless scene captured in the poem: "I went for a walk on the beach + Jane + Mildred eventually fell asleep by the fire, while Jo went to bed, I got a candle + sat down on the hearth + wrote two poems. One is pretty bad I fear + the other one is not so worse but bad enough. It is something to write anything though" (*MB/Parents*, date unknown).

"green wood"—Barnard revised this from "wet wood."

"Were I not so convincingly green"—a feeling Barnard carried around quite heavily in her years in metropolitan New York. "I was still so green that

I had not yet learned why people stand up at cocktail parties. I sat down and was immediately trapped by a woman poet who had had a bit too much scotch and wanted to tell me the story of her life," she remarked of "the first and last time" she went to a party in 1941 hosted by anthologist Oscar Williams, for example (*AMH* 194).

See, also, note to 134 ("the many-voiced sea") of Barnard's *TI*. Poem listed in *MC*.

Ms/Ts: *U*

"A cloud comes down . . ."
1934
PNC dates this poem as from 1934, with this year also given for copyright registration. Possibly an early version of "In Praise of Potted Plants," but *PNC* also speculates that it may be a later version of an older poem/older two poems Barnard wrote about clouds, respectively "Clouds" from 1926–1927 and "Sunset Clouds" from 1927 (no copies of these poems have been found). Poem appears in *MC*, where it is listed in the contents by its first two lines ("A cloud comes down Like the purple lid of a box" [*sic*]). See, also, comments for "The Carver" and, with reference to the color play in this poem, the note to "Fire, snow, and the night. . . ."

Ms/Ts: *U*

For a Collection of Suburbiana
1934
PNC gives the following: "dated by author 3/22/34" and "Astoria housewife of 12 children," suggesting that it may have been inspired, to some extent, by a true story in Barnard's locale.

Ms/Ts: *U*

Letter from the Country
1934
PNC dates the poem as "1/26/34." The poem foreshadows the ways in which Barnard's later *CC* poems would attribute human qualities and dramas to the landscape, here reaching towards traditional form before a more concerted shift into free verse. While not quite a sonnet, it's useful to note that Barnard was experimenting with sonnets around this time particularly in relation to poems that explored college social life such as "Laughter" and "The Late Party"

(to be found in her papers) as well as (in more romantic tones) "Sonnet for Dorothy," printed in this volume.

Ms/Ts: *U*

Fable
c. 1934

While there is no clear date for this poem, it's one of many poems that Barnard appeared to give to her friend Mildred Cline in the early 1930s (see *MC*). Barnard also sent it to T. C. Wilson and Genevieve Taggard for comment in the summer of 1934 (with 1934 given for copyright registration). Poem also titled "Fable of a Career."

"she hashed and learned"—this refers to Barnard's time as a student at Reed College, Portland, Oregon, 1928–1932, an experience detailed in Barnard's *AMH* 31–42, including that of her last two years as the Depression hit of "hashing three meals a day"—waiting tables in order to cover her board (*AMH* 45) because, as she told one of her professors, " '[m]y father is in the lumber business, if that means anything to you.' And he said, 'Oh!!! He's lucky he's not hashing himself, or washing dishes!' " (*EA* 18).

"commons"—dining hall at Reed College.

"Buttercup"—possibly a reference to a nickname for Barnard at Reed, as indicated in a note to her by her college friend Xenia Kashavaroff (see note to "Cream"); in the homonymic play, there's a clear connection to another version of apprentice-poet self, the "Butterfly" who appears two lines later.

"Butterfly, she overturned / the pedagogic juggernaut"—a reference to Barnard's choice to submit a creative thesis in place of a critical thesis at Reed College where "the very few creative theses in the past had been disappointing" (*AMH* 40). Titled "The Horae of Mary Ethel Barnard" (*H*), the thesis bucked the trend and was described by Professor Rex Arragon as "A beautiful example of the pedagogic juggernaut being overturned by a butterfly" (*AMH* 42). See, also, note to "Confessional."

"lamp her"—Barnard annotated this with an asterisk on the original manuscript, noting "First version: 'Behold her.' Changed out of deference to E. P.'s remarks."

"She wrote to Ezra"—a reference to the beginnings of Barnard's lifelong correspondence with Pound, at her instigation, in the autumn of 1933: "I decided that Pound was the poet I wanted to write to" Barnard wrote in *AMH* (52).

"Light [. . .] / Leaps the timorous gazelle"—a reference to Pound's response to Barnard's concern at the "lightness" of her poetry: "Don't worry about LIGHTNESS," Pound wrote; "shall the gazelle mimic the hippo / 'be yerrsellf!'" (*AMH* 69–70; see also *SB/MBAI* 26). It was a persona Barnard also used to describe herself in comparison to Marianne Moore. "I think Miss Moore is with me," Barnard told her parents, referring to her sense of feeling a lack of experience of the world and its impact on her poems, "but she obviously thinks I don't use my head enough or to good enough purpose (vide 'extended thinking') [*sic*] I admit the defect but still enjoy being a gazelle" (*MB/Parents*, 5 June 1936).

"Parnassian wild"—reference to Mount Parnassus, the sacred Greek mountain said to be the home of poetry, literature, and art. See, also, Barnard's "Ursus Parnassius" and "Two Visits."

Ms/Ts: *U*

Drama
c. 1934

BKNB notes that a poem called "Drama" was sent to Pound on 28 July 1934—it may be this version, or the version that appeared in *CC*, but a definitive answer has yet to be found. See, also, note to the *CC* poem entitled "Drama" that appears earlier in this volume.

"After a statement of no consequence"—this is correctly punctuated (i.e., no question mark is given at the end of the sentence where this appears, which begins with "And I ask him").

"We sweat"—Barnard's TS gives this as "we sweating," which appears to be a typo. With thanks to Ellen K, Stauder for assistance with this correction.

Ms/Ts: LBN

Beyond Medusa
1935

This poem was part of a group of fourteen selected for *WQ* (where it was reprinted) but presented here as it first appeared alongside "Cassandra" and "Lethe" in *NEW*. *BKNB* notes that Barnard sent the poem to Pound the year prior to its publication on 28 July 1934 and also to T. C. Wilson on 31 August 1934. On Barnard's contributor's copy of *WQ* it appears she has made several corrective annotations in black ink to this poem, which appears on page 30—so "Beyond Meduca" is given as the title, but the erroneous "c" is amended to "s"; in St 3, L2, the vowels in "Found" have been clarified; and in the last line of the poem an erroneous "e" added to the end of

"Eyes" has been crossed through. *WQ* version also gives "carven" as "cavern" (see, also, notes to "Chanson Pathetique" and "Lament from the Shores of the Boorzh-wah Zee").

Amid Barnard's unpublished poems held by Bell, a shorter (almost certainly earlier given the appearance of the TS) version exists, reproduced here by way of comparison:

Beyond Medusa

I stared beyond the mask that petrifies
Into the living eyes,
Which, starred with beauty and sorrow,
Woke my own.
Sickening, I felt my blood released
From the cold stone
And sensed in flesh fragility of bone,
And hair moving.
Now am I sure the mouth
Behind the writhed mask is sweetly bent,
And the eyes dearly known.
I have learned transformation, not
What these things meant.

Ms/Ts: *U*

Published text: *NEW* 354 and *WQ* 30.

Cat
1935

As with "Beyond Medusa," this poem was part of a group of fourteen selected for *WQ*—and similarly afflicted by copy error. Here, the second line, "When she handled them" is erroneously presented in *WQ* in the wrong tense, thus "When she handle them." The editor has corrected this, making what is presented here in line with the version as transcribed by Bell from a handwritten copy once in the possession of Thomas J. Donovan, a good friend of Barnard's.

Published text: *WQ* 31.

Dormitory
1935

As with "Beyond Medusa" and "Cat," this poem was part of a group of fourteen selected for *WQ*. Again, the poem is affected by copy error: St 1, L 12 in *WQ* version gives "curled" as "curltd." As with "Cat," an editorial correction has been made, again, presented in line with how this line is given in a version as transcribed by Bell from a handwritten copy once in the possession of Thomas J. Donovan.

"Joinville"—Jean de Joinville, French author famous for his biography of Louis IX (*Histoire de Saint-Louis*) whom Joinville accompanied on the Seventh Crusade to Egypt (1248–1254), chronicled in detail in the book.

Published text: *WQ* 31.

Lament from the Shores of the Boorzh-wah Zee
1935

Another poem part of a group of fourteen selected for *WQ*. On Barnard's contributor's copy of *WQ* it appears that in St 3, L1 she has crossed out "seeing" between "this" and "life"; thus "A little more of this seeing life" becomes "A little more of this life." I have gone with Barnard's correction, not least because she has corrected several apparent typos and mistakes on this copy (see, also, notes to "Beyond Medusa" and "Chanson Pathetique.") In *MB/IC* the title of this poem was spelled slightly differently, with "Boorzh-Wah" given as "Bouzh-wah" (thus "Lament from the Shores of the Bouzh-wah Zee").

Published text: *WQ* 30.

Lyonesse Sub Mare
1935

Another poem part of a group of fourteen selected for *WQ*. As with "Cat" and "Dormitory," an editorial correction has been made, again, with commas restored to St 2, L1 and L2, presented in line with how this line is given in a version as seemingly typed by Barnard found amid *MB/TD*.

Published text: *WQ* 31–32.

Study
1935

Another poem part of a group of fourteen selected for *WQ*.

Published text: *WQ* 30–31.

Trefoil
1935

Another poem part of a group of fourteen selected for *WQ*. See, also, note to "Blanchefleur," which includes a note about the group this poem appeared in that was sent to Marianne Moore for comment. *MB/IC* says it was previously sent to *Hound and Horn* and *Yale Review* in 1933 (returned).

Published text: *WQ* 30.

"Waiting for a waning moon to rise . . ."
c. 1935

PNC dates the poem as 1935 but also says it's from *MC,* which collates slightly earlier work—nevertheless, it's typical, in its style, of Barnard's early 1930s debt to her studies of the troubadours and the Greek lyric poets at Reed, while also evocative of the kind of Imagism she was developing in her initial years corresponding with Pound.

Ms/Ts: *U*

Of Possession
c. 1935–1938

PNC dates the poem as "1935 EB" (referencing Bell), although Bell has given two other dates on two sets of TS, which respectively date it as 1937 and 1938. It's also possible that the poem was included in the MS given to publisher Florence Codman, of Arrow Editions, in 1936, at Codman's request when Barnard first arrived in New York in the spring of 1936 (see *AMH* 90–92). In a letter to Pound of 15 April 1938, Barnard wrote: "I think you must have misinterpreted the poem about the man and his hat. It's a pity that a lady poet can't use a masculine pronoun without being suspected of romantic urges. It was inspired by my relief clients in general, and an Old Age Pensioner in particular" (*MB/EP*; Barnard worked as a social worker for the Emergency Relief Administration, intermittently, between 1934 and 1937). *PNC* furnishes some interesting wider context: noting that it was "also called 'The Pensioner,'" Bell writes that the poem tells a "story with a similar theme: possibly <u>The Shadow</u> [*sic*]," referring to a short story of that name published in *Harper's Bazaar* in 1946 as one of Barnard's "Boundary Stories" (*BTS*). Omitted from the published version of "The Shadow"—a mystery story concerning a woman who loses part of her memory—is the protagonist's reflection on hats and the nature of the human condition, which bears strong resemblance to the narrative and emotional arc of "Of Possession." The deleted reflection is excerpted here for reference:

She remembered a man's hat. An old man, worn and humble and nervous about the business he had to do with her, laid his hat on the desk as he sat down. It was a very old hat, and, as her eyes fell on it, she read its history in the uneven brim, the soiled spots and creases, dents, bulges, weather. Her memory, playing tricks again, had claimed it for her own. She had taken it down from a nail (she could see the nail, and the board beside the kitchen door where the nail was driven) morning after morning, until, if a new hat hung there, she would not know this herself. She remembered the rainy days that had run off its brim and the August sun from which it had shaded her eyes. She felt the sweat of the lumber yards and the freight yards that had soaked into its band. She had taken it off in deference to people who sat behind desks as she sat. She had fumbled its brim with her fingers as he did now, while humbly, nervously asking for help.

Oh my dear, she wanted to say, how can I help you when I <u>am</u> [*sic*] you. (*TSMS*)

"Who, living at once within and without, / Wears"—Barnard's TS omits a comma after "without"; error corrected by the editor.

Ms/Ts: *U*

The Colored Stone
c. 1935–1939
PNC first dated the poem as "1937," subsequently crossed out in favor of "12/3/39 dated in *BKKNB* by MB" (*BKKNB* assumed to be *BKNB*). Bell has circled on one TS version of the poem "Dec 3, 1937," an annotation apparently by Barnard on the overleaf to the poem; on another TS, Bell has written "1935." *BKNB* notes that the poem was sent to Pound on 15 January 1938, as well as to other mentors in early 1938, including Babette Deutsch and Williams. On the TS with Bell's "1935" annotation, it's possible that this is from the MS that Barnard gave to Florence Codman (see note to "Of Possession," above). Parts of this manuscript seem to have been preserved—if scattered—within Barnard's archive. Barnard showed a version of this manuscript to Marianne Moore but also Williams, who told her he thought it heralded the beginning of her best work (see *AMH* 91). In this selection, "Of Possession" was on pages 17–18 of the manuscript and "Ursus Parnassius" on page 51. All three poems are laid out in the same way, with "Mary Barnard, Vancouver, Wash." in the upper left corner, and, with the exception of "Ursus Parnassius," "Unpub." in the bottom left.

Ms/Ts: *U*

Cold Heaven
1936

First published in *ND* 193, reprinted in the same year in *ND ONE* (no page). *PNC* suggests the poem was written on 2 January 1936, directing the reader to the "Blue Diary." *BKNB* notes that the poem was sent to Pound on 20 January 1936, along with other poems that appeared in *ND* the next month ("Provincial," "Epicure," "Mechanism," and "A Defense of the Poet's Method"). The poem also appeared on the back page of a letter sent to Barnard's parents of 31 August 1938 (see *MB/Parents*). Poem appears in *LBN*. The second stanza reads partly like an anticipation of the final stanzas of both "Height Is the Distance Down" and "The Rock of Levkas."

Published text: *ND* 193.

Curly Locks
1936

First published in *ND*. In the second stanza there appears to be a grammatical error; "Somewhere there are" can be followed by "Very high rocks" but not "Very cold rain." *BKNB* notes that the poem was on a list of poems titled "sent to Rapallo."

Published text: *ND* 193.

Eavesdropper
1936

First published in *ND*. A draft took the first line as a title—"The room is full of a sour foliage"—and offered a slightly expanded set of last lines, thus:

> The slurring sibilant answers heard
> Through an open doorway. Quieter.
> Quieter. Coals whisper together. Do
> Coals also kiss?

(Ms/Ts: *U*)

"Eavesdropper" was never subsequently collected and may well have been revised into "In Praise of Potted Plants," published in *CC*—for further discussion of the significance of this, please see the note to "In Praise of Potted Plants."

Published text: *ND* 194.

Epicure
1936

Poem appears in *MC. BKNB* notes that the poem sent to Pound on 20 January 1936, along with other poems that were published with it in *ND* ("Provincial," "Cold Heaven," "Mechanism," and "A Defense of the Poet's Method.")

Published text: *ND* 193.

Mechanism
1936

BKNB notes that the poem was sent to Pound on 20 January 1936, along with other poems that appeared with it in *ND* the next month ("Provincial," "Epicure," "Cold Heaven," and "A Defense of the Poet's Method").

Published text: *ND* 193.

North Window
1936

PNC dates the poem as "Feb. 4, 1936, by MB."

Poem discussed extensively in *SB/MBAI* (see 5–8, 17, 21, 27–29, 33–34, 54, 69, 78, and 136).

Ms/Ts: *U*

Point of Departure
1936

Although published shortly before Barnard's first trip to New York, the second stanza of this poem is remarkably prescient of the kind of nomadic lifestyle experienced on her second trip (from which she didn't immediately return West) in 1938. There, after Barnard's mother had empathized "'how deadly dull it is for you'" in Vancouver (*AMH* 116), Barnard experienced a housing crisis. She was put up by several friends from Reed and Yaddo and ended up sleeping a good while on a folding bed courtesy of her Reed friends, window-dressers Charlotte and Rex Heaton-Sessions, who lived on West 23rd Street. "They were in a loft," Barnard recalled, "most of which was their display studio, with their (illegal) living quarters at one end and the office, containing a desk, filing cabinets, and a telephone, at the other" (*AMH* 130).

Published text: *ND* 193.

The Silk Leaf
1936

"salal"—waxy evergreen plant native to the Pacific Northwest coast.

This poem was not reprinted in book form; it appears as it did upon publication alongside "Without Benefit of Tragedy" in *AP* whose introduction namechecks Barnard and fellow poet-contributor Kenneth Patchen as "two of the outstanding young American poets" (*AP* 50). Poem discussed in *SB/MBAI* 34, 108; appears in *MC*. See, also, note to "An Evening by the Sea."

Published text: *AP* 61.

Tourist
1936

Poem appears in *MC*. The poem perhaps conveys some of the frustration that Barnard felt in the years after graduating from Reed around balancing writing with the need for an income. Certainly some of Barnard's early correspondence complained to Pound of such tensions as found in the last stanza, where the keen traveler to the "resort" of poetry "frequently does not arrive, / And never stays as long as she planned to." "Dear Mr. Pound," she wrote six months into their correspondence, "I had not intended to send you any Sapphics until I had written more of them, but a job has descended upon my neck [. . .] I'll not be writing Sapphics for a little while" (*MB/EP*, 1 April 1934). A fortnight later Pound was telling her to write them anyway—and that she should also try translating Catullus, too, for good measure—barking "NO 'job' (if by that you mean money earning) can use 24 hours a day of yr/ time/" (*AMH* 58). In a letter of 28 July 1934, Barnard rejoindered "[m]y job lasted three months, and maybe you could write sapphics after working in the bedlam of a relief office for even eight hours, but I can't. Like every other indigent college student I turned social worker and budgeted for shoes and potatoes," (*MB/EP*).

Published text: *ND* 194.

Without Benefit of Tragedy
1936

"The Eumenides"—play by Aeschylus (c. 525–455 BC), the third part of a series of Greek tragedy plays.

This poem was not reprinted in book form; it appears as it did upon publication, alongside "The Silk Leaf," in *AP*.

Published text: *AP* 61.

Ursus Parnassius
c. 1937

  LBN on reverse of this poem gives the date of "Aug. 19, 1937," in Barnard's hand. *PNC* dates it as "8/14/3Z MB" (underlining Bell's—with an August 14 date as opposed to Barnard's August 19) but also specifies a "slightly different version 1/15/38 sent to EP (Bk. N.B.)" ("Bk. N.B." assumed to be *BKNB*). However, as with "Of Possession" and "The Colored Stone," the poem was possibly included in the MS given to Florence Codman in 1936 (see note for "The Colored Stone"). Sent to Pound on 10 February 1937 and to Williams in January 1938.

  "Ursus"—Latin name for bear.

  "Parnassius"—a type of butterfly. However, the wider context suggests that, unusually, this may be a typo and that Barnard meant to write "Parnassus," as featured in "Fable." This latter reading is supported by comparing the poem to a much later poem, "Two Visits," especially the second part entitled "E.P.: Sant'Ambrogio, 1964." There, Pound is overtly situated "standing high, high on Parnassus."

  "Ursus Parnassius"—a more playful interpretation is to read the possible typo on Mount Parnassus as a deliberate slip. If, in "Fable," Barnard presents herself as a "butterfly" who "overturned / The pedagogic juggernaut," and in "Two Visits" specifies "*we* were standing high, high on Parnassus" (italics mine), then perhaps Barnard intended to compound the bear/Pound persona ("Ursus") with the butterfly/Barnard persona ("Parnassius"). That is, the title both evokes Mount Parnassus *and* Barnard and Pound's poetic kinship.

Ms/Ts: *LBN*

"The slenderly poised clean shaft of your fir . . ."
c. 1937–1938

  Bell suggests, in an annotation on a copy of the TS, that the poem is possibly from 1937, which would make it shortly after Barnard left the Northwest in 1936 to meet poets in New York; this estimate would certainly fit with the poem's content of a significant departure. However, it's perhaps more likely that the poem was from 1938 or afterwards—Barnard's initial trip in 1936 took her via California and New Orleans by train, then up to New York by sea (*AMH* 82). Barnard's next trip "contrarily eastward" was to Yaddo in 1938, via a "long train journey (three days and three nights) from the West Coast" (*AMH* 120). Regardless, the 1937–1938 estimate is sound enough if we consider the poem's form. While the content evokes the mood and narratives of Barnard's 1934–1935 Sapphic exercises (see later notes to "Tranquil and shallow, spread across the flat stones . . ." and "A Defense of the

Poet's Method"), there is also discernible use of the balanced line that Barnard was refining in free verse following her experiments into Greek quantity, as in poems published over 1937–1938 such as "Logging Trestle" (metrics discussed in *SB/W*) and "Roots" (metrics discussed in *SB/MBAI* 109–110). Poem discussed in *SB/MBAI* 83. See, also, note to "Inheritance."

"Great Northern rails"—company that owned the western railroad that ran from Seattle through to St. Paul in Minnesota from the late 1880s through to 1970, when it underwent merger. Barnard rode its passenger train, the Empire Builder, which ran between Chicago and Seattle, as part of her journeying between east and west. It was during a free afternoon in Chicago in July 1936 waiting for the midnight departure for Seattle that Barnard called up Harriet Monroe in the *Poetry* office and met her for the first time, having dinner with her that evening before traveling home (*AMH* 108).

"Wind River"—thirty-mile-long tributary off the Columbia River, WA.

Ms/Ts: *U*

Altitude
c. 1937–1940

Dates differ across different TSs and *PNC* but place the poem within the late 1930s. One of several poems Barnard wrote drawing on the Columbia River Gorge landscape (see *PNC*), a huge river canyon that, in Barnard's locale, divides Washington from Oregon. Like Ocean Park, this northwestern geographical feature formed the backdrop to Barnard's formative years. The sense of experiencing the world from a gorge-induced height is a recurrent motif in Barnard's poetry (see, for example, "Height Is the Distance Down" in *AFP*, which also references the "altitude" of this poem's title, as well as "The Rock of Levkas," as well as "The Gorge," "The Pump," and "The River Under Different Lights" in *CP*).

"congoleum"—manufacturer of linoleum and other floor coverings.

A tantalizing, former last line of this poem reads: "The more lonely, the more comradely they are." As *PNC* noted, this line has been "crossed out lightly with question mark"; it's not too hard to see why—for Barnard, it approaches overstatement, rather than the characteristic restraint of other poems at this time, but nonetheless emphasizes the theme of loneliness that courses through so many of her poems. *PNC* also records an entry in *JSN*, which reads "2/20/38 Tried again to revise Altitude," suggesting that Barnard struggled with it to some extent.

Ms/Ts: *U*

Road to Xanadu
1939

Poem submitted, unsuccessfully, to *Furioso* on 8 May 1939, with a letter declaring "My own productions are always pianissimo, but I hope you'll find something you like in the inclosed [*sic*] group" (*MB/F*). *Furioso* was established in 1939 by two Yale undergraduates, James Angleton and Reed Whittemore, at Pound's encouragement. Along with *Poetry, The Nation, New Republic,* and *Partisan Review, Furioso* was a periodical that Barnard saw as having modernist sympathies and, like the others, they were similarly receptive to her work, publishing "In Praise of Potted Plants," "Prometheus Loved Us," and "The Rapids" in 1940 and "Inheritance" in 1947 before the magazine ended in 1953. Barnard appears to have attempted to revise this poem much later in her career; a version of it appears in an undated, but more modern typescript (possibly word-processed as opposed to typed), along with a draft of the final section of what was to become "The River Under Different Lights." Barnard comments at the foot of the manuscript: "Note. The fish [in the final section] are from last fall somewhat revised. The peas [in "Road to Xanadu"] are my favourite but not polished up yet. Middle section isn't right." Barnard never did publish either version of this poem. Poem discussed in *SB/MBAI* 113–14.

Ms/Ts: *MB/F*

Fire
1940

Early versions of this poem began "Clouds turn the light to lizard" or were titled "Forest Fire," the latter a poem Barnard sent to Williams and discussed in *AMH* 178. *PNC* notes that the TS for this poem includes Barnard's Buffalo address (16 Winspear Ave., Buffalo, NY). "Fire," as *PNC* goes on to note, is the name of one of the fables in *TF* that Barnard went on to publish first as a sequence in *The Kenyon Review* in 1948 then as a book in 1983 (published by Breitenbush Books). The poem evokes the Judeo-Christian prophecy of the lion and the lamb, and the place of children in leading the way to peace, as recounted in the Bible, with Barnard's line "[t]hey shall lie down together" a direct allusion to Isaiah 11:6. See, also, note to L52 ("thick on the beach the pyres of the dead burned always") of Barnard's *TI* and the tenth fytte of *TIME* ("The shepherd will pipe to his sheep / and the lion will lie down beside them"). Poem explored as an example of a late Imagist war poem in *SB/P.* See, also, the poem "Low Tide," which appears in the note to "Height Is the Distance Down" as well as the note to "Convalescence."

Ms/Ts: *U*

Convalescence
1943–1944

PNC dates the poem as from 1944, yet Barnard told her parents that it was a poem she started on her birthday in a letter of 15 December 1943 (*MB/ Parents*; Barnard's birthday was December 6). As with "The Accounting," (see below), Barnard gives her New York Minetta Street address in the upper left corner of the typescript for this poem. During the fall of 1943 Barnard experienced some strenuous dental work, which likely furnished the frame narrative of this poem. It was during this time she was attending a reading series organized by May Sarton at the New York Public Library, which seemed so vital that even a debilitating session at the dentist wasn't to deter Barnard from attending. At the after party to a reading by Reuel Denney and Kenneth Patchen, Barnard recounted to her parents how "I was having chills, so I wore my fur coat even if it was a bit unseasonable" and how "I was supporting myself with sherry and cigarettes and mostly wishing I'd never been born" when she was introduced to: "a very nice young man in uniform who turned out to be Selden Rodman, poet, anthologist, and once editor of Common Sense, and now with the army air force, and stationed of all places at the University of Buffalo. He has, of course, been seeing Mr. Abbott, and the poetry collection, and says he has decided to give his collection of letters" (*MB/Parents*, 31 October 1943). This entwinement of painful dentistry with reminders of war may account for the surprising way that the poem tips into social critique. The references to "the world's death," "those that did not die," and the idea of "the soul's crisis"—along with the idea of waking "Years after" suggests a kind of meditation on World War Two, resonant with the oblique way the American experience of it is rendered in Barnard's late Imagist war poem "Fire" (see note above). After all, Barnard wrote of the May Sarton reading series, which triggered this encounter with Rodman, that: "Interest in modern poets and poetry had quickened during the war years, whether because of the war or not, I do not know; perhaps nobody knows, but it is at least probable. Poetry is more easily portable, in the pocket or in the mind, than the novel; and the concentrated, more intense form suited the need of the times" (*AMH* 211).

Barnard made the following amendments in ink on the TS to the last stanza:

"Always with Pain"—appears in the TS with "Pain" as uncapitalized.

"in his clasp"—this originally appears in the TS as "to his night," thus the last line first read "Years after, to his night, at daybreak." Barnard appears to be referencing the clasp of the dentist's tools.

Ms/Ts: *U*

The Accounting
c. 1943–1957

While there's no date given by Barnard on the TS of the poem, she does give her long-term New York address ("5 Minetta Street, New York City 12"). It was in this Greenwich Village apartment where Barnard was resident, as *PNC* notes, between 1943 and 1957, with time away for traveling and, in the early 1950s, recuperation at her parents' northwestern home after a serious bout of illness. Bell dates a copy of the TS as 1944.

Ms/Ts: *U*

Crossroads
1944

Published text: *Poetry* 63.5 (February 1944): 263; (later *CP* 56) **Differences from *CP*:** *Poetry* version has initial capitals at the start of run-on lines. *CP* version replaced "place"—in the first line of the third stanza—with "spot."

Preacher
No date; post-1963

This poem is followed by a note on the manuscript copy: "June 3/Really June 2, after reading TLS review of Poet in Exile." *Poet in Exile* was a book on Pound by Noel Stock, published in 1963; *TLS* refers to British periodical the *Times Literary Supplement*.

"at the end of the garden path"—see Barnard's account of her discussions with Pound on the lawn at St Elizabeths in *AMH* 264–67, which may be the inspiration for the setting of this poem. It was during the course of two visits on such lawn, over a long weekend of fine weather in October 1949 following Barnard's first trip to Italy, that Barnard was inspired by Pound to begin a new project, *A Pagan's Guide to Italian Frescoes*. Planning to include around ten essays, each on a different painter of frescoes painted in situ in Italy between 1435 and 1505, inspired by her own trip following Pound's itinerary, Barnard intended the work as a kind of cultural recuperation for American travelers like herself. "The world which the paintings mirrored has vanished," wrote Barnard in the work's introduction, "and the modern American tourist, usually a pagan, barbarian, or heretic by Quattrocento standards, is imperfectly acquainted with the stories illustrated on the walls. This book is intended to extend the capacity of intelligent, generally educated traveller for this kind of enjoyment his predecessors could take for granted" (*APGIF* 1). It was an important work for Barnard. "Of course Pound was always thinking up projects for people, most of them completely unsuitable, and I may as well say at once that nothing came of this one, so far as publication went," recalled Barnard, "but it was a god-send to me at the moment, when the impetus that had carried me through several years of fiction-writing had failed, and the impetus towards poetry had not returned" (*AMH* 266). See, also, note to "Eternal She."

Ms/Ts: *U*

Travel Notes
1982

Subsequently published in *The Prescott Street Reader*, ed. Vi Gale (Portland, OR: Prescott Street Press, 1995), 128–29.

"John Montague at Carron"—Montague was an Irish poet, translator, and writer (1929–2016); Carron (also Carran) is a small, rural village in Clare County in "the West of Ireland," to quote L7 of the poem. Montague is mentioned in Barnard's correspondence with Myrna and Erik Haugaard, the American-Danish writer couple who later relocated to Ireland and whom Barnard appears to have visited—perhaps generating the material for this poem that, she told John Sheehy in a letter of 19 October 1981, was the only poem she had written since the 1979 publication of *CP* (*MB/JS*). In a letter of 9 February 1981, Barnard informed the Haugaards of her plan to visit Ireland that summer, with her friend Claudia Lewis, "a specialist in children's literature and an admirer of Erik's work," while also enclosing a draft of "Travel Notes," of which Barnard said:

> I wrote [it] last summer. It has been rejected by Atlantic, New Yorker, Poetry, American Scholar, and has now gone to Cincinnati Poetry Review, which has asked for something for a special issue featuring Elliston Award Winners. I wrote to John Montague and sent him a copy, asking for permission to use his name. I know that his poem and book-title "The Poisoned Lands" must have been in the back of [my mind] when I was writing it, and I felt that was in order, but not if he thought it was a bad poem. (*MB/MEH*)

Clearly, Montague did not think that and the poem was accepted by *Cincinnati Poetry Review*. It's possible that Barnard met Montague in Ireland in the summer of 1979 at a creative writing workshop at New Quay, County Clare. "I've never taken part in one of these things (the country is lousy with them, of course), but this interests me," Barnard told Myrna Haugaard in a letter of 17 February 1979 when trying to make arrangements to call in at the Haugaards' further south in Balleydehob after the workshop, adding "[s]ome Irish writers are invited to read and discuss their works (Kinsella, John Montague and Benedict Kiely" *(MB/MEH)*. So far, the editor has been unable to verify if the visit eventually took place, but researchers are directed to the Mary Barnard Papers at the Yale Beinecke Library, which includes some of Barnard's travel diaries as well as the *MB/MEH* correspondence.

"But I have been here before, / not in Ireland, in Greece"—Barnard first traveled to Greece in 1953, where she spent the winter, having that summer finished the first full draft of her *Sappho* (see *AMH* 288–89).

"stony hills of the Burren and Attica"—the Burren is an Irish national park in County Clare, known for its rockiness (the etymology of "Burren" comes from the Irish word for "rocky place"); Attica is the Greek peninsula where Athens is situated.

"masonry like that of Mycenae"—the ancient Greek civilization of the Myceneans, emanating from the city of Mycenae, was esteemed for its Cyclopean masonry, so named because of its use of gigantic stones (the belief being only a mythical creature as mighty as the Cyclops could have hoisted them into place).

Published text: *CPR* 47.

On Arriving
1987

Subsequently published in *OE* 73. See notes to "The Carver" and "Shoreline."

"Morton Zabel"—Morton Dauwen Zabel, poet, editor, and critic, who selected Barnard's "Shoreline" for *Poetry* making it her first—and much-desired—publication in *Poetry* in 1935. Zabel attended Yaddo at the same time as Barnard in her first residency there in 1936; her disappointment in meeting him, finally, after the exhilaration of breaking into national print because of him, is recalled with touching humor in *AMH* (106–107).

"Harriet"—Harriet Monroe (1860–1936), poet and founder and editor of *Poetry* who took a year away from *Poetry* over 1934–1935 to spend time in China.

"the Levinson"—Helen Haire Levinson Prize, which Barnard won in 1935. See, also, note to "Ondine."

Published text: *P* 1–2.

A Dedication
1999

This poem prefaces *EA* and, as such, is a fitting tribute to Barnard's alma mater, Reed College, and specifically the Old Dorm Block with its French medieval Gothic sally port entrance at the center (see https://www.reed.edu/ facilities_services/buildings/old-dorm-block.html, date last accessed 22 May 2024).

"those two knowing owls"—there is only one owl associated with Reed, the "Doyle owl," a large, concrete garden sculpture that rapidly became the unofficial college mascot (in place of the official griffin), the "theft," possession, and display of which has been the subject of much pranking over the years. The only "two" creatures above the Old Dorm sally port are, in fact, statues of beavers (signaling the college's locating in Oregon, the beaver state), who Barnard switches for owls here—either knowingly or unknowingly, for it appears that such mistakes of perception are fairly common in Reed mythology.

"Fat Nox and Lux smug in their stone cowls"—reference to other statues that flank the sally port, which point to the Old Dorm Block's purpose as a space for recreation and sleep. Grotesques on this building emphasize its use for recreation and sleep. Lux (meaning "light") is a figure who greets the day and Nox (meaning "night") displays closing eyes for sleep.

"Under the entrance light, under the sun dial"—renowned sun dial, just above the sally port to the Old Dorm Block.

Published text: *EA.*

POEMS INSPIRED BY SAPPHO

The Fool's Serenade
No date

Bell dates this poem as from 1930 on one copy of the TS. Poem discussed in *SB/MBAI* 66, 100.

"The foam upon the beach" and "A rose"—possible allusion to Aphrodite; see note to "Anadyomene." Foam is an image that appears in a range of Barnard's poems; see, for example, "The Pathetic Fallacy," "An Evening by the Sea," "Sonnet for Dorothy," "Ondine," "Storm," "Lai," "Departure," "The Rock of Levkas," and "The River Under Different Lights."

"And kissed its petals"—Barnard's original typescript reads "An kissed its petals"; typo corrected by the editor.

"petals.—Every poet knows"—punctuation retained as used by Barnard.

"But would you think the moon could throw a rose?"—Barnard's original TS contains this underlining, probably for emphasis; thus, it is duly retained.

See, also, note to L34 ("the many-voiced sea") of Barnard's *TI*.

Ms/Ts: *JUV*

"In the bridal . . ." (four fragments)
No date

These fragments appear together on a TS divided by the pen marks "X X X" in Barnard's hand, as retained here, with Barnard's name (also in pen) at the foot of the page. While the fragments do not directly match those that appear in *S* there are some links and resonances, for example, the first of four fragments beginning "In the bridal . . ." relates to Barnard's fragment 10, "Six out of seven stars" relates to Barnard's fragment 64.

"If only I'd been . . ."—Barnard originally began this with "Ai! Ai" followed by a space, using a first line as a title, as she does in *S*.

"Thetis"—see note to "The Pathetic Fallacy"; see also L358 of Book 1of *TI*, where Thetis first appears in the text, as well as the notes to L359–60 of the text.

"The short-stemmed rose"—one TS seems to present an earlier version of this poem entitled "The Red Rose"; two versions of this fragment appear, concurrently, on the TS that informs the printing in this volume. I have gone with the second version on the basis that it might represent a later, and thus preferred, attempt.

"sail high overhead"—a reference to the star cluster of the Pleiades, of ancient importance in determining navigation in the Mediterranean sea.

"sister"—the Pleiades are also known as the Seven Sisters.

"lost wings"—see Barnard's poem "The Pleiades" (later included in *TIME*), which compares the stars to a "flock of wild swans."

Ms/Ts: *U*

Love Poem
No date

The poem is at least from 1930, since it was included in the set given to Lloyd Reynolds that year for critique (*MB/Parents*, 27 October 1930). While there is no direct correspondence between this poem and the fragments in *S* there are again some links and resonances. For example the first line ("Oh plaguing Aphrodite, hear my prayer!") reads like a condensation of Barnard's fragment 38—or Fragment One as it is commonly known—which is a translation of the one fragment that has survived intact out of Sappho's fragments, also known as "Prayer to Aphrodite." Poem discussed in *SB/MBAI* 66, 68.

Ms/Ts: *U*

Blanchefleur
1933

Poem first published in *CV 2.7* along with "Bay Road" and "Inspiration," but also, as Bell notes on her copy of *LBN*, was folded inside the back cover of *LBN*, with "Noon Hour," a version of "Chronos" titled "Khronos," as well as "Late Roman." One of a group of poems sent to Pound on 28 July 1934, notes *BKNB*. It was also sent to Marianne Moore, who commented on it in a letter of 11 September 1934 (quoted in full by Barnard in *AMH* 63–64 and cited in discussion of the poem in *SB/MBAI* 66). In this letter, Moore also commented on "Shoreline" and "Trefoil," reprinted in this volume, as well as some other poems not collected here ("Life Class," "College Scene," and "The Sheltered Flower").

"marges"—edge or margin.

"white flowers," "wax-white flowers," and "each petal a white / Polished flake"—possible allusions to Aphrodite, goddess of love and flowers, birthed from the sea in a cloak of white foam; see note to "Anadyomene."

Published text: *CV 2.7* 17.

Fatigue
c. 1934

Again, this is another poem apparently given to Barnard's friend Mildred Cline in the early 1930s with 1934 given for copyright registration (see *MC*). In *JSN*, Barnard's entry for 17 February 1934 included the note: "Worked on sapphics—<u>Fatigue</u>" ([*sic*], punctuation Barnard's). An additional stanza is included in the only known draft; the stanza is enclosed in square brackets with a note, seemingly in Barnard's hand, which says "omitted in revision." Situated between the third and final stanzas, this omitted stanza veils an eroticism that we see a little more explicitly—if simultaneously cooled—in Barnard's other early landscape poems, such as the poem that begins "The slenderly poised clean shaft of your fir." The additional stanza repeats a little on the last and reads:

Over and over and over and over
Benumbing the tired brain
Did I think that another lover

Would drown in floods of exquisite sound
The silly refrain?
It is there,
Repeating its inane
Phrase—sun striking
Rhythmically upon bright hair.

"Marked"—appears in the TS as "murked," which, given the context and the later line "Mark well the beat," seems almost certainly a typo, so has been corrected here.

Ms/Ts: *U*

"Tranquil and shallow, spread across the flat stones . . ."
c. 1934

Bell's annotations on one TS speculate that this poem is from 1934, the same TS where Barnard marked this poem as a "Sapphic exercise." For specific exploration of Sapphic meter in this poem, see *SB/PhD* 73 and 216. See, also, notes to "A Defense of the Poet's Method," below, for discussion of poem's origins and context and, earlier, to "The slenderly poised clean shaft of your fir . . ." Around the time of composition Barnard was newly-immersed in Sapphics, as evidenced in her correspondence with Pound, noting in *JSN* on 8 February 1934 that she had "[w]orked all day on Sapphics. Who wouldn't! Wrote the firelight poem in that form. Had dinner late. Listened to symphony and finally retired to my desk to write to Ezra Pound."

Ms/Ts: *U*

Commerce
1935

Appeared as a free verse version in *LBN*; on reverse of this poem is the date of "Dec. 10. 1932," in Barnard's hand. *BKNB* notes that the poem was on a list of poems titled "sent to Rapallo"; next to the poem's title on the list, Barnard wrote "Sapphics" in brackets, for on 28 March 1934, Barnard said she "[r]ewrote Commerce in the Sapphic form. Quite successful" (*JSN*; underlining Barnard's). Barnard told Pound in a letter of 19 January 1936 that she had received some feedback on the poem by classical scholar W. H. D. Rouse (whom Pound had encouraged her to contact): "He thought Commerce was pretty bad, which it certainly is if you try to read it quantitatively. Of the [A Defense of the] Poet's Method he said he thought it was quite good enough to justify more trying. He also though it was 'clever and ingenious in managing the accent' " (*MB/EP*).

See, also, reference to Rouse in the introduction and the notes to Barnard's essay, *ACOG* (reprinted in this volume). In a letter to editor T. C. Wilson ahead of this poem's first publication in *WQ*, Barnard wrote: "Mr. Pound suggested some changes in <u>Commerce</u>, but I didn't send them to you because I thought they were intended to help me in writing more sapphics, not in getting the poems ready for publication. Will you please change 'Rich am I' to 'I am rich,' and 'sculptor' to 'sculptors'?" (*MB/TW*, TS dated 25 January 1934—although this year seems incorrect; 1935 seems more chronologically accurate; n.b., these changes were made in *WQ*).

See, also, note to "A Defense of the Poet's Method." Poem discussed as an example of Barnard's early Sapphic exercises in *SB/MBAI* 103, 109.

Published text: *WQ* 38.

Departure
1935

Barnard marked this poem "29A35" suggesting 29 April or 29 August as the date of composition, with *PNC* suggesting the latter is correct, recording "8/29/35." See, also, notes to "A Defense of the Poet's Method" for discussion of poem's origins and context; as with this poem, *BKNB* notes that "Departure" was on a list of poems titled "sent to Rapallo," (to Pound). For specific exploration of Sapphic meter in this poem, see *SB/PhD* 70 and 217 and, as an example of Barnard's early Sapphic exercises, *SB/MBAI* 68, 100.

"white Cytherean maiden"—Aphrodite; "Cytherean" relates to Venus/ the goddess Cytherea. See, also, notes to "Fire, snow, and the night . . ." and "The Fool's Serenade."

Ms/Ts: *U*

Mask
1935

Appeared on separate page of *WQ* to the majority of poems published in that volume, alongside "Commerce" and "Lai," two other poems in Sapphics.

"Hurt but still untracked her desirous mouth lost"—as with so many of the poems presented in Barnard's section in *WQ*, "Mask" carried an error, in this instance quite glaring: this whole line was omitted and in its place was a repeat of St 1, L8 ("Hands of grief oppressing her cheek and forehead." The erroneous line was marked with a check in Barnard's hand in her contributor copy; as editor I have restored the correct line, as it appears in an early TS version (and appears also in a later copy Barnard typed up for her good friend Thomas J. Donovan, see *MB/TD*).

Published text: *WQ* 38.

A Defense of the Poet's Method
1936

BKNB notes that the poem was sent to Pound on 20 January 1936, along with other poems that appeared with it in *ND* the next month ("Provincial," "Epicure," "Mechanism," and "Cold Heaven"). *PNC* records that "3 Sapphics sent in to the *Westminster Review*. [I]n 1934 MB sent to EP her own experiments in Sapphics on her own subj. (don't know which ones)" [*sic*]. A TS version of the poem is dated "Nov. 21 1935?" in Barnard's typeface, with British spelling in the title ("A Defence . . ." as opposed to "A Defense . . ."). This poem is thus clearly one of a suite of Sapphic exercises that Barnard worked on over 1934–1935, following Pound's encouragement (see notes to "Commerce," "Departure," and the untitled poem beginning "Tranquil and shallow, spread across the flat stones . . ." as well as *SB/MBAI* 100–104). But, as later poems show, Barnard soon began to manage Sapphics differently. "Did you mean I should make the translations in metres original with the Greek [as attempted here] or original with me?" she asked Pound in a letter of 10 February 1937 (*MB/EP*). For specific exploration of Sapphic meter in this poem, see *SB/PhD* 70–72 and 218. See, also, notes to "Commerce," and, earlier, to "The slenderly poised clean shaft of your fir . . ." The poem seems to have been inspired by Multnomah Falls in the Columbia River Gorge, which pour over steep rock into two pools. Several of Barnard's photographs of these falls can be found in albums among the Mary Barnard Papers.

Published text: *ND* 194.

Later: Four Fragments
1972; 1979

First published under the title of "Fragments" as part of a suite of poems in *ODY* (no page), along with "E.P.: Sant' Ambrogio, 1964," "Fable of the Ant and the Word" and "The Spring"; for publication details of "E.P.: Sant' Ambrogio, 1964" see notes to "Two Visits." Also published as part of group of poems in *ENC* 8 in a postcard format, with the third and fourth fragments in the upper half, the first and second fragments in the lower half in an attempt to impose a temporal span on the group (and an added comma after "Tired").

Such reordering may not have come from Barnard, for, according to *MB/IC*, there was an incident where the fragments were "run together as one poem, and not in the right order" in *The Columbian*, Sunday, May 28, 1978—and also reprinted in *HAT* 38. Published as a set of four postcards (Portland, OR: Prescott Press, 1975), with woodcuts by Charles Bigelow.

Published text: *CP* 57.

Ceremony
1979

Published text: *CP* 67.

Chronos
1979

One draft of this poem gives the title as "Khronos" and omits the comma from the first stanza, which gives the effect of the words being weighed equally, as per Barnard's balanced line prosody (*U*; but also see note to "Blanchefleur").

"Chronos"—god of time; see Barnard's note to Lines 35–38 of the tenth fytte—*Song for the Millenium*—of *TIME* and, also, the note to L502 in *TI*.

"Electra"—mythological figure featured widely in Greek tragedies; daughter of Agamemnon and Clytaemnestra (see notes to *TI*, L7) also known as "Laodice." Sophocles's play *Electra* tells the story of Electra's search for justice after the murder of her father, hence the "scales" in this poem. See, also, notes to "The Pleiades."

Published text: *CP* 65.

Late Roman
1979

A draft of this poem omits all punctuation except the capitalizations, enhancing the sense of the poem as a pared-down single utterance (*U*; but also see note to "Blanchefleur").

Poem discussed in *SB/MBAI* 21, 82.

"Mr. Achilles"—hero of *The Iliad*. See, also, note to L1 of *TI*.

"Gibbon's"—Edward Gibbon, author of *The History of the Decline and Fall of the Roman Empire*.

"ME"—possible reference to Barnard's first initials, "Mary Ethel." In her youth she signed off her poems as "MEB" or "Mary Ethel Barnard."

Published text: *CP* 66.

Now
1979

See note to L52 ("thick on the beach the pyres of the dead burned always") of Barnard's *TI* and note for "The Pump."

Published text: *CP* 85.

The Rock of Levkas
1979

Named after the rock (also known as the Leucadian rock) from which Sappho is said to have leapt to her death, this poem was published as part of a group of poems in *WP*, which were scheduled to be published ahead of *CP.* Poem discussed in *SB/MBAI* 70. An undated—presumably earlier—version was titled "Not at the Leucalian Rock" [*sic*] and ran to a mere seven lines, evocative of the final stanza of "The Rock of Levkas." In a handwritten draft, Barnard wrote:

> Not at the Leucalian Rock
> Fearing the noisy
> sea under the cliff
> she climbed always
> higher summits to
> find that foam was
> now snow: a death less
> quick but colder

(Ms/Ts: *U*)

See, also, notes for "Cold Heaven" and "The Fool's Serenade."

Published text: *CP* 31.

Soft Chains
1979

Subsequently published as a bus poster by *Streetfare Journal* (no date other than listed under 1987 in *BIB* 197). See, also, note for "The Pump."

Published text: *CP* 84.

Static
1979

Poem was published as part of a group of poems in *WP*, which were scheduled to be published ahead of *CP*; reprinted in *AP V2* 658. Poem discussed in *SB/MBAI* 70.

"her stringed shell"—Sappho's lyre, reputedly made from tortoiseshell; see Margaret Reynolds, *The Sappho Companion* (London: Vintage, 2001), 5.

"Greek pterodactyls"—pun on the dactyl, common to ancient Greek quantitative meter/Sapphics.

Published text: *CP* 64.

II. TRANSLATIONS

FROM *SAPPHO: A NEW TRANSLATION* (1958)

1. "Tell everyone . . ."
1958
> Barnard's translated fragment is discussed in *AC* 34–35 and *SB/MBAI* 123.

Published text: *S* (no page).

37. "You know the place: then . . ."
1958
> Barnard's translated fragment is discussed in *SB/MBAI* 120.
> "Queen! Cyprian"—Aphrodite.
> See, also, "Cupbearer," which dramatizes the final stanza of this fragment, possibly from the point of view of Aphrodite.

Published text: *S* (no page).

53. "With his venom . . ."
1958
> Barnard's translated fragment is discussed in *AC* 51 and, with relation to questions of movement in Greek poetry, in the second paragraph of Barnard's essay *FN*, reprinted in this volume.

Published text: *S* (no page).

61. "Pain penetrates . . ."
1958
> Barnard's translated fragment is discussed in *AC* 52–53.

Published text: *S* (no page).

100. "I have no complaint . . ."
1958
> Barnard's translated fragment is discussed in *AC* 60–61.

"the golden Muses"—mountain-goddesses (*TGM* 60) associated with poetic inspiration; their home was Mount Helicon (*TGM* 82), after which Barnard named her memoir *AMH*.

Published text: *S* (no page).

OTHER TRANSLATIONS

Adonis Dying
No date

Poem is named after Aphrodite's mortal lover. Upon dying, Adonis is asked by the shades in the underworld what he will miss the most—this poem is his response. *PNC* suggests the poem is possibly from 1932. There exists another version that was sent to Ezra Pound and that, at its foot, attributes the poem to Praxilla, a Greek lyric poet from 5 BC, who was said to have written a hymn to Adonis—see the facsimile draft in the opening to this book, with Pound's annotations. It was Pound's lines on Adonis that Barnard was impressed by from the close of section VI of his "Homage to Sextus Propertius" when she was introduced to his work at college (*AMH* 39):

> Since Adonis was gored in Idalia, and the Cytherean
> Ran crying with out-spread hair,
> In vain, you call back the shade,
> In vain, Cynthia. Vain call to unanswering shadow,
> Small talk comes from small bones.
>
> (*PER* 215)

Ms/Ts: *U*

Book 1 from Homer, The Iliad
No date

Barnard's translation appears in a manuscript totaling 123 A4 pages (all unpublished); Book I runs to 25 A4 pages. Where Barnard made a clear change by hand on the TS, I have gone with her change; but the original text as Barnard had it (where legible) is noted in the notes that follow. Barnard's basic proofing changes regarding spacings, spellings, and so on have been carried over to this edition without any further note. Excerpts from Barnard's translation of Books III, IV, and V appear in Barnard's essay on her use of metric in her

Homer translations in *FN*. Reprinted in full in this volume, *FN* also explains the motivation behind Barnard's translation, even if these five books only went to a first draft (see *SB/MBAI* 129–30 for additional context).

L1 "Achilles"—leading warrior in the Achaean army, son of a divine mother, the sea goddess Thetis, and a mortal father, Peleus, referred to as "Zeus-born Peleus" (L488), therefore making Achilles "beloved of Zeus" (L74). The legend goes that Thetis attempted to make Achilles fully immortal by dipping him in the river Styx as a child; since she held him by the heel, his heel was not dipped, rendering this area vulnerable. Toward the end of *The Iliad*, it is this heel that receives the arrow from Paris, which proves fatal. Achilles is often referred to as "fleet-footed" (as in L84), "swift of foot" (as in L58), "godlike" (as in L121), and generally considered "the noblest Achaean" (L244). It is Achilles's rage against Agamemnon—his "death-dealing anger" as we are told in the opening line—that lights and fuels the narrative of the poem; and from the very first book, we are left in no doubt of the outcome—that Achilles's anger will bring "disaster upon the Greeks" (L2), rendering him destined, as his mother Thetis says to Zeus, "to live / but the briefest time" (L505–506). Barnard's poem "Late Roman" invokes Achilles, as well as provides testament to the importance of Homer in Barnard's career, as does her unpublished fragment beginning "In the bridal . . ." (four fragments), which fantasizes about being a poet in the time of Thetis's wedding. Thetis is referenced, also, in the previously-unpublished early poem "The Pathetic Fallacy"; see also the note to L34, below, which cites this poem.

L7 "Agamemnon"—king and commander of the largest body of the Achaean army (see also note to L14), son of Atreus, husband to Clytemnestra (see note to L113), brother of Menelaos (sometimes spelled "Menelaus").

L9 "Apollo"—god and son of Zeus and Leto, twin brother to Artemis; god of medicine, the arts (especially music and poetry), and prophecy; associated with the lyre and the military bow. One of Apollo's recurring epithets in Barnard's translation excerpted here is "Lord of the Silver Bow"; in her translation of book 4, he is known as "the Light-Born, the Prince of Archers." Because of this skill, Apollo is also known as "the son of Zeus, far-striking Apollo" (L21). Also associated with "fillets / and golden staff" (L13–14) as god of crops and herds. His forename was "Phoebus" (meaning "bright" and "pure," as in "Phoebus Apollo" [see L43]—therefore associated with the sun. Seen in *The Iliad* as a divine ally of the Trojans [see notes for L37–38]). See also note for L10.

L10 "Chryses"—a priest of Apollo, whose daughter (Chryseis) has been captured by the Achaeans. In these opening lines, Chryses is shown bringing a ransom to the Achaean camp in exchange for her release. Agamemnon initially refuses to give her up, a decision that invokes Apollo's rage, induces a plague that ravages the Achaean army, and leaves Agamemnon with no choice but to return the daughter to Chryses—but not before demanding that Achilles compensates him through surrendering "at once a prize / to replace her" (L118–119). By "prize," we learn, he means the girl Briseis (see also notes to L185 and L429), to be found in Achilles's tent. See also notes to L37–38.

L13 "fillets"—headband; in antiquity, could be made of cloth or leather or be in the form of a garland worn around the head.

L14 "the Achaeans"—Greek and allied opponents to the Trojans, led by King Agamemnon. See also note for L254.

L15–L16 "Atreus's sons, both Menelaos and / King Agamemnon"—see note to L7.

L16 "his daughter Chryseis"—see note for L10.

L19 "Priam's city"—the wealthy, fortified city of Troy, ruled over by Priam, the king and father to Hector and Paris.

L22–23 "Almost all the Achaeans expressed their approval and said / they should honor . . ."—amended by Barnard from "The other Achaeans expressed their approval and said / they should honor the priest and accept his glittering ransom— . . ."

L26 "oldster"—amended by Barnard from "sir."

L30 "Argos"—city in the general region of the Achaeans.

L34 "the many-voiced sea"—the association of the sea and voice was strong in Barnard not just biographically, but also poetically—see, for example, "The Fool's Serenade," "Uninspired to the Uninspiring," and "The Pathetic Fallacy."

L36 "Leto"—mother of Apollo and Artemis by Zeus; daughter of the Titans Coeus ("intelligence") and Phoebe ("moon") (*TGM* 60–61).

L36 "whom"—amended by Barnard from "who."

L37–38 "Lord of the Silver Bow, who bestridest / Chrysa, protector of Cilla"—Apollo (see note to L9 above); Chrysa (also known as "Chryse"); and Cilla are Greek towns. The town of Chrysa is home to Chryses.

L39 "Tenedos"—island off the coast of Troy.

L42 "Let the Greeks pay for my tears under thine arrows"—amended by Barnard from "Under thine arrows, let the Greeks pay for my tears"; editor has further removed the comma in keeping with the smoothness of the syntax Barnard finally opted for.

L52 "thick on the beach the pyres of the dead burned always"—another image that Barnard seems to have drawn on in various poems with funereal beach scenes such as "Bay Beach," "Fire," "Moonstone," "Ondine," and "Shore-line." See, especially, note to "Fire."

L55 "Hera"—goddess wife of Zeus; seen in *The Iliad* as a divine ally of the Achaeans.

L65 "hecatomb"—public sacrifice of one hundred cattle to the gods.

L66 "Or does he require [. . .]?"—amended by Barnard from "Perhaps he requires [. . .]?"

L68 "Calchas"—prophet of the Achaeans who advises Agamemnon to return Chryses's daughter in order to placate Apollo.

L73 "The seer, a man of good will, addressed them"—amended by Barnard from "He, being well-disposed, addressed them."

L76 "I shall obey you, but you must hear me and, speak this"—Bell agrees with the editor that "speak" seems the correct the word in this instance.

L76–79 this has been amended by Barnard, from "I shall do as you say, but listen, and promise me this: / that you will gladly defend me both by action / and speech, for I think I shall anger a man who holds sway / over the Argives."

L78–79 "a man / ruling the Argives"—Agamemnon, the "Argives" being an alternate name for the Achaeans.

L88 "no man"—amended by Barnard from "no one."

L97–100 "He will not protect the Greeks from this pitiless plague / until, without ransom, we give up the bright-eyed girl / and send her home to her own dear father in Chrysa / and send a hecatomb with her. Then he may hear us"—amended by Barnard from "He will not ward off from the Greeks this pitiless plague / until, without ransom, we give up the bright-eyed girl / sending her home to her own dear father in Chrysa / and a hecatomb with her. Then he may hear our prayer."

L101 "With this, the seer sat down"—amended by Barnard from "With this, he sat down again."

L113 "Queen Clytemnestra"—wife of Agamemnon (see note to L7).

L114 "for she is in no way inferior"—amended by Barnard from "since she is in no way inferior."

L138 "Ajax"—an Achaean commander; "Odysseus"—Achaean commander of Ithaca; son of Laertes; father of Telemachus; and speaker in Barnard's poem "Odysseus Speaking."

L139 "*he* will be furious!"—Barnard's typescript uses underline for emphasis on "he," updated to italics by the editor here.

L145 "Idomeneus"—Achaean commander of Crete.

L155 "Phthia"—home of Achilles in south Thessaly, kingdom of Peleus.

L180 "your Myrmidons"—large contingent of the Achaean army, led by Achilles.

L185 "Briseis"—see notes for L10 and L429.

L194 "Athena"—defender of the Achaeans. See also "The First Chorus from Oedipus King, from Sophocles, *Oedipus Rex*" note to L15.

L200 "Pallas Athena"—alternative name for Athena.

L203 "O daughter of Zeus Aegis-bearer"—Athena; "Aegis" was an emblematic shield or breastplate that was associated with both Zeus and Athena.

L225 "Sot"—archaism for person who is frequently drunk.

L243 "Hector"—leader of the Trojans, son of King Priam of Troy, who eventually kills Achilles's closest friend Patroclus, resulting in his own death at the hands of a vengeful Achilles who, for a time, tethers Hector's corpse to his chariot.

L248 "Nestor [. . .] the clear-voiced speaker of Pylos"—Achaean king of Pylos.

L253 "The old king, a man of good will"—amended by Barnard from "He, being well-disposed."

L254 "Achaea"—collective name for mainland Greece; see also note for L14.

L263–64 "Peirithoos and Dryas [. . .] "Kaineus, Exadios, Polyphemus the Lapith."—Peirithoos (sometimes known as "Pirithous") was king of the Lapiths (a Thessalian tribe) as well as son of Zeus: Dryas, Kaineus (sometimes known as "Caeneus"), and Exadios were all Lapith heroes of Nestor's generation, as was the warrior Polyphemus.

L265 "Theseus son of Aegeus"—king of Athens.

L273 "And they always"—word order amended by Barnard from "And always they."

L280–81 "It is true you are stronger, but you had a goddess for mother, [*sic*] / and he has the greater power"—amended by Barnard from "Although you are stronger, you had a goddess for mother, / but he has the greater power."

L283 "for he is a bulwark"—amended by Barnard from "since he is a bulwark."

L298 "although I shall not fight either you"—amended by Barnard from "although I shall not fight with you."

L306 "Patroclus"—Achilles's closest friend, killed by Hector, whose death Achilles seeks to avenge.

L310 "Chrysa"—see note for L37–38.

L320–21 "Talythybios [. . .] Eurybates"—Agamemnon's heralds; ("Talythybios" is sometimes known as "Talythybius").

L349–50 "he knelt at the edge of the gray sea /and looked out"—amended by Barnard from "he knelt at the edge of the gray sea, / looking out."

L358 "her ancient father"—Nereus, the sea god, father of Thetis; known as the "Old Man of the Sea."

L359 "Quickly she rose up out of the sea like a mist"—Thetis, Achilles's mother. This image bears remarkable correspondence to Barnard's poem about Aphrodite rising from the sea in mist in "Anadyomene" where a "Cloudself [. . .] / Touching the warm stone / Distils radiance."

L366 "Theba"—Greek city ruled by Eëtion, sacked by Achilles (sometimes known as "Thebe").

L367 "Eëtion"—king of the Cillicians in Theba (sometimes known as "Eetion").

L399–400 "Hera, Poseidon / and Pallas-Athena"—Hera, wife of Zeus; Poseidon, sea god, younger brother of Zeus, and son of Cronus (see note for L502) and Rhea. Hera and Athena are united in their hatred of the Trojans.

L403–405 "the Hundred-armed [. . .] Briareos [. . .] Aigaion"—giant of hundred hands known as "Briareos" (sometimes as "Briareus") to the gods and "Aigaion" (sometimes as "Aegaeon") to mortals.

L405–406 "his glory; /and so the gods"—amended by Barnard from "his strength / so the blessed gods."

L413 "Thetis"—sea goddess and Achilles's mother, also referred to as "silvery-footed" (L555) "the Old Man of the Ocean's silvery-footed daughter" (L538); see, also, note for L1.

L420 "Zeus, the thunder-bolt wielder"—husband of Hera, considered the father/king of all gods and men, and to whom Thetis appeals on Achilles's behalf as part of his quest for revenge on Agamemnon. Like Poseidon, Zeus was the son of Cronus (see note for L502) and Rhea. "Thunder-bolt wielder" refers to Zeus's associations with the sky and weather.

L429 "the trim-waisted girl"—Briseis (see notes for L10 and L185); amended by Barnard from "the trim-waisted woman."

L444 "that we may appease the god"—amended by Barnard from "that we may appease him" who now afflicts the Argives with bitter sorrow."

L477 "the rose-fingered child"—amended by Barnard from "the pink-fingered child."

L500 "her left hand clasping his knees"—amended by Barnard from "clasping his knees in her left hand."

L502 "son of Cronos"—god of time, father of Zeus but also Demeter, Hera, Hades, and Poseidon. Sometimes known as "Cronus" but also "Chronos." "The later Greeks read 'Cronus' as *Chronos*, 'Father Time,' with his relentless sickle," writes Graves (*TGM* 45), which may be said to be inspiration for

Barnard's poem "Chronos." See, also Barnard's note to lines 35–38 of the tenth fytte—*Song for the Millenium*—of *TIME*.

L530 "the deathless head"—this idea of immortality of the head is evoked in Barnard's poem about Ezra Pound, written around the same time, in Pound's later years. The first visit in "Two Visits" may lament Pound's "death-mask" of ageing in 1961, but there's something Zeus-like about the "deathless" ways in which his eyes and jaw are described: "The eyes, alive, look sharply [. . .] his jaws unhinged by death will sing."

L547 "no other"—amended by Barnard from "no one."

L552 "Cronides"—son of Cronus, here, of course, Zeus.

L570–71 "Hephaistos / the glorious artist"—god of fire, son of Hera, associated with artistry (sometimes known as "Hephaestus").

L580 "Olympios, god of lightning"—Zeus, whose home, as with other gods, is the mountain Olympus.

L593 "Lemnos"—Greek island, in the northeast of the Aegean Sea.

L594 "The Sintians"—inhabitants of Lemnos who tended to Hephaistos when he was thrown down to the island from Olympus by his mother Hera.

Ms/Ts: *TI*

The First Chorus from Oedipus King, from Sophocles, Oedipus Rex 1932

In the manuscript from *H*, where this translation appears in its own section titled "Monad," words of each Strophe and Antistrophe appear on separate pages, achieving a similar kind of ribbon-like fragment quality as that Barnard later refined in *S*.

L2 "The sweet-voiced god" (Strophe I)—Apollo, associated with song, poetry, and music. See fuller note on Apollo in *TI* note for L9.

L4 "shining Thebes" (Strophe I)—city of the Thebans.

L8 "Paean Delos!" (Strophe I)—a "paean" was a choral chant to a god (here, Apollo); Delos was a cult site associated with Apollo.

L15 "immortal Athena" (Antistrophe I)—goddess daughter of Hera and Zeus. Associated with wisdom, human ingenuity, and resourcefulness, such as that exemplified by handicrafts (e.g. the skill of spinning), or by skill in human relations, such as that recognized in Odysseus. "Although a goddess of war," writes Robert Graves, "she gets no pleasure from battle [. . .] but rather from settling disputes, and upholding the law by pacific means" (*TGM* 98). See also *TI* note for L195.

L16 "Artemis" (Antistrophe I)—goddess of the hunt and the moon, sister to Apollo, daughter of Zeus and Leto. See also *TI* note for L36.

L20 "far darting Phoebus" (Antistrophe I)—Apollo's forename. See fuller *TI* note for L9.

L43 "To the coast land of the god of the evening" (Strophe II)—this line appears (in Greek) in Barnard's later poem "Storm." There are other resonances between this translation and "Storm," such as the references to "well-plumed birds" (L38 here) and "well-plumed music" ("in "Storm"), as well as images of dead birds, disease, and decay.

L44 "furious Ares" (Strophe III)—son of Hera and Zeus, god of war, protector of the Trojans.

L49–50 "the great sea / Chamber of Amphitrite" (Strophe III)—Amphitrite was a sea goddess, married to Poseidon. See also *TI* note for L400–401.

L52–53 "Thracian waters that refuse / Haven to strangers" (Strophe III)—sea surrounding Thrace, home to Trojan allies the Thracians.

L58 "From bound to bound" (Antistrophe II)—this line is indented in Barnard's typescript.

L62 "Stretched out on the ground" (Antistrophe II)—Barnard's typescript gives "Stetched" in place of "Stretched"; error corrected by the editor.

L73 "Lycian King" (Antistrophe III)—Apollo. In *TI* (book 4) he is known as "Lycegenes," "born in Lycia" (*TGM* 61). See fuller note on Apollo in *TI* note for L9.

L84 "Euios Bacchos of the ruddy face" (Antistrophe III)—Dionysus, son of Zeus and Theban princess Semele; associated with wine.

L87 "Maenads" (Antistrophe III)—Dionysus's female followers.

The motivation for this translation may have come from the Greek class Barnard took in her last year at Reed, where she made some early forays into Greek metric: "One day [. . .] my Greek instructor had said, 'We really *ought* to be saying something about metric, but to tell you the truth, I don't understand it myself.' We were reading Sophocles at the time; he put on the blackboard a few lines of one of the choruses, and said 'It's something like this . . .' Having learned about dactyls and spondees, I had supposed this was all" (*AMH* 54). Of course, it wasn't until Barnard came under Pound's instruction that her entire view was to change, as she went on to recall of the moment she first read the chapter on Greek metric in the *Encyclopédie de la musique* edited by Laurencie and Lavignac. "Now I discovered," Barnard wrote, "that there were glyconics, epitrites, Aeolian tripodies, in short, that the whole matter was much more exciting and complicated than I had ever imagined" (*AMH* 54). See Barnard's later essay on the subject in section III, *ACCG*, as well as the notes to "Playroom," "The Rapids," and "Roots."

Ms/Ts: *H*

Odysseus Speaking (from The Odyssey, *opening of Book IX)*
1966; 1979

First published in *AFEST* 60. Presented here as it appeared in *CP*, with the accompanying note "from the *Odyssey,* opening of Book IX." Odysseus's short biography, as discussed in this poem, is given in the note to L139 of *TI*. That Barnard felt this translation to be a suitable honor for her former Reed professor Lloyd Reynolds is telling of both Barnard's and Reynolds's complex sense of "home"—both found "richer homes," as the translation explores, away from where they began their careers, Reynolds across faculties, Barnard across the continent. Reynolds, *AMH* tells us, had begun teaching at Reed as "a young man [. . .] at the beginning of my second year [1929]" (*AMH* 36). Barnard recalls:

> He had only recently received his M.A. in English from the University of Oregon. In contrast to both [Barry] Cerf and [Victor] Chittick [Barnard's other Reed professors] he was in no way bird-like and only faintly academic, never even attempting (so far as I know) to get a Ph.D. Always a bit more of a guru than a professor, he stayed on at Reed, moving from literature into graphic arts and calligraphy, with excursions into other arts visual and theoretical until his retirement. (*AMH* 36)

See, also, the introduction to this volume, which cites Pound's advice to Barnard about translating Homer. It appears that Barnard did no other work on *The Odyssey* other than this poem.

Published text: *CP* 97.

Three Translations from the Greek
1979

First appearance in print in *CP.* In a letter to her editor, James Anderson, as she finalized the manuscript for *CP,* Barnard said: "I have never sent out the three Greek translations, although I like them, since most magazines don't want translations" (*MB/JA,* 4 March 1979).

"Ball Game"—translation of a poem called "Love" by Anacreon, originally in two stanzas, unlike Barnard's expansion into three as an act of "thinning" the poem out, perhaps, into the kind of economic sparsity exemplified by her *S*.

"red sandals"—arguably an expression of the imagistic concreteness Barnard brought to the translation, in contrast to the "fancy shoes" of the "motley sandalled girl" suggested by David Campbell (*TGL* 21). Curiously she offers a "bright ball" in place of Campbell's "purple ball" (*TGL* 21)—perhaps as a signal of "Love's" ultimate elusiveness, as opposed to the concrete colors attached to the couple caught up in "Love's" "game."

"another man"—Campbell writes that the last line in the original Greek has no gendered noun as "no noun is needed in the Greek, so that the point [that the speaker only has eyes for another girl] is the more concisely made" (*TGL* 22)—which is clearly a subjective view. Richmond Lattimore has similarly gendered the object as female [*RL* 29], but curiously Barnard opts for the male gender, perhaps to flag the irresolution of the original. T. F. Higham and C. M. Bowra opted for the more generic "someone" (*TFH* 221).

"Anacreon"—ancient Greek poet b. c. 570 BC, who famously died by choking on a grape, according to *A Garden of Greek Verse: Poems of Ancient Greece* (London: Frances Lincoln, 2000), p. 70. Such a death proves also the inspiration for the second translation in the series, "Terpander," where the poet figure dies not through some honorable drama concerning "arrow" and "sword," but by choking on a fig.

"Terpander"—Greek poet famous for his death where "[s]omeone threw a fig into his mouth as he was singing, and this killed him" (*GA* 272).

"Tryphon"—Greek poet whose poem about how the harp player "Terpes" (clearly a version of Terpander) "died" "by a fig on the lips" appears in volume 3 (The Declamatory Epigrams) of *The Greek Anthology*—number 488 (*GA* 273).

"The Anthology"—*The Greek Anthology*, revered by Pound, Aldington, and H. D. in their Imagist phases, and model for some of Pound's poems in *Lustra* (London: Elkin Matthews, 1916). See, for example, W. R. Paton, trans., *The Greek Anthology*, vol. 1 (London: Heinemann, 1916).

Published text: *CP* 61–63.

III. SELECTED PROSE

"Confessional"
1932

This piece first appeared as the preface to *H* (Barnard's senior thesis at Reed College, "this book [. . .] the little window of the confessional" as described in the first paragraph); presented here as it appeared in *EA* (Barnard's account, in letters home, of "Writing a Creative Thesis at Reed College in 'The Golden Age,'" to quote the subtitle of *EA*). As a literature major, Barnard was required to write a critical thesis. Yet she struggled with "an inability to write critical papers largely because of her unwillingness to judge the work of writers she [didn't] feel qualified to critique," as John Sheehy wrote in his foreword to *EA*, adding that "[t]he faddish tutorial style of the times, which place[d] her one-on-one with erudite professors, only exacerbate[d] the problem" (*EA* 10)—so instead broke with precedent and wrote a creative thesis. See, also, note to "Fable."

"my fathers in learning"—Barnard's professors at Reed, noted and contextualized by Sheehy as those "who were recruited during Reed's early years and who [remained] there until retirement—Knowlton, Cerf, McKinley, Chittick, Arragon, Woodbridge, both the Griffins—[and were] mid-career of what will later be referred to as Reed's 'golden age'" (*EA* 9).

"four years of sin"—Barnard's four-year undergraduate career at Reed.

Published text: *EA* 27–29.

"Creed"
1932

As with "Confessional," "Creed" initially appeared as the preface to *H* and is also presented here as it appeared in *EA*. Discussed in *SB/MBAI* 25 (in relation to Imagism), 27 (in relation to omitted material—see below), 91 (in relation to Sappho), and 114 (in relation to metric).

"Jocelin of Brakelond"—Benedictine English monk (fl. c. 1163–1225); noted for his chronicle of his abbey (1173–1202).

Barnard omitted the following two beliefs from her "Creed":

I BELIEVE that most poets and students of poetry have essentially the same ideas about what is good poetry; but they become stubborn about the words they use to describe it.

I BELIEVE that good poets who have theories forget about them when they write. (*UH*)

Published text: *EA* 31–32.

"A Note on Poetry"
1940

Discussed in *SB/MBAI* 18–19, 91.

Published text: *CC* 5.

"A Communication on Greek Metric, Ezra Pound, and Sappho*"*
1978/79; 1994

First appeared in *Agenda* (London) 16.3–4 (Autumn–Winter 1978–1979): 62–68. Reprinted in *Paideuma* in 1994 (see *ACOG* in abbreviations), which is the version presented here since the manual scansion marks are clearer for reproduction purposes. Most of the differences between the two versions appear to be in terms of house style and some occasional, non-controversial punctuation changes (e.g. colon supplied before a quotation in place of a comma). Where there has been a change of phrasing, it is identified below. Discussed in chapter 4, " 'A New Way of Measuring Verse,' " of *SB/MBAI* 93, 103, 118, 133. In a letter to Myrna Haugaard ahead of publication, Barnard described this essay as "a very brief, odd article," although why she thought it "odd" wasn't clear (*MB/MEH*, undated).

"W. H. D. Rouse"—English Classics scholar and translator who had a brief correspondence with Barnard when she was first attempting Sapphics. See also, the reference to Rouse in the introduction and notes to "Commerce."

"I wrote an ill-fated verse play in dimeters, but failed to introduce enough variation"—very possibly a reference to *The Trap* (unpub.), which Barnard worked on in the 1940s; see *SB/MBAI,* "Chronology," (XVII).

"Each line would have to balance against the others" (in paragraph beginning "The brevity of the fragments reminded me," sixth from the end)—in the *Agenda* version "One" was used originally in place of "Each," thus "One line would have to balance against the others."

"It seemed to me impossible to get these effects in English, as I wanted, if I used a Sapphic meter" (in paragraph beginning "Some of the longer poems I translated," third from the end)—in the *Agenda* version, the original line read "It seemed to me impossible to get these effects, which I wanted, in English if I used a Sapphic meter."

Published text: *ACOG.*

"Meeting Marianne"
1982

First appeared in *The Iowa Review* in 1982, a version of which was printed in *AMH* 86, 88, and 99–102; presented here as it appeared in *The Iowa Review.*

"T. C. Wilson"—New York-based poet and editor of *WQ* and friend of Barnard, to whom she sent a number of poems in the 1930s; see notes to "Fable," "Ondine," "Shoreline," "Lethe," "Cassandra," "Chanson Pathetique," and "Commerce" and reference to T. C. Wilson in the descriptor for *LBN* in abbreviations.

"Katherine Cornell"—critically-acclaimed American actress and producer (1893–1974).

"the (Sheed and Ward) Henry W. Wells edition of Piers Ploughman"—edition of Langland's Middle English allegorical narrative poem, rendered into modern English by Henry W. Wells and published in London in 1935 by Sheed and Ward.

"Kagawa's novel, *A Grain of Wheat*"—novel by Toyohiko Kagawa (1888–1960), a translation of which from Japanese into English was published in 1936 in New York by Harper.

"What Are Years?"—in both printings of this essay (*MM* and *AMH*), Barnard omitted the question mark from the title of this poem; it has been restored, as in Moore's version in her *Complete Poems* (London: Faber and Faber, 1968; first published 1967), 95.

Published text: *MM*.

"Ezra Pound, Sappho and My Assault on Mount Helicon"
1983

Appeared in *The Malahat Review* in 1983, a version of which was printed in *AMH*; presented here as it appeared in *The Malahat Review*, which included a note at the end acknowledging that the essay is "excerpted from *Assault on Mount Helicon / A Literary Memoir*, to be published by the University of California Press early in 1984" and acknowledging permissions given for the two letters by Ezra Pound, which are reproduced here as they appeared in Barnard's reproduction in the essay with respect to layout, spelling, and punctuation.

"I wrote to friends in Italy"—editor of Pound's *Selected Letters*, D. D. Paige, and his wife, who assisted Barnard with settling into Italian life and traveling on to Rapallo where she met Pound's lover Olga Rudge in her first trip to Italy in 1949.

"when I ceased to write poetry a number of years before"—Barnard's poetry publications decreased in number in the second half of the 1940s when she turned to focus on fiction writing, including mysteries in the short story form. However, she did not strictly "cease" to write poems; as she says in *AMH* 201, she "wrote a few poems after my return to New York [in 1943, following her stint at Buffalo], but I had never been so dissatisfied with my work. I put most of them aside after much revision and never published them. I read no poetry at all."

"Fordie"—Ford Madox Ford (1873–1939), editor and novelist.

"Sternberg made Antheil do a fugue a week"—Constantin Sternberg (1852–1924), musician, composer, and Director of the Sternberg Conservatory, Philadelphia, and George Antheil (1900–1959), avant-garde composer.

"*Frankly I"—reference to material that would become Barnard's Fragment 42 in *S*.

"Cleis"—Sappho's daughter.

"waaal the chink does without a damLot"—Pound's reference to doing without "a damLOT [of syntax]" emanates from his observations of the Chinese ideogram as he interpreted it through unfinished work by Ernest Fenollosa. Editing and publishing this work as an essay in 1918, Pound emphasized that the ideogram offers a "shorthand [. . .] thought-picture" where there's "this quality of vividness in the structure of detached Chinese words," (Pound, ed., *The Chinese Written Character as a Medium for Poetry*, [San Francisco: City Lights, 1991], 8–9). The phrasing Pound chooses to use to make this point in a letter to Barnard resonates with that identified by Fiona Green in an essay concerning his correspondence with Marianne Moore over 1918–1919. Writing of how, in one letter, Pound "lurches wildly [. . .] between stereotypes and racial slurs," Green remarks it is a "reminder of the entangled relationship between modernist experiment and race" of the kind problematized in Michael North's work (Fiona Green, " 'Black obsidian Diana': Moore, Pound, and the Curation of Race," *Yearbook of English Studies* 50 [2020]: 61–80: pp.61–62; see, also, notes to Barnard's poem "Two Visits").

Published text: *EPS*.

"William Carlos Williams and the Poetry Archive at Buffalo"
1983

Appeared as part of *WCW* in 1982, a version of which was printed in *AMH*; presented here as it appeared in *WCW*.

"Honor Tracy"—British novelist and travel writer (1913–1989).

"Charles Abbott"—see note to the poem "Thinking of Yeats" (in notes to *Uncollected*); also Iris Barry's brother-in-law. In *AMH* Barnard describes how Pound introduced her to Barry when in New York in May 1939. Recalling a visit to Barry's workplace at the MOMA after Barnard had had tea with Pound, Barnard observed that Barry "handed Pound some mail that had come for him, care of the Museum. As he took it, he said casually, 'Now, while I look over my mail, give Mary a job' " (*AMH* 161). A couple of months later Charles Abbott wrote and offered Barnard the new position of Poetry Curator at Buffalo.

Published text: *WCW*.

"Further Notes on Metric"
1995

Discussed in chapter 4, "A New Way of Measuring Verse," of *SB/MBAI* 90.

"After a hiatus of about ten years when family responsibilities interfered with writing, I began again [. . .] I realized that the book I was trying to write"—"the book" became *TIME*.

"And what kind of metric would accommodate the instructions for finding the meridian as found in the *Panchasiddhantika*? I remembered then that these instructions were written in verse in the original Sanskrit"—the original printing included a typo on "accommodate" and an unnecessary comma after "I remembered then," which the editor has respectively corrected and omitted here.

"From Christmas Eve to night of the Magi's visit [. . .] the turning round of the year"—the original printing of this essay gave the reference in the same language and style as the previous excerpts from Barnard's Homer, as follows: "(author's trans.; V. 54–60)." While the line numbers from the relevant fifth fytte of *TIME* are correct, the lines are not a translation, nor does the work refer to its sections in roman numerals. This error is therefore corrected here.

"these were days when time was at rest"—the original printing introduced another error here giving *TIME*'s "these were days" as "these were the days." This error is also corrected, dropping the definite article from the phrase.

"I really wonder, though, what happens to them if they are read aloud by a Briton? A recent royalty report included a payment from the BBC"—the original printing omits the required definite article from before "BBC"; it is restored here.

Published text: *FN.*

Afterword

Elizabeth J. Bell

Complete Poems and Selected Translations preserves for posterity the brilliant tapestry of Mary Barnard's total life's work. During her lifetime, especially during the years she was in New York City, Mary Barnard had many important and auspicious supporters, like Pound, Williams, and Moore. Since 1958, her successful and continuous publication of her Sappho translation has been well-known. Although Mary Barnard had a small group of ardent admirers in both Portland and in her hometown of Vancouver, Washington, the depth and scope of her intellectual talents were not, at the time, fully realized. Not prone to push herself forward socially or professionally, she was often regarded as rather reclusive and aloof by her community. Although recognized nationally in her day by such awards as the Elliston Award for her *Collected Poems*, or the Western States Book Award of the National Endowment for the Arts for *Time and the White Tigress*, Mary Barnard remained a poet rooted in the Pacific Northwest by a fierce love of her home territory.

My link with Mary Barnard began in the early 1980s. A neighbor who lived down the road in my hometown of Vancouver, knowing I was studying modernist poets at Reed, invited me to a luncheon where Mary was present. That contact with Mary was the beginning of a twenty-year friendship, which included driving Mary to chamber music concerts in Portland, trips to Europe, and entertaining some of her friends at our home to mark certain accomplishments in her writing career. Before she died, Mary Barnard had asked me to be her literary executor. Not really knowing what this would entail, I agreed, and after her death I found myself in charge of her papers and books. Pat Willis of the Beinecke Library was a great help, even personally organizing and transferring

Mary's papers to that library, where Mary had already deposited her letters to and from Pound. Before numerous papers were transferred to the Beinecke, and with their consent, I copied many of Mary's writings and papers with the goal of registering the unpublished works with the help of an intellectual property attorney. At Mary's insistence, I kept the original small publications in which her poems first appeared, which turned out to be an invaluable source. I could not have done so without the help of Maggie Bennett Halpin, a former piano student of mine, who spent countless hours at the Xerox machine, and, more recently, helped with Sarah Barnsley's research for this book.

Sarah Barnsley, not unlike Mary Barnard's ancestors, made a trip from England to the US in 1994, not by way of Nantucket, but directly to the Northwest, specifically to Reed College where Sarah, an undergraduate, was taking a year abroad from the University of East Anglia. Her assignment to write a paper about a local person who was somehow related to her major field, American literature, started Sarah along the path to *Complete Poems and Selected Translations*. Sarah's advisor at Reed, Professor Ellen Stauder, suggested she explore the works of Mary Barnard, mentioning that I was someone who knew Mary. In 2003, two years after Mary's death, Sarah was on another trip from England, this time to the Beinecke Library at Yale to do research for her doctoral thesis on Barnard. She decided to extend her trip to Vancouver, Washington, to see Mary's home. Sarah wrote to me "it seems strange that Mary Barnard has been a strong presence in my academic work since 1995, yet I never met her." As close friends of Mary Barnard, my husband and I were delighted to help Sarah explore the area where Mary grew up, taking a trip to the shores of Mary's beloved Long Beach, a ride along the Columbia River Gorge, and an excursion to the country home in Buxton where Mary spent significant early childhood years. Sarah and I became better acquainted as we spent several days examining the many papers and manuscripts Mary had left behind. Some of Barnard's friends gathered for tea with Sarah. The result was a strong network linking academic research and friendship, started by Professor Stauder, centered around rediscovering and rounding out the complete picture of Mary Barnard.

Complete Poems and Selected Translations rescues Barnard from being "one of the inadequately acknowledged treasures of our time" (W. S. Merwin). With the thoroughness and dedication that Mary Barnard herself showed in her work, Sarah Barnsley has woven together the many intricate threads of Mary Barnard's unique creative process, to give us a lasting record and narrative of Barnard's complete work—and giving Barnard a rightful place in the canon of American literature.

Index of Titles and First Lines